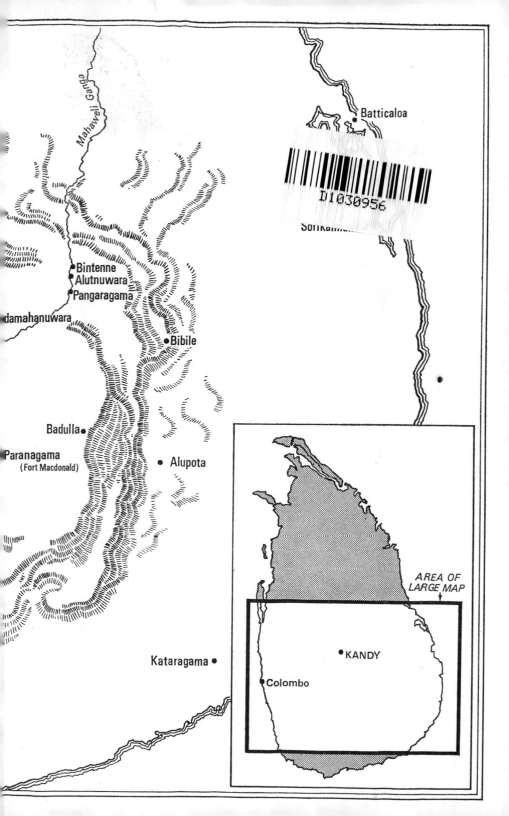

Mahaweli Ganga

Batticaloa

Sorrkamm...

D1030956

Bintenne
Alutnuwara
Pangaragama

damahanuwara

Bibile

Badulla

Paranagama
(Fort Macdonald)

Alupota

Kataragama

KANDY

Colombo

AREA OF
LARGE MAP

The
Kandyan
Wars

19TH CENTURY MILITARY CAMPAIGNS

The Kandyan Wars
THE BRITISH ARMY IN CEYLON
1803 – 1818

by
GEOFFREY POWELL

LEO COOPER · LONDON

First published in Great Britain 1973
by LEO COOPER LTD
196 Shaftesbury Avenue, London, W.C.2

Copyright © by Geoffrey Powell 1973

ISBN 0 85052 106 8

Printed in Great Britain
by Ebenezer Baylis & Son Ltd.
The Trinity Press, Worcester, and London

CONTENTS

ACKNOWLEDGEMENTS

The author and publishers would like to express their thanks to the following for permission to reproduce the illustrations listed opposite: To Mrs Olive Paterson for Nos. 1–9; The Scottish National Portrait Gallery, No. 11; The National Army Museum, No. 12; Mr James Fairfax, Sydney, Australia, No. 13; The Director, the Department of National Museums, Ceylon, Nos. 14, 15, 16, 17, 18, 21, 22; The Royal Asiatic Society, No. 15; The Black Watch Museum, Nos. 19, 20; The Thorvaldsen Museum, Copenhagen, No. 23; The National Portrait Gallery, No. 24; The Trustees of the British Museum, No. 25.

ILLUSTRATIONS

THE PROVINCES
OF THE
KANDYAN KINGDOM
in the early 18th C.

BOMBAY

MADRAS

CEYLON

Provincial
boundary
The Maritime
Provinces

0   5 10   20   30
miles

J A F F N A
Jaffna

VANNI
Manaar

NUVARAKALAVIYA
Anuradhapura

TAMANKADUVA
Lake Minneriya
Polonnaruwa

Trincomalee
Fort Ostenburg

Puttalam

SEVEN
KORALES
Dambulla
MATALE

BINTENNA

Batticaloa

Chilaw

DUMBARA
Kandy

FOUR
KORALES
INNER
PROVINCES
VALAPANE
VELLASSA

Negombo

THREE KORALES

Colombo

Mahaveli Ganga

SABARAGAMUVA
Kataragama

UVA

Galle
Matara
Tangalla
Hambantota

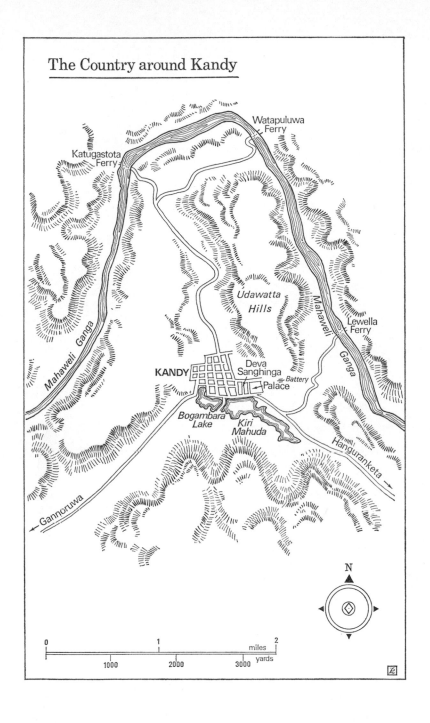

The Country around Kandy

Watapuluwa Ferry

Katugastota Ferry

Udawatta Hills

Mahaweli Ganga

Lewella Ferry

Mahaweli Ganga

KANDY

Deva Sanghinga

Palace

Battery

Bogambara Lake

Kiri Mahuda

Hanguranketa

Gannoruwa

N

0   1   2

miles

1000   2000   3000

yards

GLOSSARY

adigar: abbr. *adigarama*: chief officer of state, chief minister.

appuhami: gentleman-in-waiting; a guard of *appuhamis* protected the king's person.

atapattuwa: the name of a class of militia which acted as the king's bodyguard. A similar body was the *maduwa*.

bhikkhu: a Buddhist monk.

burgher: an inhabitant of Ceylon of European or partial European descent.

dagoba: a dome-shaped Buddhist relic-shrine.

dalada: tooth-relic of the Buddha; *Dalada Mandapa*, the Temple of the Tooth, lit. the Building of the Tooth; sometimes *Dalada Maligava*, the Palace of the Tooth.

devala: abode of the gods, temple.

dissawa: governor of a province or *dissawane*; *dissawa* is often used also to describe the latter.

diyo: god; the word was also used to describe a member of the royal family.

fanam: a copper coin, twelve of which equalled a *rix-dollar* which was worth two shillings.

gingal: a locally made light-artillery piece of about one inch calibre, fired from a tripod: also called a grasshopper gun.

kurakkan: eleusine coracana: a poor-quality cereal.

lascarin: a soldier; in early British times used to describe Ceylonese auxiliary troops.

madige: the pack-bullock or transport organization of the king.

maha: great; hence *mahadigar*, the first or principal adigar.

maduwa: q.v. *atapattuwa*.

mohindiram: a title of rank: a senior official.

moor: a Mohammedan inhabitant of Ceylon.

mudaliyar: a senior official, higher in rank than a *mohindiram*.

ola: palm-leaf on which writing is inscribed with a stylus and afterwards rubbed with a solution of lamp-black and gum.

11

GLOSSARY

pali: language of the sacred books of the Buddhists.

parangi: from *ferengi* (foreigner); used to describe the Portuguese and the disease of yaws; the symptoms of the latter are similar to syphilis which the Portuguese were accused of having introduced into Ceylon.

perahera: a procession or pageant, the most important of which was the *esala perahera* of Kandy.

rajakariya: the king's duty, extended to any service performed for the king, a lord or a temple.

rix-dollar: q.v. *fanum.*

rodiya: the lowest caste, members of which performed the most menial duties.

sangha: the associated brotherhood of the Buddhist monks.

sinha: a lion, hence Sinhalese, the people of the lion.

salagama: the caste of cinnamon workers: also *halagama: challia* was previously used but this word is distasteful to the Sinhalese.

tuppoti: a fine muslin waist-cloth, as many as eight of which were worn by Sinhalese of rank in ceremonial dress.

utun kumaraya: the grand prince, a title offered by North to Pilima Talauva.

yakka: the indigenous aboriginal inhabitants of Ceylon, whom the Sinhalese invaders considered to be demons; in Sinhalese literature, the *yakkas* are a class of malevolent superhuman beings, devoted to the arts of music and dancing.

wesak: the festival of the celebration of Buddha's birth, enlightenment and death.

wewa: an artificial irrigation reservoir.

PREFACE

ALTHOUGH I cannot recall the context, a phrase which I read some years ago in a book-review has stuck in my memory: 'This book could hardly escape being English-orientated'. I have tried hard to avoid incurring similar strictures, but this is still not the book which I would like to have written. It tells the story of the occupation of Kandy primarily from the viewpoint of the British, Asian and African soldiers who invaded that ancient kingdom, and it has far less to say about the Sinhalese villagers who defended their hills against their assailants. This I could not avoid. The British story is well-documented: there is no lack of official documents or private memoirs. But the Kandyans left little or nothing in the way of written records of their misfortunes. If any comprehensive account of the events seen from their standpoint does exist, it has still to see the light of day. Inevitably, therefore, this book tells the story as the British participants saw it, and more often than not they were bedevilled by the prejudices of their kind.

Perhaps I may be chided for dignifying these skirmishes with the status of wars. Certainly they were not wars as the term was then understood, with armies equipped and organized to a similar pattern manœuvring towards a climax of formal battle or siege. But the fighting cost a multitude of lives—Sinhalese, British, Malay, Indian and African, and was in many ways a portent of the type of conflict in which European-type armies were to become more and more involved during the subsequent century and a half, a trend which continues to develop. Time and again, an unsophisticated people, by making good use of its terrain and climate, has managed to defend itself against an army superior in technology and training, but designed for a different purpose.

One of the pleasures of writing a book such as this is the friends which one makes in the process. In Kandy, Professor Kingsley de Silva and Mr Justin La Brooy of the Department of History of the University of Ceylon and Mr Ian Goonetileke, the University Librarian, all took my wife and myself into their homes and were unstinting with their help and advice. In Colombo, Mr Ray Wijewardane was generous with his hospitality and found the time to read and comment upon several chapters of the typescript. Professor de Silva and Mr Labrooy read it all, producing a variety of helpful comments, as did Professor E. F. C. Ludowyk, late of the Department of English of the University of Ceylon, whose help at all stages of my work was, without any exaggeration, invaluable. Mr Goonetileke checked the bibliography, as well as giving me the run of his excellent Library and showering me daily with a gentle rain of fresh sources, culled from the depths of his awe-inspiring but modest erudition. They were among the friends I made. None of them are in any way responsible for any errors which may remain or for any of the opinions which I have expressed.

How is it that curators and librarians are such an amiable race? If you enter an unexplored museum or library, you can be confident that your inquiries, however puerile or time-consuming, will be answered with gracious enthusiasm. To all who helped me, I must pay tribute and offer thanks. The Library of the University of Ceylon I have mentioned already. I also had unsparing help from the staff of the Black Watch Museum, the Ceylon National Museum and Library, the Green Howards' Museum, the India Office Library, the Kandy Museum, the Light Infantry Museum, the London Library, the Ministry of Defence (Central) Library, the National Army Museum, the National Portrait Gallery, the Public Record Office, the Royal Asiatic Society Library, the Royal United Services Institute for Defence Studies Library, the Scottish National Portrait Gallery, and the York and Lancaster Regiment Museum. Other individuals whom I must mention are Dr R. L. Brohier of Colombo, Miss Vijita de Silva of the Ceylon National Library, Professor Tennakoon Vimalananda of Vidyalankara

University, Brigadier T. F. J. Collins, who advised me upon the subject of uniforms, and Mrs Olive Paterson, who was generous in her help in arranging for me to reproduce some of the drawings of her ancestor, Dr James Paterson. Lastly, my wife found the time in her busy professional and domestic life to read the typescript, chapter by chapter, and supply her kind but trenchant criticism.

I am also grateful to the following for allowing me to publish copyright material: Messrs Faber and Faber for the quotation from *The Story of Ceylon*; the Director of the Department of National Museums of Ceylon for quotations from *The Pybus Embassy to Kandy* and *The War with the Singalese*; and The Historical Association for the quotation from *Lord North*. Unpublished Crown copyright material in the Public Record Office and the India Office Library appears by permission of the Controller of Her Majesty's Stationery Office. The Editors of *History Today* have kindly allowed me to use material previously published by them in my article *Johnston's March to Kandy*.

For the spelling of place names I have been guided by the United States Department of the Interior's *Ceylon: official standard names approved by the U.S. Board on Geographic Names*. Proper names have proved more difficult. All my Sinhala-speaking friends gave me excellent advice on the subject, usually conflicting. One offered me the consolation that it was impossible to be consistent and that there were nine ways of spelling *Pilima Talauva*.

The regimentation of the plantation industry has transformed Ceylon's southern and central landscapes, but she still remains an enchanting island, her beauty intensified by the delicacy of her proportions and the smallness of her scale. To think of Asia is to visualize vast spaces, either empty or packed with jostling multitudes; for many Ceylon conjures up a picture of a rather smaller India. So the discovery that the island is just three times the size of Wales, and that only five times as many people live there comes as a surprise. No place in Ceylon is above seventy miles from the sea. By contrast, the Indian peninsula is sixty times as large, and sixty times as many people live there.

The history of a country is usually the product of its geography —the interplay of its climate on its geology. Of Ceylon this is particularly true. Shaped like a mango—some say a mole or even a Westphalian ham—the uppermost tip lies only nine degrees north of the equator. Separating her from India are the Palk Straits, about as wide as the English Channel, but so shallow that boats of only the slightest draught can navigate Adam's Bridge, the chain of rocks and reefs that all but joins Ceylon to the mainland. A country so placed does not have to be rich to invite invasion, but Ceylon was always wealthy: a treasure-house of spices and gems, elephants and rice. As a result, waves of invaders from the south of India tied Ceylon's history to that of her larger neighbour until the control of the Indian Ocean passed to the Portuguese at the start of the sixteenth century. These Portuguese invaders, with their Dutch and their British successors, greedy not only for the riches but also for the excellent harbours of the island, so strategically placed at the cross-roads of the sea routes of the Orient, transformed this relationship between Lanka and India. Their navies made the island safe from invasion by anyone but rival European powers, thus isolating her from the influences of the mainland, an isolation that was furthered by the effects of alien rule and culture on a comparatively small and concentrated population. Nevertheless, this isolation never became absolute. Ties with southern India, exercised through trade, religion and the family relationships of the ruling dynasties continued to influence many aspects of the life of the island.

A traveller landing on the south-west coast of Ceylon in the

CHAPTER 1
The Early Conquerors

I

'WHEREFORE Ceilão is by her position the Crown of the whole of India, and God would appear to have created her to be the Mistress of that great world, giving her a healthful and benign climate with the greatest treasures which He has distributed over the whole earth.'[1] So Captain João Ribeiro, a soldier of Portugal, in the seventeenth century saw Ceilão, the name by which his countrymen knew the island which was called proudly by its Sinhalese inhabitants 'Sri Lanka'—the Blessed or the Auspicious One. In similar superlatives, Ribeiro's successors enthused about the island's beauties, each newcomer groping for fresh adjectives to describe its fascinating tropical exuberance. 'Woods, water and mountains, woods, water and mountains!' welcomed Captain Herbert Beaver of the 19th Regiment of Foot, as he landed in Ceylon one hundred and fifty years later. 'Adjoining to the verandah, before my room at the Governor's, is the garden—all verdure. At the bottom of it is a sheet of water, varied in its form by luxuriant groves stretching into various parts of it, which renders its irregularities lovely. At about forty miles distant a hilly range arises, sometimes below, sometimes above the clouds, and at seventy miles, the majestic Adam's Peak rears its lofty head. This mountain, when visible, which it generally is in the early morning, is almost always so high above the cloudy region as to look like a pyramidal black cloud.'[2]

eighteenth century would have seen ahead of him a landscape that, from the distance, was much the same as it is today. The spider-like catamarans of the fishermen lay under the coconut palms, safe from the waves breaking in from the Indian Ocean. As he moved inland the colours were fresh and clean: the green-blue of the lagoons, spotted with white egrets; the paddy-fields shaded from lime to deep yellow according to the ripeness of the crop; the browns and greys of the scattered huts of the villagers and the buffaloes glistening as naked boys washed them down; the primary colours of the clothes of the women and the blossom on the trees; and the wayside fruit stalls (possibly the brightest of all) with melons and brinjals, bananas and pomegranates, golden king-coconuts and carpets of scarlet chillis laid out for sale. The backdrop was the blue mountains, rising more than 8,000 feet above the sea shore; and as our stranger moved towards them he soon found himself in the lowland hills, covered with a dense tropical rain forest that thickened as he climbed. Higher still, as the gradients steepened, sheer valleys barred his way, and he marvelled at the paddy fields of the infrequent villages running in minute and regular steps down the contours of the hills. Soon he felt the chill of the high country where the forest thinned to stark rocky outcrops and grassy slopes studded with stunted lichen-clad trees and rhododendrons, a land that could remind a Scot of his native heaths. As he crossed the central plateau, he saw the 200-mile-long Mahaweli Ganga starting on its journey down to Trincomalee, and mountains now dropping in a rather more gradual slope towards the Bay of Bengal. The south-west monsoon had drenched the western escarpment, but here the hills were not so lush, drier because they collected only the sparser rain of the north-easterly monsoon. Then, as our stranger came down once more towards the sea, he found a coast in parts bolder and more rocky than the shore where he had landed, its deep water providing the safe harbour of Trincomalee.

In strong contrast to the mountainous southern half of Ceylon, the northern part of the island was a flattish plain, watered only by the short-lived north-east monsoon, a thirsty land, covered with a thirty foot-high bush, dignified by the title of jungle, and harbouring leopard, elephant and bear. Two thousand years earlier, however, this had been a land of rich villages and great cities.

II

Between the sixth and third centuries B.C., an Aryan race, the Sinhalese, who probably had their origin in north-west India, crossed the Palk Straits into the northern plain of Lanka. The heroes of this early people are part history, part myth, their deeds handed down by word of mouth or recorded in lost chronicles which provided the source material for the Mahavamsa, the tale of the ancient Lanka kings, written somewhere around the fifth century A.D. in the sacred Pali script by a *bhikkhu*, one of the yellow-clad monks of the Buddhist faith.

In their language *sinha* signified a lion, and so the Sinhalese were the People of the Lion. Vijaya, the first of their national heroes, was the son of one Sinhabahu, who was sired by a lion on a princess of south India and, as a consequence, favoured with extremities resembling the paws of his father. Vijaya conquered the *yakkas*, an indigenous race of aboriginals, whom the new-comers called demons. A few of the descendants of these people still exist—the Veddas, a stone-age australoid hunting community, akin to the Bhils and Gonds of south and central India. The early Sinhalese invaders, who subjugated the ancestors of the Veddas, were Hindu by religion, but Buddhism overspread this older faith during the second half of the third century B.C., failing, however, to displace the worship of the Hindu pantheon, elements of which many Sinhalese incorporated in their Buddhism, that most tolerant of all faiths. The Gautama himself is said to have visited Lanka on three occasions, and his death in 483 B.C. coincided with Vijaya's arrival in the island. Although the Buddha's teachings spread widely during the next two centuries, 247 B.C. is held to be the date of Lanka's acceptance of the faith. This is the year in which Asoka, the great emperor of south India, recommended to the Sinhalese ruler Tissa that he should adopt the Buddhist faith, and sent his son (though some say it was his brother), the *bhikkhu* Mahinda, to preach at Anuradhapura, then the capital of the Sinhalese kings.

For close on one thousand years Anuradhapura was the capital of Rajarata, the Country of the Kings, as this northern land was called, a pleasant and abundant haven during the peaceful intervals when invasion or civil conflict was not tearing it apart. The fierce but short north-east monsoon, and the rivers that flooded down from the central uplands after the rains could do little for the country unless the precious water could be conserved. This the Sinhalese kings did in the finest irrigation system of the ancient world. In vast man-made inland seas, called by the British 'tanks', from the Portuguese word *tanque*, or lakelet (the Sinhala *wewa* is more euphonic), the water was collected and stored. Below these giant reservoirs were hundreds more, great and small, on which cities and villages depended for their water, the whole joined together by a wonderful complex of canals, some with a fall as small as six inches in a mile. It was engineering work of a high order: some of the immense main tanks covered as much as 4,000 acres with retaining banks three miles long and three hundred feet wide; the concrete was harder even than that of the Romans.

Then as now, rice supplemented by fish, vegetables and fruit made up the diet of the Ceylonese, and the *wewa* provided the water to flood the fields in which the rice could be grown. With this ample water and the sun, these early kings, of whom Tissa was the first, were able to channel the spare labour of their people into building yet more superb public works, that beautified as well as enriched their land. Anuradhapura, the capital, could be likened as a water-city to Venice or Bruges. Surrounded by its complex of tanks, great and small, in which were reflected the glistening white, conically shaped *dagobas*, Anuradhapura was one of the great cities of the world. Fa-Hsien, the fifth-century Chinese traveller, described one of the *dagobas* rising four hundred feet into the sky, decorated with gold and silver and every other kind of precious substance, and served by an army of 5,000 priests.[3]

But the Sinhalese peasant enjoyed only intermittent peace. Time and again, the Dravidian races of south India erupted into his country to ravage and destroy, sometimes as invaders, but often invited by the Sinhalese rulers, either as mercenaries or as allies to help them in their tangled dynastic disputes. From time to time the Indians established themselves in Ceylon, but until the ninth century the Sinhalese were able to withstand the worst of the pressure from their powerful neighbours. By 992 A.D., however, they had been forced to abandon Anuradhapura, its glorious temples and palaces in ruins; Rajarata had become a principality of south India; and the Sinhalese were being forced southwards. First they built a new capital at Polonnaruwa, then another at Dambadeniya, and then they were pushed further south still, to Kotte, just outside the present Colombo. Finally they retreated from the Portuguese up into Kandy,[4] the country of the central mountain massif, a wild forest-clad land which had always been a home for lost causes and outlaws. Now it became the refuge of the last remnants of Sinhalese independence, while the ruined northern cities disappeared into the jungle until amateur British antiquarians arrived in the nineteenth century to rescue them. As the tanks were breached and the canals fell into ruins, the handful of survivors were stricken by malaria, spread by the proliferating mosquitoes which bred in the stagnant pools formed by the wreck of the irrigation system. Some of the Dravidian invaders remained and the north of the island became Tamil, with the capital at Jaffna, and Tamil it remains to this day.

Ceylon's wealth attracted traders as well as invaders. Both the Greeks and the Romans knew the country. Onesicritus, one of Alexander's admirals, describes the size and courage of its war-elephants. Arab dhows usually carried this eastern trade, and the west had long been familiar with the details of Ceylon's geography even before a Roman ship was blown off course in the first century A.D. while collecting tribute on the Arabian coast. Making landfall in Ceylon, the crew so fascinated the King with their tales that he decided to send four envoys to Rome. These ambassadors astonished Claudius's court with their description of the just and gentle government practised by their kings, although Pliny treated their eulogies with a proper measure of scepticism.[5]

Over the centuries a polyglot succession of merchants visited Lanka—Chinese and Cambodians, Arabs and Indians, Malays and Persians. Usually these strangers came to trade in spices and gems, but others visited the island as pilgrims to the many famous shrines. More than once the Chinese reached out to invade the country. Their ships descended on the coast to carry the local ruler into captivity as late as the beginning of the fifteenth century, a foray that resulted in the Ming Emperors exercising a loose form of suzerainty over the island. This was the last time the Sinhalese were to be subjugated by an oriental neighbour. Lanka's future oppressors were to arrive from the west.

III

First came the Portuguese. Towards the end of the fifteenth century, the recovery of the Iberian peninsula from the Moors was all but complete, and the energies of this small but talented nation were about to be released for their extraordinary maritime and colonial enterprises around the world. Their advances in the sciences of shipbuilding and navigation enabled Bartholomew Diaz, in 1487, to round the Cape of Good Hope. In 1498 Vasco da Gama reached Calicut in India, five years after Columbus had carried the flag of Spain to America and only thirteen years after Richard III's death at Bosworth had brought the Wars of the Roses to an end in England.

The motives for this sudden expansion were complex. The spice trade from the east was in the hands of the Arabs and the Venetians. The former controlled the sea routes that stretched across the Indian Ocean into the Red Sea and the Persian Gulf, and they also ran the caravans which wound across the deserts of the Middle East into the Mediterranean ports where the Venetians took delivery of the goods. The Portuguese hated the Muslim Arabs and envied the Venetians. To open a sea route around the Cape would divert this trade from their rivals into their own hands and would give them direct access, not only to the spice trade, but to the other fabulous riches of the east, tales of which had been brought back by Marco Polo and his fellow travellers. This wealth the Portuguese could exploit both by trade and by plunder, but it was not only avarice that inspired them. There were other spurs—scientific exploration for its own sake; the missionary zeal of the Catholic faith; even the hope that they

23

might find the fabled Prester John and enlist his help as a Christian ally in their struggle against the Muslim.

In November, 1505, the first Portuguese vessels were seen off Ceylon. Dom Lourenço de Almeida, the son of the newly appointed Viceroy of the Indies, was blown off course and anchored his nine ships outside Colombo while trying to intercept a fleet of Moorish spice ships reported to be sailing for the Red Sea by way of the Maldives. As yet the Sinhalese had no reason to fear these Europeans. The Portuguese were few in number, and it was still their policy to maintain friendly relations with the local rulers, whose coasts they could guard from attack by sea in exchange for the protection of their trading factories. For this reason the King of Kotte made a show of offering them tribute in exchange for protection, both against his local enemies and his rival claimants to the throne. Kotte was only six miles from Colombo but the King arranged for the Portuguese envoys to be led there by a circuitous route that took five days to travel, a naive and rather pedestrian ruse that failed to deceive the strangers. It did, however, produce two results: the seed of the legend of Sinhalese chicanery was planted in the Portuguese mind and the Sinhalese gained a new proverb, 'As the parangi went to Kotte', to describe a roundabout route.[6]

The hundred years prior to the arrival of the Portuguese had been a quite peaceful period in Ceylonese history. It was a prosperous and happy land. Galle, the ancient sea-port on the south-west coast, in the words of the epic poem, Paravi Sandesaya, was a place 'where the shops were resplendent with gold and gems and pearls, as if the depths of every ocean had been searched to procure them'.[7] When the Portuguese left the island a century and a half later, the Sinhalese had, in the words of P. E. Pieris, been reduced to 'a broken race with their ancient civilization brought to the verge of ruins, and their scheme of life well-nigh destroyed'.[8]

At first, however, the Portuguese were too busy consolidating their scattered possessions around the perimeter of the Indian Ocean to pay much attention to Ceylon. Their miniscule forces had the task, not only of sweeping the Moors (their generic term for their Muslim rivals) from the seas, but also of manning and maintaining a ring of forts extending in an arc that swung from

East Africa to Macao by way of the Persian Gulf. Although they were well aware of the riches waiting to be won in Ceylon and of its strategic importance at the centre of their eastern empire, they first established a fort at Colombo only in 1518. For most of the first century of their occupation they were content to confine themselves to trade, extending their influence by their shrewd manipulation of the complicated dynastic struggles of the Sinhalese royalty. Sometimes they would make a sharp raid into the interior, but often they would have to defend their position against a race still militarily powerful. Only towards the end of the sixteenth century did they make a deliberate attempt to conquer the island. Jaffna they took with little trouble but the mountainous southern state of Kanda Uda Pas Rata, with its capital at Senkadagala, known to Europeans as Kandy, stayed independent, the last stronghold of the Sinhalese people, although the Portuguese occupied, looted and burned the capital several times.

Like the *conquistadores* in South America, the Portuguese fought their battles with minute European forces. These they supplemented with their native allies and with *lascarins*, or native troops, but both were likely to prove unreliable. It was rare for the Portuguese themselves to be numbered in more than hundreds. They were frequently pardoned criminals and sometimes boys as young as nine years of age. Shipped to the Indies in filthy and disease-ridden caravels, it was not surprising that the morale and discipline of such troops was often poor. Nevertheless they usually fought bravely, but it was possibly the bravery of despair, knowing as they did what would happen to them if they fell alive into the hands of the Sinhalese. As the maintenance of its vast empire became an increasing burden on the small population of Portugal, even soldiers of this calibre became scarce and it was found necessary to encourage the troops to form alliances with local women in order to provide the missing manpower.

For many years the Sinhalese fought their European enemies in open warfare. But in time they learned that the jungle-covered mountains and the discomforts of the climate were weapons in themselves. Making proper use of the natural advantages of their country, they started to fight in a fashion later known as guerrilla warfare.

The advanced state of the development of sixteenth-century Kanda Uda Rata and the extent of her military strength is shown in the Portuguese description of the forces of the warlike King Raja Sinha I, gathered to besiege Colombo in 1587:

'Raju now took the field. He had fifty thousand men of war, sixty thousand workmen and camp followers, two thousand and two hundred elephants, one hundred and fifty pieces of bronze artillery, large and small, four thousand draught oxen, ten thousand axes, three thousand bill-hooks, two thousand picks that are called in India *codeli*, six thousand hoes, a large quantity of spare arms, four hundred smiths to prepare arrow heads and other implements, one thousand carpenters, four hundred gunners—Javas, Caffirs and of other nationalities, the greater part of whom had deserted from the Portuguese,—a vast quantity of timber large and small, of which he made two cars resembling castles each on nine wheels and others of the height of a man, a large quantity of sulphur, saltpetre and gunpowder, with much lead and shot; while sixty-five fustas and caturas and four hundred smaller boats were also ordered to be got ready at some of the seaports.'[9]

For seven months a handful of Portuguese and *lascarins* defended Colombo against this host of Sinhalese, displaying a bravery that was matched by their enemies. Ravaged by plague the Portuguese had to counter not only the most modern weapons and tactics of Western Europe, of which Raja Sinha appears to have been master, but also the traditional war-elephants of the East, tearing and trampling down the city fortifications and brandishing large swords in their trunks. The Sinhalese even used mines, a branch of warfare unknown to the Great Mogul a century later.

The story of the Portuguese attempts to subjugate Ceylon is a long nightmare of cruelty and carnage, varying from the deliberate to the capricious, from the slaughter of every male over fourteen years of age to bizarre and esoteric horrors. The notorious Dom Jeronymo de Azavedo made mothers watch their babies spitted on pikes or mashed between millstones; men were hacked in two with axes; women's breasts were torn off or their wombs split open and their infants forced back inside their bodies. The Sinhalese, by nature rather a gentle people, retaliated but in a rather lower key. Sometimes they refrained from killing their prisoners, preferring to mutilate them. After the ambush of a

Portuguese column, the commander of which had been guilty of a particularly despicable piece of treachery, they returned fifty prisoners to Colombo, castrated, their ears clipped like village curs and with a solitary eye left to each five men to guide them back.

The Portuguese *lascarins* could be as cruel as their masters, but the Sinhalese dreaded most the Kaffir troops their enemies had imported from Africa. On one occasion, it is said, in order to strike terror into a surrendered district, the Portuguese handed over a villager to their Kaffirs who then cut a man up and ate him in the presence of his wife and children.

What the Portuguese could not carry away they destroyed. The Portuguese writer who described Raja Sinha's forces outside Colombo recounts how his comrades subsequently ravaged the south-west coast of the island. After burning in turn the string of coastal towns, with their glorious shrines and their monasteries, they came to the famous temple of Devundara, known from China to Arabia, whose great copper-gilt roof served as a landmark for mariners:

'The temple itself was vast in size, all the roofs being domed and richly carved; round about it were several very handsome chapels and over the principal gateway was a tall tower entirely roofed with copper, gilt in various parts. Within was a large square with verandahs and terraces with a handsome gate on each side, while all around were planted sweet-smelling flowers which were used during the processions. . . . We burst in the gates and proceeded to destroy the idols of which there were more than a thousand of different figures of clay and wood and copper, mostly gilded. We destroyed the domes and colonnades and sacked the stores where we found a vast accumulation of ivory, fine cloths, coffee, pepper, sandalwood, jewels, precious stones and all the fittings of the temple, which we plundered as we desired and set the rest on fire. As the greatest affront that could be offered to the place we slaughtered within some cows, this being a stain which could not be purified without the most elaborate ceremonies. We also burnt a magnificent wooden car built like a tower of seven stories and beautifully painted and gilt—a magnificent vehicle in which they were accustomed to convey the chief idol around the city.'[10]

In this manner the Portuguese marched backwards and forwards across the island, destroying or looting its treasures, murdering and torturing its people, and leaving behind them a waste of burnt houses, ruined cultivation and felled fruit trees. Each time they captured Kandy, it gained them little or nothing. Knowing now the futility of trying to defend their homes against soldiers of the calibre of the Portuguese, the people disappeared into the jungle, leaving their enemies to vent their spite on empty buildings. Attempts to pursue the Kandyans into the forest brought only fatigue, ambush and disease. Faced with the problem of maintaining their lines of communication to the coast, over one hundred miles away, the Portuguese soon discovered that they could neither bring their supplies and reinforcements up into the hills nor evacuate their casualties to Colombo. A retreat to the coast followed and again the lesson was learned that the forests, the rivers and the easily defended mountain passes needed little in the way of human help to destroy troops already weak from disease and encumbered with their sick and wounded comrades.

On three separate occasions Portuguese armies were destroyed in this manner. Manoel de Sousa, retreating from Kandy in 1594 towards Balane,[11] the key pass commanding the main route that runs from Colombo into the hills, was himself killed and his army annihilated. As the heavily laden Portuguese soldiers struggled towards safety along the rough and narrow forest track, time after time they found felled trees blocking the path ahead. Then behind them, further trees, which had been skilfully cut through but held erect by giant creepers, crashed down to cut off their retreat. Arrows and bullets then poured from the tangled undergrowth into the exhausted men and stones smashed down on them from the cliffs above. This was the pattern of de Sousa's disastrous retreat.

In 1630, Captain General Constantine de Saa was surrounded in Uva and his army wiped out. On the battlefield the Sinhalese built a pyramid of severed Portuguese heads and laid at the feet of their King, Raja Sinha II, the grisly trophy of de Saa himself. This the ruler addressed with the words 'How often have I prayed you not to make war on me and destroy my realm, but to let me live in peace, while you kept the best part of Lanka: but if your successors follow in your footsteps, you will not be the last'.[12] De Saa was not the last. Eight years later General Miego Melo de Castro, following in de Sousa's footsteps after a further foray on

Kandy, was surrounded at Gannoruwa and his army of over 6,000 Portuguese, *lascarins,* and Indian and African mercenaries, was destroyed. It was the last pitched battle fought by the Sinhalese people, and is remembered by them in their epic poem, *Parangi Hatana,* The Story of the Foreigners,[13] a terrible tale of courage and carnage, of torture and of death:

'They cut and slash and stab and bind and wrench away their chains; they shoot and feel and seize their swords; they chase and leap and raise their shouts; for was not this Raja Sinha's mighty host? They wrench the muskets and *pedreneiros* from their hands to smash their bones therewith, and while one halts to cut their throats, another seizes the spoil.'

Now it was the turn of the Sinhalese to loot:

'Like raging wolves on a herd of kine our gallant host lay about on the Parangis; their cushions and rugs and packages—who can recount the plunder of that fight? Silver trays and poniards, water jugs with silver tops, sabres wrought with lion heads, coats and *jaggalat* hats—they made a glorious spoil.'

The terrified porters had thrown away the stores they carried before the battle started and the poem provides a picture of the supplies the Portuguese troops had with them:

'The palm leaves which they bore, the copper vessels in which their rice was cooked, their powder, the loads of butter and chickens which many a coolie carried on his shoulders, all were cast away in their deadly panic fear; Their bread and biscuits, boxes filled with sweet things, flasks and jars of maddening arrack, rice bags by the thousand, all manner of food and drink—all were thrown aside and trampled under foot.'

The Portuguese occupation of Ceylon was nearing its end. The decline of Portugal as a world power had started as long ago as 1578 when the Moroccans defeated her at the battle of Alcacer Quibir, nine years before Raja Sinha tried to take Colombo by storm. Through the peculation of corrupt officials, her empires in Brazil and the East had brought little to the treasury. Then, when the Aviz dynasty came to an end in 1581, the crown went to

Philip II of Spain and the so-called Sixty Year Captivity by her more powerful neighbour started. This Spanish domination of Portugal had two effects. It hastened her decline and it brought her into conflict with the Dutch, who were in the process of freeing themselves from their Catholic rulers.

It was extraordinary that a country so small and poverty-stricken as Portugal could for so long have retained her grip on such a vast overseas empire. In the end control slipped from her grasp. No longer could she find enough men to garrison her forts or fight her battles, and the losses she had suffered in Ceylon had much to do with this.

CHAPTER 2
The Hollanders and the British

I

WHEN, in their turn, the Hollanders went adventuring towards the East, they had two aims—to enrich themselves and to harm their enemies, the Portuguese. Their enterprise as seafarers, their astuteness as merchants, and their efficiency as administrators brought them swift success. In 1597, they established their first trading factory in Java; five years later, representatives of their United East India Company were being received at the Kandyan court, and the Sinhalese, as usual too eager to find allies, invited the new arrivals to join them in an attack on the Portuguese in Colombo.

These early negotiations between the new arrivals and the Kandyans broke down after a somewhat unfortunate incident. Drink was the weakness of the Dutch (as it was of most Europeans), and their envoy, Admiral Spilbergen, while in his cups, insulted the King. The error cost him his life and those of his men. As a result, the control of Ceylon, for the time being, remained in Portuguese hands; but the Dutch, as they expanded their influence over the rest of the Indian Ocean, never lost sight of the march of events in the island. At length in 1638, the year when Raja Sinha II overwhelmed General de Castro at Gannoruwa, a treaty was concluded by which the Dutch agreed to help the Sinhalese in exchange for a monopoly of the overseas trade of the country. One of the articles of this treaty stipulated that the Dutch would

31

be allowed to garrison any forts they might succeed in capturing only if the King so desired it, a vital clause that was deliberately omitted from the Kandyan copy of the document—a piece of roguery considered to be ethically justifiable by the European moral standards of the day. Treaties concluded with pagan potentates were thought to lack the binding power of those negotiated between fellow Christians.

By 1640, the Dutch had established small forts on the east coast at Trincomalee and Batticaloa; they had also captured Galle and Negombo from the Portuguese on the west side of the island. Their refusal to hand these two forts over to the Kandyans when asked for them quickly disillusioned Raja Sinha; his new allies, it dawned upon him, were no more to be trusted than their rivals. Nevertheless, the Sinhalese could not dispense with Dutch help if they were ever to rid themselves of the hated Portuguese. There followed a short respite while the two powers were at peace in Europe, but the outbreak of fresh hostilities in 1656 provided the Dutch with their excuse to take Colombo. Two years later they had Jaffna as well, the last Portuguese stronghold in the island.

The exit of the Portuguese from Ceylon was as savage as it was gallant. For seven months Colombo resisted a large Dutch force, fighting alongside 20,000 Sinhalese, commanded by Raja Sinha in person. A handful of Portuguese, starving and racked by plague, fever and dysentery, held an over-extended perimeter against the repeated assaults of the Dutch and their allies. No pity was shown. When the Portuguese tried to smuggle out their starving non-combatants, the Dutch turned them back. The defenders then refused to allow them to re-enter the city, and the poor wretches were left to die, watched by their relations and friends, in the no-man's-land between the fort walls and the batteries of the Hollanders. When even this failed to stop the exodus, the Dutch flogged their victims before returning them. In the end they produced the ultimate in horrors. One of their soldiers, Johann Jacob Sarr, relates:

'When we had no means of driving them away from our camp, we had to strike still greater terror into them. Therefore when a woman came and brought small children, we forced her to put her child into a wooden mortar and to pound it to death with the pounder, and then to go away with the dead child.'[1]

There was nothing spontaneous about the Dutch behaviour; their conduct possessed a unique quality of methodical cruelty. Cannibalism also is said to have been rife within the city; certainly two of the women marooned between the lines were found to have devoured their newly-born infants.

In the end the Portuguese were compelled to capitulate. At three o'clock on 12 May, 1656, they marched out of Colombo, their drums beating and their colours flying, none of the brutalities so recently perpetrated being allowed to interfere with the traditional ceremonial of war. Past the astounded Dutch and Sinhalese soldiers marched, or rather staggered, seventy-three wrecks of men, the survivors of the siege, some dragging themselves on crutches and some supported by their comrades, but their stubborn pride driving them to haul four of their cannon as far as the gate. Among the survivors was Captain João Ribeiro, and to him we owe the description of the gallant end to an inglorious chapter of Portuguese history.[2] It was some little time before the Sinhalese and Dutch were able to realize that this pitiful handful of men was all that had held them at bay for so long.

Profit was, of course, the driving force behind the colonial exploits of the Portuguese. This was reflected in the intense greed shown by both soldiers and officials, and this, in turn, was the cause of much of the cruelty suffered by the hapless villagers. Nevertheless, this avarice was easy to understand. Selfless officials were rare in any country, and the poverty-stricken Portuguese fidalgo, like the starving peasant, ventured to the Orient or the Americas to make his fortune. But although avarice was the primary spur, there was indeed an element of altruism in their conquests; it was necessary to convert the pagan to the Christian faith. The widespread success of the Portuguese priests and monks in this missionary field was due, in some degree, to the material advantages that conversion brought in its train; on the other hand, to many Sinhalese the Christian religion held out a genuine appeal.

Unfortunately for Ceylon, the intolerance of sixteenth-century Catholicism paid no regard to the beliefs, the culture or the

C

traditions of either Sinhalese or Tamil. The destruction of a magnificent Buddhist or Tamil temple was, to these bigoted Christians, a praiseworthy act.

Paradoxically, the general detestation felt by the Sinhalese for the Portuguese was often accompanied by a close and familiar relationship between individuals. The foreign culture was attractive, at least to the wealthier classes, who adopted in a large measure the language, sometimes the dress, the music, and even the names and titles of their oppressors. Characteristic though this may be of the attitude of subject races towards their rulers, seldom has it taken such an acute form among a people whose civilization and traditions were so highly developed as the Sinhalese. Nor were these influences rejected as soon as their conquerors left. The Catholic religion and, indeed, Portuguese names still survive, after three hundred years.

II

Any doubts the Sinhalese may have had about the intentions of the Hollanders were clarified as soon as Colombo fell. Not only did the victors settle the terms of the capitulation without consulting Raja Sinha, but they then refused his forces permission to enter the captured city. For a quarter of a century the King had struggled to rid his country of the Portuguese. Now he had done no more than exchange them for the Dutch. As the Sinhalese say, he had 'given pepper and got ginger'. Utterly disillusioned by the Dutch chicanery, Raja Sinha withdrew to his mountain stronghold, there to nurse his hatred and harry his enemies to the best of his ability for the remaining twenty-one years of his reign.

The Dutch had inherited a wasteland. The rich paddy fields were ruined and abandoned, the people poverty-stricken and the countryside deserted. Only by the avoidance of war and efficient management could the newcomers make a profit from this run-down estate and to these twin tasks the United East India Company turned its business-like talents. Acknowledging that they had no legal right to be in the country and accepting the fact that most Sinhalese saw Raja Sinha as the legal ruler of the whole island, the Dutch held to the fiction that they occupied their territory only as its protector. To the uncompromising Raja Sinha and to his rather more tractable successors, they paid the empty compliment of acknowledging formal vassalage to the Kandyan throne, obsequiously accepting insults and pinpricks, not least of which was the ignominious ceremonial to which their ambassadors were subjected by the ritualized formality of the Kandyan court. Even when the Kandyans proferred the ultimate injury by actually detaining their ambassador, the Dutch resisted the temptation of allowing themselves to be provoked to violence. It was a policy both intelligent and successful. Armed conflict was rare and the Dutch were able to cut their military spending in the island to the minimum. An uneasy balance of power resulted. The King, when he so wished, was able to interfere with the Dutch as they gathered their cinnamon or areca-nut crops in the forest, or he could make it difficult for them to engage in the profitable occupation of elephant trapping. To counter this the Dutch controlled most of the coast and could, when they wanted, impose an economic blockade on the Kandyans.

The richness of the Ceylonese soil, allied to the efficient management of the Dutch, speedily brought the occupied areas back to a state of comparative prosperity. Repairs were carried out to tanks and irrigation systems, and wells were reopened. Cattle were imported from India, together with Tamil slaves to assist in the hard work of reclamation. The growing of cash crops was encouraged, the administration of justice was reorganized on the basis of Roman-Dutch law, and the work of local government was placed on a sound footing. Schools were opened to provide a training for the junior administrators demanded by the expanding bureaucracy. But despite its apparent efficiency, the Dutch rule was a rigid tyranny, its edge dulled by the corruption of the officials who administered it, both Dutch and Asian.

The Kandyans were now ruled by a dynasty of pure Dravidian blood. Because the Sinhalese ruling family had long been in the habit of finding its brides in southern India, the kings had always been more Indian than Sinhalese. When Raja Sinha II's grandson died without an heir in 1739, the throne passed to the dead King's brother-in-law, a Dravidian who adopted the Buddhist faith. Buddhism had suffered a sad neglect during the reign of Raja Sinha, but the new dynasty, with the enthusiasm commonly found in converts, led a remarkable religious revival, to which was united an implacable opposition to the Dutch, far surpassing that shown by Raja Sinha's immediate successors.

In 1761, full-scale war broke out.[3] The initiative came from the Kandyan King, Kirti Sri, who saw his opportunity to support a wave of rebellion and unrest that had been festering in the Dutch provinces during the previous year. Neglect of their military forces had left the Dutch ill-prepared for the war which swept across their settlements. The south coast was overrun, Negombo resisted only with difficulty, and Colombo itself was threatened by the Kandyan invasion. Faced, therefore, by a ruler with whom there seemed to be little hope of reviving the *status quo* of peaceful hostility, and worried also by his approach to the British, now the paramount European power in the Indian Ocean, the Dutch decided to complete the subjugation of Ceylon by capturing Kirti Sri's kingdom. The arrival of reinforcements in 1762 had enabled them to re-establish and consolidate their control of the coast by the end of the following year. In 1764 six columns marched on the capital but none succeeded in finding their way there. Some lost their way, some disintegrated through the ravages of disease, and some were repulsed by the Kandyans with disastrous losses. Concealed among the trees and undergrowth, their native sharpshooters, armed with home-made guns and bows, took a steady toll of the heavily-laden troops laboriously carving their way through jungles devoid of any type of path or track. First to be picked off were the conspicuously-clad drummers and officers, the casualties among the latter becoming so severe that they adopted the uniform of their men, one of the earliest recorded instances of a practice the necessity for which had regularly to be re-learned in the early stages of many future wars. Once again European soldiers cowered at the bottom of cliffs as boulders crashed down on them from above; once again they found themselves trapped in narrow defiles by barricades of felled trees. The Sinhalese still remembered the tactics that had proved so successful against the Portuguese.

The experiences of the 1764 campaign caused the Dutch Governor, Baron Van Eck, an experienced and accomplished soldier, to make many changes in the composition and equipment of his troops. A corps of Jagers was raised, armed with special muskets; three-quarters of them were either Germans or Swiss as was usual in the Dutch European units. About two-thirds of the fighting troops were Malays. Many of these men, who were usually referred to as Easterners, took their wives with them; inveterate gamblers, some of them even weighed down their haversacks with their fighting cocks. Machetes were substituted for swords and bayonets, both equally useless in the jungle, and Van Eck dressed his troops in a new and practical field-service uniform consisting of a double-breasted coat and long trousers made out of sail-cloth; for headgear they were given soft hats with flaps that could be lowered to protect the ears and the nape of the neck, the crowns being the colour of the regimental facings. Van Eck was clear about the qualities he expected to find in his officers. His instructions read:

'Officers who cannot adapt themselves to circumstances and endure the discomforts of the men, satisfying themselves with simple clothing, food and drink, living like the soldiers and setting a good example— should stay behind with the women.'[4]

With this new army Van Eck again invaded Kandy in January, 1765. Taking the northerly route that involved capturing the twin hill forts of Galagedara and Girihagama, he crossed the Mahaweli Ganga on 19 February and entered a deserted capital. Three days were needed to sack the palace of its booty of gold, gems, rich fabrics and silver-plated doors. Three columns were then sent out into the surrounding countryside to ravage the villages and attempt to cut off the retreating Kandyans, one of which burned the royal palace at Hanguranketa, lying to the westward. Nothing was achieved by these raids except to exhaust the men and spread disease among them. With illness now rife, the monsoon approaching and his communications harried by enemy bands, Van Eck realized that no longer could he maintain such a large force among the mountains. Withdrawing the greater proportion of his troops to the coast, he left some 1,800 men and a multitude of women and children belonging to the Malays and Indians in Kandy. As the months passed by, sniping, raids, starvation and disease took their toll of the garrison and it became apparent that their position was untenable. Hopes that the Dutch had placed in the Siamese puppet they had produced for the Kandyan throne proved to be misplaced and, on 31 August, the retreat from the capital began. After hard fighting about 1,000 stricken survivors managed to claw their way back to the coast; few of the coolies and none of the women or children seem to have arrived.

By 1766, with his country ruined, and anxious to end the carnage, Kirti Sri was persuaded to sign a peace treaty that left the Dutch firmly in charge of the entire coastline of the island; at the same time they obtained full sovereign rights over the provinces they controlled. But the war had proved, if proof were necessary, that nothing was to be gained from trying to subdue the final mountain refuge of the Sinhalese people.

Thirty years remained to the Dutch before they, in their turn, gave way to the British. They used it to consolidate the administration of their maritime provinces and develop the trade of the island. The Sinhalese peasant living under their jurisdiction had the infinite blessing of a peaceful existence, some measure of personal security and the protection of a not too corrupt judicial system. Poor he was, but he rarely starved; since the expulsion of the Portuguese his condition had improved beyond recognition. The upper classes also prospered materially. The substantial Dutch stone houses filled with good furniture, porcelain and even Venetian glass were being copied by the wealthier Ceylonese. On the other hand, the Dutch did not mix socially with their subjects in the same easy manner as the Portuguese. Asian and northern European had little in common.

In contrast to the Maritime Provinces, the half-million or so Kandyans stagnated in their encircled mountain kingdom. Their old culture was nearly in ruins and they were cut off from contact, not only with the rest of the world, but in many respects from their own littoral as well. The effects of this separation of the Kandyan from his low-country compatriots have not been eradicated even today, and is one of the two main marks the Dutch set upon Ceylon. The other was their foundation of a sound administrative system upon which the British were later to build.

III

The Portuguese had no cause to worry about any external threat to their interests in Ceylon until the last fifty years of their stay in the island. By contrast, the Dutch felt the first slight breeze of menace from their trade rivals only sixteen years after they had ousted the Portuguese.

In 1672, a French fleet, commanded by Admiral de la Haye appeared in the Indian Ocean. A base was set up near Trincomalee, but the French stay was brief. No sooner had de la Haye departed with his ships than the Dutch compelled the small garrison he had left behind to surrender. In one respect only is the incident memorable.

In the time between the departure of the ships and the arrival of the Dutch, the newcomers decided to send an embassy to the Kandyan court. The results were unfortunate, the fate of the leader of the embassy, M. de la Narolle, bearing a painful resemblance to that of the inebriated Dutch admiral who had headed a similar mission seventy years before. Unable to forget that he was the ambassador of the Sun King, the Frenchman showed such an arrogant contempt for the complicated etiquette of the Kandyan court that Raja Sinha had him put in chains. Afterwards restrictions were relaxed, but he and his suite were fated to be detained permanently in the interior where they joined the thousand-man-strong menagerie of Europeans which the King whimsically collected around himself. Among the captives was a young man called Robert Knox, the son of the captain of a British vessel. Seized with his father and several other members of the ship's crew, Knox was held captive in Kandy for nearly twenty years. He managed at length to escape and his account of his life in the island, published as *An Historical Relation of the Island Ceylon in the East Indies*, furnished material for Defoe's *Robinson Crusoe*. Knox's book provides fascinating insight into seventeenth-century Ceylon, its peoples, its customs, and the court of the great Raja Sinha. So long as they did not venture to conspire against him, the King treated Knox, de la Narolle, and the rest of his assorted bag of French and Dutch, British and Portuguese, Danes and Germans, kindly and generously, quartering them on his villages and allowing them freedom to move about his kingdom. Some of them he employed as soldiers, some as officials, but he built up his troop with the zeal of a true collector indulging an entertaining hobby rather than for strictly utilitarian reasons. The presence of this large body of men is said to have produced a not insignificant strain of European blood among the Kandyans, and even today some of their names, including de Lanarolle [sic], are to be found.

To revert to Trincomalee—as the British struggled with the French to control India, the value of this magnificent harbour on the east coast of Ceylon became increasingly apparent. Although Clive's victories had shifted the weight of British power from the west coast of India to the east, the main naval base had to remain at Bombay because of the lack of a suitable harbour on the other seaboard. Calcutta lay 100 miles up the Hooghli, and Madras was a dangerously open anchorage. Often during the north-east monsoon, the British were obliged to seek Dutch permission to allow them to use the natural harbour at Trincomalee; as H. A. Colgate points out, between 1746 and 1795, the British fleet spent fifteen winters there.[5] But Trincomalee was Dutch, and the Dutch were becoming steadily weaker, overshadowed in Europe and Asia by both the French and the British, with their East India Company near to bankruptcy. The temptation to the British to lay their hands on the port grew steadily stronger, and as a lure far outweighed the rich trade of the island. Equally well placed as it was to support operations both in the Indian Ocean and the Bay of Bengal, the British had to ensure that they, and not the French, controlled the harbour.

In 1762, during the Seven Years' War, the British made their first tentative move, sending John Pybus, a choleric member of the Madras Council, on an embassy to Kandy in response to a request from King Kirti Sri. At that time, the Kandyans still held a small part of their country's coastline, and Pybus was instructed to discover whether the King would grant the British a harbour and allow them a share in the cinnamon trade. Pybus found the Kandyans happy enough to grant these concessions. In return, however, they wanted military aid in their struggle with Van Eck, and to this Pybus lacked the authority to agree. The Kandyans very soon realized that the British were ready to offer little or nothing in return for the privileges they were seeking. Not surprisingly the negotiations proved abortive and Pybus was returned to his ship with due ceremony. Pybus's report vividly captures the rigorous and time-consuming formality of the Kandyan court that enraged him as it did so many others both before and afterwards; it tells us also what the capital city looked like three years before Van Eck sacked it.[6] But the mission did more harm than good. It served only to alarm the Dutch and to give the Kandyans cause to mistrust the British intentions.

Twenty years later, Dutch embroilment in the American War of Independence gave Britain no choice but to seize Trincomalee. This they did in 1782, and from their foothold on the coast despatched another embassy to Kandy, this time in charge of Mr Hugh Boyd. He was a more patient man than Pybus and had a clearer brief, but he met with no more success than his predecessor. Disillusioned by their previous experiences, the Kandyans informed Boyd that they were not prepared to deal with an envoy from the East India Company; they wished to see an ambassador from the King of England himself, a not unreasonable request in the circumstances. On his return voyage Boyd was unlucky enough to be captured by the French fleet which, a little later, wrenched Trincomalee back from the British. The valiant Admiral Suffren was in command and Captain Hay Macdowall, the British commander, capitulated after only a token resistance. Impregnable though the fort at Trincomalee appears, perched on its sheer cliffs above the sea and having a landward frontage of only 150 yards to defend, the place always fell with startling ease to its attackers. To some extent the British fears proved to be groundless; at the end of the war the French were constrained to hand the port back to the Dutch.

A decade later Europe was at war once again and the armies of Republican France were surging across Europe. Most of the Dutch welcomed their revolutionary conquerors with enthusiasm and co-operated with them in setting up the Batavian Republic in the Netherlands. The Stadtholder, Prince William V, fled to

England, where his hosts persuaded him to urge the Governors of the Dutch possessions in the East Indies to accept British protection for the duration of the war. The Stadtholder's message was passed to Madras and transmitted from there to the authorities in Colombo. No time was allowed for the Dutch to reply. Hard behind the message came an expeditionary force directed against Trincomalee. It was an unscrupulous but understandable move. War with the Mahrattas and Mysore was imminent, and a French fleet might arrive at any time to support the Indian princes. Mindful that the Dutch in Ceylon might throw in their lot with the Batavian government, the British could hardly risk their enemy forestalling them at Trincomalee.

On 26 August, 1795, Colonel Stuart, an old and experienced officer of the Madras Army, who went by the nickname of 'Old Row', captured Trincomalee at the head of 1,100 British infantry and two Indian battalions. Its defence by a garrison composed primarily of 'quiet merchants and mechanics'[7] was derisory. The Dutch were both militarily and psychologically unprepared for war.[8] Loyalties were split between the Stadtholder and the Batavian government, and the supporters of the former were doubtful about the meaning of the instructions he had sent to them, the vagueness of which was possibly deliberate. Of the defenders of Trincomalee only a party of Malays acquitted themselves with credit. Stripped naked they crept out of the fort in the darkness to spike the guns of a British battery and dispose of the men on duty with their krises.

The ineffective resistance of the Dutch at Trincomalee set a pattern that was to be repeated everywhere. After taking Fort Ostenburg, which commanded the entrance to the harbour at Trincomalee, and then Batticaloa, the British forces sailed round the coast in large open boats, capturing Jaffnapatam and the string of Dutch coastal stations that stretched southwards towards Negombo, twenty miles short of Colombo. The campaign was not too unpleasant: every night the boats were pulled up on to the open beach where the soldiers cooked their evening meal, only the nightly rain marring what otherwise could have been a relatively comfortable voyage.

After receiving reinforcements at Negombo, Stuart started

south by land towards Colombo on 7 February. His route ran through a rich and beautiful country along the bank of a vast lagoon, separated from the ocean by a spit of coconut-clad land that somehow resisted the solid breakers swept in each year by the monsoon. But attractive country nearly always poses thorny tactical problems for advancing troops. The defiles, the numerous streams and the two broad rivers which bisected Stuart's path provided the Dutch with copybook opportunities for ambushing and delaying the British. But to their astonishment the British met with no resistance until they were nearing their destination. Then, just outside Colombo, a force of some 300 Malays, commanded by a gallant French officer named Colonel Raymond, rushed the British camp at dawn. After a short and bitter struggle, the British troops repulsed the Malays, killing and wounding half of them at a cost of only fifteen casualties. Raymond himself was mortally hit. Afterwards the British discovered that those few Dutch soldiers who had marched out of Colombo with the Malays had melted away as soon as the city gates closed behind them.

The Dutch might have done better if the machinations of Professor Hugh Cleghorn of St Andrew's University, and also a secret service agent of the British Government, had not deprived them of the services of one of their best regiments. This was a corps of Swiss mercenaries which had been raised by the Comte de Meuron in 1782 for service with the Dutch East India Company. De Meuron, who had returned to Europe in 1786 after handing over the care of his regiment to his brother Pierre, had met Cleghorn and been persuaded by him to transfer his command to the British service in exchange for the sum of £4,000. The Colonel's debts were a little pressing. In September, 1796, Cleghorn and de Meuron arrived in India after an adventurous voyage down the Red Sea in an Arab boat. When Pierre in due course received his instructions (which in true cloak and dagger fashion had been concealed in a Dutch cheese), he was only too pleased to fall in with the plan. Lacking the strength to prevent them leaving, the Dutch had no alternative but to allow the Swiss to sail for India. The Regiment de Meuron gave good service to the British until, in 1816, it was disbanded in Canada. Cleghorn was rewarded with the sum of £5,000 and the post of Crown Secretary of Ceylon. For £9,000 and a little duplicity the British had bought a sound regiment and reduced the Dutch garrison by a quarter of its fighting troops, and the best quarter at that. It was a considerable achievement for a single professor.

When the British appeared before Colombo, Van Anglebeck, the Governor, who had served with Van Eck in Kandy just thirty years before, wasted little time in capitulating, and the British took possession of the city on 16 February. Van Anglebeck had little alternative. A large part of his European troops, few of whom were Hollanders, were unreliable; his Malays were disgusted with the pusillanimous conduct of the Europeans; and many of his officers were active Jacobins who were conspiring against him. It is, nevertheless, hard to avoid contrasting the final days of the Dutch occupation of Ceylon with the way the Portuguese had fought for Colombo one hundred and sixty years before.

Reading the accounts of the campaign, one is left with the impression that the British had little sympathy with the lack of fight shown by the Dutch. A certain frustration that the campaign had not been rather more bloody can be detected. Nevertheless the British soldiers had learned to respect the razor-sharp krises of the Malays, much in the same way that their descendants esteemed the Gurkha soldiers of the Indian Army for their skill with their savage kukris. But it would have been a hard siege if the Dutch had decided to resist. One hundred and seventy-three brass guns and mortars were found in the fort, as well as one hundred and eighty-seven iron guns. Exclusive of ships and stores, the prize money added up to £300,000, an adequate compensation to the officers and soldiers for any lack of excitement.

CHAPTER 3

The Sinhalese

I

Despite the prejudices inherent in Knox's Puritan background, his twenty years' enforced stay among the Kandyans did not give him cause seriously to criticize either the character or the customs of his captors. Living for so long as one of them, speaking their language as if it were his own, and free to travel about the country, Knox's *Historical Relation* is a uniquely accurate and sensitive travel book. Because the standard of living and outlook of the seventeenth-century Sinhalese and English villager were far from disparate, Knox's understanding of his hosts (for they were this rather than jailers) was peculiarly perceptive. What is more Knox could view the Kandyans as his equals. As S. D. Saparamadu points out in his introduction to one of the latest editions of this perenially attractive book, the better living conditions brought about by the industrial revolution had not yet persuaded the European to condescend towards the East. The British Empire and its associated concepts of superiority were still unborn.[1]

The natural dignity of the Kandyans appealed particularly to Knox:

'Their ordinary Plow men and Husbandmen do speak elegantly, and are full of complement. And there is no difference between the ability and speech of a Country-man and a Courtier. . . . They bring up their Children to speak after this manner, and use them to go with errands to great men; and they are able to tell their tale very well also. . . . In

45

their speech the people are bold without sheepish shame facedness, and yet no more confidence than is becoming.'[2]

Knox approved also of his hosts' gentleness of disposition:

'They are not very malicious one towards another; and their anger doth not last long; seldom or never any blood shed among them in their quarrels. It is not customary to strike; and it is very rare that they give a blow as much as to their Slaves;'[3]

There is possibly some exaggeration here, but a natural gentleness existed in the Sinhalese character that was never erased despite the provocation of the horrors to which they were subjected over the centuries. As mentioned earlier, their abassadors to Imperial Rome, when depicting the luxury and wealth of their homeland, had related to an undoubtedly cynical audience that their king was elected by the people on the unusual grounds of age and gentleness of disposition; thirty governors were then assigned by the people to the king and capital punishment could be awarded only by a majority of these governors, a final appeal to a people's court being available to the accused.[4] Nearly two thousand years later, European writers could still note the Sinhalese distaste for cruelty and draw comparison between the harsh and often revolting brutalities of their own penal systems and the comparative leniency practised by the Sinhalese towards their malefactors. Dr Henry Marshall, writing about his experiences in Ceylon during the early days of British rule, commented:

'The general feelings of the people seems to be unfavourable to acts of cruelty. When executions took place in the vicinity of Kandy, whether of indigenous or Malay delinquents, scarcely an inhabitant repaired to the spot to witness the scene, while, perhaps, not a European wife of a soldier of the garrison was absent.'[5]

This is not to suggest, of course, that the Sinhalese were quite devoid of that singular human vice—deliberate cruelty towards their own kind. Although they do not seem to have taken as much pleasure as many races in cruelty for its own sake, they were capable of maltreating their fellows when the need arose. In normal times the death penalty was reserved to the King, and it usually seems to have been used sparingly, although treachery could be punished mercilessly, not unnaturally so in view of the political history of the island. Raja Sinha II, for example, who had been famous in his youth for chivalry and gallantry, degenerated into an embittered tyrant in later years, half demented by his hatred of the Dutch who had so duped and cheated him. His consequent neglect of his kingdom aroused the antagonism of his people and produced a succession of plots, all of which he crushed with remorseless ferocity. According to Knox, specially trained elephants were usually used to kill condemned criminals:

'The King makes use of them for Executioners; they will run their Teeth through the body, and then tear it in pieces, and throw it limb from limb. They have sharp Iron with a socket at three edges, which they put on their teeth at such times;'[6]

Impaling malefactors on sharpened poles was another traditional Sinhalese punishment. But it was a fact that during the last forty years of Kandyan rule, there were only two recorded cases of maiming having been used as a punishment, and serious whippings were the prerogative of the King. Throughout Kandyan history there was scarcely a precedent for the execution of women.[7]

II

It is difficult to avoid the conclusion that the Sinhalese were naturally rather less cruel than most of their fellows, either Asian or European and this absence of basic savagery in their nature probably owes much to Buddhism, one of the main tenets of which forbids the taking of human life, either human or animal. Despite centuries of domination by Hindu or Christian rulers and the material benefits accruing from apostasy, the mass of the Sinhalese people have held fast to their ancient faith, so much so, in fact, that the modern Marxists have found it necessary to make some sort of common cause with this opiate of the people.

A philosophy rather than a religion, Buddhism springs from an acceptance of the basic Hindu dogma that an individual continues to be re-born in some other body, either human or animal, according to the quality of his previous life. Gautama, the Buddha, had stipulated that human suffering stemmed from man's ceaseless craving for things material: his greed, his sensuousness, his avarice and his ambition. Only by relinquishing these desires could he be re-born into a higher state, and to attain this enlightenment he had to follow the Eightfold Path of mental uprightness, right aims and speech, right conduct and honest livelihood, combined with proper effort, mindfulness and concentration. Although the complicated metaphysics of the philosophy are beyond the comprehension of the unsophisticated, its essence forms a background to the colourful ceremonies, the superstitions and the devil-worship that Buddhism has taken under its wing for the spiritual satisfaction of simpler people. Buddhism is, in fact, an integral part of the Sinhala way of life. Delighting in the beauty of simple things, the people find their pleasure in its daily rituals and its periodic ceremonies: the processions on the nights of the full moon, particularly *Wesak* in May, the celebration of Buddha's enlightenment, when paper lanterns are hung outside the houses; the vivid *Esala Perahera* in Kandy when gaily dressed and good-tempered crowds gathered for the processions of magnificently ornamented elephants, accompanied by teams of untiring dancers and musicians; above all, perhaps, the pilgrimage to Sri Pada, the sacred footprint of Buddha on the summit of the 7,000 foot mountain known to the West as Adam's Peak, described so accurately by Marco Polo,[8] and up whose slopes crowds toil before dawn to view the rising of the sun.

The Buddhist *bhikkhus*, like the mediaeval Christian monks, have played a major role in the growth and defence of the culture of their country, a culture derived from the Indian mainland and influenced over the years by changes originating there, but one that has nevertheless developed its own strong native characteristics. Scholarship, based on the classical *Pali*, had been maintained by the *bhikkhus*, and, as in pre-Renaissance Europe, the decorative arts are rooted more in religion than in war or daily life. To Buddhism we owe the glories of Lanka's religious sculpture, its architecture, its decorative carving and the wall-paintings of its temples. Little remains of what secular arts there may have been. Only the palace-fortress of fifth-century Sigiriya, perched

1. A Soldier of the Ceylon Regiment about 1820

2. A Kandyan Chief. The Dissawa of Vellessa

3. A Dissawa administering justice

4. An Adigar in Procession about 1820. This is probably Molligoda.

5. Kandyan music and dancing

like the Jewish Masada on an unscalable rock, has survived in an easily comprehensible form.

For other than spiritual or cultural reasons, the influence of Buddhism on the daily life of the Sinhalese is as vigorous today as it has been in the past. Not only is the *bhikkhu* often the village schoolmaster, but the ideal of service vested in the faith has led its priests to take a leading part in public affairs. With the aristocracy, from whose ranks many were drawn, they were in the habit of exercising a temporizing influence on the excesses of an absolute monarchy. In recent years the *Sangha*, or Buddhist church, has once again become a potent factor in the political life of the country, as has happened in other countries such as Tibet and Vietnam.

III

The dignity of the individual Sinhalese, allied to his delight in the magic of ceremonial, was epitomized in the exaggerated formality of the courts of the Kandyan kings, a formality that not only wore the patience and physical endurance of European ambassadors, but also, as has been mentioned, at times even endangered their safety. Knox, in describing Raja Sinha when he was an old man relates that:

'His Pride and affectation of honour is unmeasurable. Which appears in his Peoples' manner of Address to him, which he either Commands or allows of. When they come before him they fall flat down on their Faces to the Ground at three several times, and then they sit with their legs under them upon their Knees all the time they are in his presence: And when he bids them to be Absent, they go backwards, until they are out of his sight, or a great distance from him. But of Christian People indeed he requires no more than to kneel with their Hats off before him.'[9]

One hundred years later, the sturdy John Pybus, described by the Kandyans 'as a man of tolerable stature and reddish complexion, with very brisk movements',[10] had no stomach for this un-English kneeling. Choleric though he undoubtedly was, he succeeded in exercising a fine self-control when faced with the frustrating discomforts of Kandyan court ceremonial.

After a six-day wait in his lodgings at Gannoruwa on the far side of the Mahaweli Ganga, Pybus was at last granted an audience. To the accompaniment of an eleven-gun salute, he set out at 7 pm in pouring rain on his five-mile progress to the palace, escorted by guards, drummers and musicians provided by his hosts. Ahead, resting on a silver tray and wrapped in folds of muslin, went his letter of introduction, carried aloft under a decorative canopy of Chinese silk. At the river, over which the party was tediously ferried with the aid of a single 'Cannoe', Pybus was obliged to leave his 'Pallenkeen', and had to complete the journey trudging damply through the mud hand-in-hand with his escorting Kandyan general. Twice the party was halted to await permission to proceed, and when at 11.30 pm, two hundred yards short of the palace, the weary, wet and famished envoy was told that he had to kneel to present his letter to the King, his mood was hardly complaisant. He protested volubly on two grounds: he should have been told earlier, and he did not come on the same suppliant footing as the Dutch ambassadors.

After a final delay outside the palace gates Pybus was admitted into a courtyard, where he found three state elephants and three horses, all richly caparisoned, waiting to receive him. Here he complied with a request to remove his muddy shoes, and he patiently listened to a series of complimentary speeches of welcome before being led into a further court where a guard of twelve men, dressed in long white linen coats and armed with halberds, awaited him. Pybus could now see a set of white curtains covering the entrance to what could only be the audience chamber,[11] but after he had kicked his heels for a further fifteen minutes, the curtains were flung aside to reveal nothing more than another set of red draperies beyond. With the silver tray now carried aloft above his head, Pybus proceeded forward, six sets of curtains being consecutively swept aside before him until at last the King was revealed, seated on a gold and jewel-encrusted throne raised three feet above the floor. The monarch was a splendid sight. Across a close-fitting vest he wore an open robe of gold tissue with a gold-embroidered belt encircling his waist. His cap, embroidered also with gold, was topped by a small crown set with precious stones. Sandals of crimson velvet decorated with strips of gold covered his feet.

As the final curtain was pulled back, the courtiers accompanying the Englishman had prostrated themselves at full length six successive times. Pybus himself, with the silver tray raised above his head, stayed doggedly upright until he was pulled down upon one knee by the skirts of his coat. Four times in all this athletic ceremony was repeated, the party advancing a few yards towards the throne after each instalment, until at last they all came to a halt at the edge of a large Persian carpet. Pybus was then led by two ministers to the throne, presented his letter to the King, and received permission to seat himself in whatever manner he found most convenient, a concession he was grateful to receive. He now had the opportunity to examine his surroundings. Except where the Persian carpet was spread, the dimly lit audience chamber, about fifty feet in length and thirty feet across, was lined with white cloth—walls, floor and ceiling as well. Muslin-covered arches, ornamented with red-spotted ruffs, divided the room into sections. On each side sat three palace officials holding the King's ceremonial golden weapons, their mouths covered by narrow slips of cloth to prevent their breath defiling their monarch. At the foot of the throne knelt the Adigar, one of the King's principal ministers, through whom the ruler addressed his remarks to Pybus. After receiving each remark the Adigar prostrated himself, passed it on to an official who sat near Pybus. From the latter it went to a Malabar doctor, from the doctor to an interpreter and from an interpreter to Pybus himself. Pybus's replies followed the same route. In a fine understatement, the Englishman described the procedure as 'tiresome and troublesome'. Only formal pleasantries were exchanged but every word was recorded by a secretary who sat in front of a square wooden stool illuminated by a wax candle. When at long last the audience concluded and Pybus was allowed to withdraw, he arrived back at his lodgings at sunrise 'never more fatigued or disgusted with any Jaunt in my Life'.

That Pybus's mission failed seems in no way due to his reluctance to undergo this wearying and frustrating ceremonial. Both the King and his officials were anxious to do business with the representative of a prospective ally and they seem to have tried their uttermost to bend their rigid ritual and etiquette to avoid inflicting too much discomfort on the envoy. Pybus's story leaves one with the impression that perhaps the procedure somewhat embarrassed the Kandyans, conflicting as it did with the good manners due to a respected guest.

For the first 150 miles of Pybus's circuitous route up to Kandy, the path led through a poverty-stricken countryside, the few villages poor and wretched-looking, with little in the way of live-stock and only just enough paddy to keep the inhabitants alive. Forty or fifty miles short of the capital, a startling change occurred. Suddenly the land was thickly populated and prosperous:

'. . . as well cultivated as so mountainous a Country will admit. Indeed the Villages between the Hills afford the most beautiful landskapes that can be conceived.'[12]

This transformation, Pybus discovered, had two causes. Not only was the land richer because the rainfall was heavier, but successive kings had made a habit of concentrating their people in the neighbourhood of the capital so as to make access to the interior of the island more difficult for invaders.

IV

So long as he was left in peace, it was not too difficult for the Kandyan peasant to live in simple prosperity in this fruitful land, even though he had to pay his share of the expense of maintaining the court and throne, his provincial government, and an expensive religious establishment. Fresh fruit and curds augmented his basic diet of rice, flavoured with well-spiced fish or unripe fruit, boiled to make 'carrees, to use the Portuguez word, that is somewhat to eat with and relish their rice'.[13] *Kurakkan*, a poor type of under-sized millet, was, however, much eaten, particularly in the poverty-stricken areas of the south-east. Meat and poultry the peasant rarely saw, although his betters might live rather more richly. But this was not necessarily so. Raja Sinha possessed:

'Geese, Ducks, Turkeys, Pigeons, which he keeps tame, but none else may. Turkeys he delights not in, because they change the colour of their heads: Neither doth he kill any of these to eat, nor any other creatures of what sort soever, and he hath that he keeps tame.'[14]

High living is, of course, rare in the tropics, even among those rich enough to afford the luxuries of the table, ceremonial communal eating being an invention of colder climates such as Europe and China where an indoor activity is needed to fill the long winter evenings.

The country was blessed with a profusion of fruit. Percival, in 1805, found pineapples, oranges, pomegranates, citrons, limes, melons, plums, pumpkins, water-melons, squashes, figs, almonds, mulberries, raisins, bilberries and bogberries. He also discovered delicacies new to him: mangoes, papayas, custard-apples, shaddock, plantain, jack-fruit and bread-fruit.[15] The coconut was cultivated but most fruit grew wild and, as an anodyne to the daily cares of life, the cultivator chewed his *bonne bouche* of betel-leaf, filled with areca nut and lime of burnt shells, a mixture that stained his lips and teeth bright red, so repellent to the European. Buddhism forbade alcohol and, as yet, the Sinhalese scorned to touch it. Wine, as his contemptuous proverb put it, was as natural to white men as milk is to children.

The villager lived in a simple clay-daubed hut, roofed with coconut leaves in the maritime provinces and with rice-straw in the hills. His chief's house would be raised on a low terrace and tiled, built in a square round an open courtyard and presenting a blank external wall. The *dissawa* or provincial governor's house could even be double-storied with narrow balconies and painted walls, but it was still a modest building. Large rooms were not needed for communal eating and drinking, and architectural magnificence was reserved for religious buildings and, to a much lesser extent, for the king's palaces.

The Sinhalese are a handsome race. Well proportioned both in build and feature, with skins the colour of an antique rosewood table, the men are trim and bear themselves in military style, while the delicate beauty of even an over-burdened peasant woman can survive frequent pregnancies and the approach of middle age. Their looks have little in common with the flaccid, limp-featured creatures portrayed in the idiom of their eighteenth-century artists, but the evidence of the European draughtsmen of the time confirms that their features have in no way changed during the past two centuries. How misleading historically an artistic convention can be! At the time the men wore beards, usually neatly trimmed, with their hair long and gathered behind in a knot. Rank was marked by the quality and quantity of wearing apparel, and differences were jealously preserved. Normal wear was a long piece of cloth reaching to the ankles. The head was covered either by a round starched hat, or by a further length of cloth wrapped like a turban but leaving the top of the head bare; only the lowest caste went uncovered. At the other end of the scale a nobleman in his best was a magnificent sight. Over narrow trousers he would wear as many as six or eight *tuppotti* of fine muslin, one on top of the other to give his hips an unnaturally rotund appearance. His short buttoned jacket, in which the influence of the early Portuguese doublet was clear, would be stuffed and puffed so that his chest matched his hips, and around his neck could be a pleated ruff, topped with gold chains, the last-named marks of distinction bestowed upon him by his monarch. On his head would be an ornate four or six-cornered hat, topped with gold finials, its shape signifying his rank. The embroidered belt around his waist, harbouring dagger and sword, still further exaggerated his girth. Such a man was all-powerful in the province he ruled, maintaining a state comparable to his king. When he progressed abroad, he was surrounded by parasol-bearers and musicians and his approach was heralded by the cracking of twenty-foot long whips.

V

In the more fertile areas of the country, little labour was needed in order to maintain a tolerable standard of living, and, in any case, much of it was carried out by the women, although the Sinhalese have never treated their wives and daughters as beasts of burden in the fashion of so many races. If a man worked too hard, he would only attract the increased attention of the tax-gatherers, so hard unrewarding labour held out no attraction to him. His inability to find virtue in toil annoyed the British as much as it had the Dutch before them, and, as happens so often in a country where simple tastes can be satisfied by an easy climate working on a fertile soil, 'indolent' was the expletive commonly levelled by the European at both the Kandyan and the lowland Sinhalese. One result of the reluctance of the Sinhalese peasant to become a day-labourer was that the traditional industries and crafts of the island tended to be in the hands either of landless labourers imported from south India or of specialist castes.

Cinnamon had been the primary attraction that brought both the Portuguese and the Dutch to the island. The high-grade variety of the spice was found in no other country, and it was still the main commercial crop when the British displaced the Dutch, although its importance had by then been somewhat diminished by the production of inferior varieties in India and other countries. The inner bark of a large shrub that grew in the dank, tropical jungle, the harsh unpleasant work of collecting the spice was the hereditary responsibility of the Salagama caste. They were serfs and had been for many hundreds of years, first to the Ceylonese kings and then to the successive European conquerors. They hated the work and avoided it as far as they could. The Dutch could only maintain production by a combination of brutal legislation and unofficial savagery. To destroy or damage a plant was a capital offence; for a Salagama to produce less than his stipulated monthly quota of cinnamon could well invoke the penalties of the whip, the branding-iron and the amputation knife. During the early days of British rule, the superintendents of cinnamon gardens continued to flog those of their labourers who failed to gather the stipulated 30 lbs monthly, and the unfortunate Salagamas were not released from their wretched thraldom until the year 1832.[16]

In their remorselessly efficient manner, the Dutch increased the productivity of their new Ceylonese estates in a variety of ways. Much of the paddy-land, ruined during the later chaotic years of Portuguese rule, was brought back into cultivation. New cash crops such as tobacco, sugar-cane, coffee and pepper were tried out; cottage industries such as the dyeing and printing of

55

cloth were developed. All this needed labour, and, faced with the Sinhalese reluctance to toil for the profit of their new rulers, the Dutch introduced large numbers of industrious workers from south India to supplement the many Tamils who already populated the north and much of the east coast of the island. During the subsequent century of British rule, a third wave of immigrant Tamils arrived to work the vast coffee, rubber and tea plantations that were to transform not just the economy but the very appearance of Ceylon.

The pearl fisheries and the gem industry were also in Indian hands. When the British arrived, both were in a state of decline, unscientific fishing and poor control having nearly ruined the former while the mining of precious stones had for many years been discouraged by the Kandyan monarchs, who had more than enough jewels for their own use and wished to discourage trade with the Dutch.

The Sinhalese were, in fact, as little interested in trade as they were in manual labour. Because of this the commerce of the country had fallen into the hands of the more recently arrived immigrant races. As well as the Hindus of south India, variously referred to as Malabars and Tamils, many of whom worked as artisans, traders and clerks, there was a sizeable Muslim population, mostly of Indian, but partly of Malay and Arab descent. Wealthier than the Hindus, they were usually either merchants or functionaries, and they commonly went by the name of Moors, a name given to them by the Portuguese who equated all Muslims with their neighbours on the North African coast. Another large minority group was the Burghers, descendants of unions between the Hollanders and the older inhabitants of the island. Because they were townsmen and were quick to forsake their Dutch tongue for English, in the early days of the British occupation they were useful as clerks, minor civil servants and policemen. Soon, however, they started to man the professions needed in a developing country (particularly the law), and with their qualities of shrewdness, application and intelligence, they quickly attained a status higher than that of any other similar community in colonial Asia.

The presence of these industrious Tamils, Moors and Burghers accentuated the impression the Sinhalese gave of being indolent. They were also accused of another vice which vexed their conquerors even more. This was treachery. Although the earlier colonial powers had denied the need for fidelity when dealing with non-Christian races, the ethical and religious awakening of the latter half of the eighteenth century had produced in the British a novel awareness of the virtues of veracity and straight dealing, even when negotiating with those they imagined to be their inferiors. It is, of course, a truism that the well-mannered Asian oils the wheels of social and business intercourse by avoiding harsh contradictions and providing his listener with what he wants to hear. Nevertheless, the so-called treachery of the Sinhalese amounted to more than the usual schism of understanding between Oriental and Occidental. In protecting their country from attack, guile was one of the few weapons in the Sinhalese armoury, other than their forests and their climate. What is more, they had met with little but deceit in their dealings with their European enemies, and they were in the habit of paying back in the coin they received. Treacherous they certainly could be. They hardly lacked justification. The Kandyan was said to be even falser than the lowlander. This may well have been so; he had suffered the more and held out the longer.

Criticize them though they did, the British found much to admire in the Kandyan people. Knox saw them as 'outwardly fair, and seemingly courteous, and of more complaisant carriage, speech and better behaviour than the Lowlanders'.[17] Dr Henry Marshall, himself a Lowland Scot, liked them because they were 'hardy, brave, and, like most mountaineers, passionately attached to their native hills; and, on many occasions, they have evinced an ardent love of liberty, or, at least, a detestation of foreign conquest',[18] all qualities that appealed to the early nineteenth-century British after their successes against Napoleonic Imperialism.

Marshall, however, thought that he could not improve on Knox's summing up of the Kandyans, written 130 years before the Scot first saw Ceylon. It read:

'In short, in Carriage and Behaviour they are very grave and stately like unto the Portugals, in understanding quick and apprehensive, in design subtil and crafty, in discourse courteous but full of Flatteries, naturally inclined to temperance both in meat and drink, but not to Chastity, near and Provident in their Families, commending good Husbandry. In their dispositions not passionate, neither hard to be reconciled again when angry. In their promises very unfaithful, approving lying in themselves, but misliking it in others; delighting in sloth, deferring labour till urgent necessity constrain them, neat in apparel, nice in eating; and not given much to sleep.'[19]

CHAPTER 4
Taking Stock

I

As Colonel Stuart's British and Indian soldiers were stumbling southwards along the ploughed-up sandy track towards Colombo, cursing as they heaved their guns across the marshy patches and waiting for the Dutch ambush that never came, inland on their left flank a large Kandyan force had been operating in parallel with them. The presence of these unexpected allies had been due to a successful diplomatic coup brought off at the Kandyan court by Mr Robert Andrews, a Madras civil servant.

Andrews had landed with Stuart's force at Trincomalee. As soon as the fort fell he had moved straight up to Kandy, arriving there on 15 September, 1795. Ready as ever to ally themselves with a newcomer in order to rid themselves of their current affliction, the Kandyans were prepared to co-operate whole-heartedly with the British against their Dutch enemies. In only a month Andrews settled the terms of a preliminary treaty of alliance and friendship, and then left for Madras, taking Kandyan ambassadors with him, where they could discuss the terms of a more comprehensive treaty with his superiors. Meanwhile the Kandyans put their army into the field and made arrangements to provision the British troops, attaching an official to Stuart's headquarters to act in the role of a liaison officer and settle the details of what had to be done. But the campaign progressed so smoothly, and the supply of rations from Madras was so well organized, that Stuart found that he had no need to take advantage of the proferred Kandyan help. In any case he was reluctant to accept it. His aim was to slip into the Dutch forts as unobtrusively as possible without the embarrassment of large bodies of Kandyan soldiery nearby. The situation was not easy. Stuart knew that the Kandyans wanted to regain some sort of foothold on the coast, and this he had to prevent without too bitterly offending them, and so destroying the cordial relations Andrews had established with their leaders. Five days after he took Colombo, he reported:

'Our lately acquired ally, the King of Candia, sent his Generals with the greatest part of his forces to co-operate with us, and considerable quantities of provisions—fortunately from the rapidity of our motions, and being amply supplied ourselves by the Madras Government, we had not occasion for either. His Principal General is now here with me, and I have desired him to send back his Troops to their own Country with all possible despatch, which he has promised me to do.'[1]

In the south the Kandyans had gained possession of Matara, but they showed both tact and discretion in evacuating it as the British approached. At this stage they were ready to concede much to avoid a clash with their allies. Probably they were hopeful of the outcome of the treaty then being discussed in Madras. In any case they would have realized the futility of provoking a conflict with the powerful British army when they were so far away from the security of their mountains. Passively, therefore, they marched back to their own country—a kingdom that had changed little since Knox lived there a century and a half before.

The return of the Kandyan army coincided with the last stages of the treaty-talks in Madras. Terms had been agreed, although not without dissension. The British were to inherit the Maritime Provinces from the Dutch, but the stranglehold this coastal encirclement represented to Kandy was to be slackened a little by the concession of what was described as a 'situation' on the coast, granted to the Kandyans for the sole purpose of allowing them to obtain supplies of salt and fish. At the same time they were to be permitted to maintain ten ships, free of search and duty, for trade with the outside world, and the commercial monopoly previously enjoyed by the Dutch was to be replaced by what amounted to little more than a trade preference for the British. Furthermore each side agreed actively to help one another against each other's enemies, a promise which the British would have found difficulty in keeping had they been obliged, by the Treaty of Amiens, to return the Provinces to the Dutch.

Both sides had two years in which to ratify the Treaty, but neither did so. The Kandyans decided that their ambassadors had obtained too little from it. They had anticipated the return of some of the territory they had conceded to the Dutch at the end of the war in 1766, together with the transfer of a proper port, not the promise of this nebulous 'situation'. For their part, the British were in possession of everything which the Dutch had enjoyed, and they had very little to gain but goodwill in acting generously towards the Kandyans. The Kandyans were the losers. Never again were they to be offered terms even as favourable as these.[2]

It was not long before Kandyan resentment took a tangible form. As a result of gross maladministration, the country districts around Colombo were in open revolt by early 1797. The unrest spread rapidly to the east coast, and soon even the placid Tamil north was disturbed. Although the coastal Sinhalese had long lost the habit of rebelling against their foreign rulers, they managed to acquit themselves with not a little credit.[3] For a year they harassed with some success the punitive columns of Sepoys which the British sent to discipline them, fighting from the shelter of the jungle which edged their villages. At times they even made ill-conceived attempts to build amateurish fortifications and boldly wait for the troops to attack them; on one occasion this happened only twelve miles from Colombo, and both sides suffered quite heavy casualties in the subsequent fighting.

The Kandyans were quick to profit from the difficulties of the British. They succoured the rebels with supplies and gave them moral backing, even to the extent of receiving one of the leaders at court and appointing him formally to rule the Colombo *dissawa* in the King's name. Even though they refrained from joining in the fighting, the threat that they might do so forced the British to scatter garrisons at focal points along the frontier to guard against the danger of Kandyan incursions.[4]

In the circumstances prevailing at the time, it is hard to see how the injustices that provoked the unrest could have been avoided. The country was under military rule, and the soldiers were understandably preoccupied by the fear of a French counter-stroke against the island and the clear hostility of the Kandyans. The few newly arrived civil servants from Madras were ignorant of the language, the laws and the customs of Ceylon, but there was no one else, other than army officers, who could administer the island. As yet the Dutch officials were not sufficiently recon-ciled to their conquerors to co-operate, while the long-term future of the Provinces was too uncertain for civil servants to be sent out from the United Kingdom. The complications of the land tenure (totally different in the Tamil and the Sinhalese areas) were too much for the newcomers; injudicious taxes were levied to raise badly-needed revenue; and, to make matters worse, the Madras Government was so wary of the powers of the *mudaliyars*, the local officials who had worked for the Dutch, that it removed many of them from office and replaced them with *amildars*, imported from India.

It was fortunate for the British that the government of the Provinces was placed, at this critical juncture, in the hands of Pierre de Meuron, who had returned to the island as a brigadier-general in July, 1797. An able and far-sighted officer, with an intimate knowledge of Ceylon, he dealt successfully with the dis-turbances. At the same time, he set about tackling the roots of the injustices that had caused the trouble. As chairman of the subsequent Committee of Investigation, which the Madras Government set up, he recommended abolishing the newly-levied taxes and reinstating the local *mudaliyars* to the rank and auth-ority they had previously enjoyed.

II

Before the news of this revolt reached Whitehall, the Cabinet had reached the conclusion that they could well ignore the possibility of ever having to hand the Provinces back to the Dutch. A permanent form of government could, therefore, be established. As a result the name of the Hon Frederick North was submitted to the Crown for the new appointment of Governor, Commander-in-Chief and Captain-General over the Territories in Ceylon. North was the third son of George III's famous prime minister, and he was destined, like his father, to succeed to the Earldom of Guildford. Wealthy, widely-travelled and well-connected, North was a not untypical pro-consul of his age. When he landed in Ceylon, he was thirty-two years of age, and his previous administrative experience had been confined to a two-year spell as a member of the Commons for a pocket-borough, a year as Comptroller of the Customs of the Port of London, and a tour as Secretary of State to the Viceroy of Corsica in 1795 and 1796, when British forces were occupying the island. North's experience might well have been less and he did not lack other qualifications to fit him for the role. He was a man of many parts, civilized and intelligent. A member of the Royal Society and a skilled Greek scholar, many years of travel in Europe as a young man had left him fluent in German, French, Romaic, Italian, Spanish and Russian. He was a near fanatic philhellene and had even been admitted to the Greek Orthodox Church. Deeply committed to the principles of Greek humanism, he was one of a new breed of colonial administrators, the members of which were soon to arrive in Asia in increasing numbers; they were attracted not merely by the possibility of feathering their own nests but by ideas of bringing sound government to those thought to be so sadly in need of its benefits. North was also a person of charm, a good conversationalist, and in most ways very honest, qualities which made it easy for him to win the confidence and loyalty of his staff. His virtues were manifold. On paper he was the perfect man for what was clearly to be a most demanding task. His failings lay in his over-enthusiasm, his impulsiveness and a lack of physical robustness, the legacy of a frail childhood.

The new Governor landed at Colombo on 19 October, 1798, accompanied by a suite of nine officials, the foundation stock for the future Ceylon Civil Service, second only in repute to the I.C.S. Among the nine were three thirteen-year-old cadets, sent out to learn the language and fit themselves for more responsible posts. One of them, George Lusignan, even at that age spoke nearly as many languages as North, a facility that probably commended itself to his new master.[5] Hugh Cleghorn, claiming his reward as Crown Secretary for his part in the de Meuron affair, headed the party. His stay was short. By 1800 he was back in Scotland, suspended by North for gross negligence, possibly amounting to connivance, in the fraudulent running of the government pearl fisheries.

In itself, North's task was difficult enough, but it was rendered more so by the terms of his appointment. The East India Company was reluctant to surrender its profitable and useful conquest, but the British Government wanted to run the newly acquired territories as a Crown Colony, unconnected in any way with the Company. The consequence was an unwieldy compromise, which came to be known as Dual Control. Although North's own appointment and those of his accompanying officials, who were to be responsible for the general administration of the country, had been made by the Crown, the Governor was to report to the Secretary of State in London through the Court of Directors, and he was also to be subject to the orders of the Governor-General at Fort William. Revenue and trade remained in Company hands, with the Madras officials who had made such a hash of things still in charge but now under North's immediate direction. North was to be Commander-in-Chief with the general officer commanding the troops subordinate to him, but his instructions in this respect were vague; the system could be worked so long as North saw eye to eye with his senior soldier, but without this goodwill it proved impossible to operate.[6]

North wasted no time in indulging his zest for reform. Basing his plans on the recommendations of de Meuron's Committee, within the year he had reorganized the executive and the judiciary. In theory at least, he separated the two, and he retained the Romano-Dutch legal code which continued to operate even after the British were in their turn to leave the island. There were few subjects the Governor did not tackle—revenue, land tenure, trade, medicine[7] and education. Inevitably the entrenched Madras civil servants resented all this change. Their standards of honesty

6. *The Fort at Badulla about 1820*

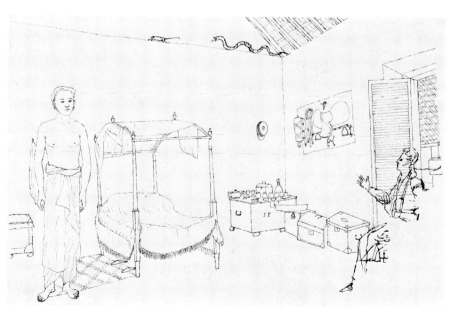

7. *'My First Day in Ceylon'—an impression of a junior officer's room*

8. *The Palace from the South-West about 1820, showing the main gateway and the Pattiripuwa or Octangular Tower*

9. *Another view of the Palace about 1820. This shows the state of dilapidation of the area after a few years of British occupation*

all but matched those of their Indian subordinates; they disliked the appointment of an outsider and they rightly feared the outcome of his investigations into their malpractices. Back in Madras, their colleagues supported them, resenting as they did their loss of control over the newly acquired territories. North's struggle against the 'Madras click', as he dubbed it, was prolonged and bitter, but after he had managed to remove the worst of its members,[8] the rest slowly came to heel, and he was able to establish some sort of authority over this section of his staff.

III

Only three weeks after his arrival, North found it necessary to direct his energies towards the problems of the kingdom of Kandy. Three months earlier King Rajadhi Raja Sinha had died and the selection of his successor had, in the customary fashion, fallen to the late King's ministers, the most formidable of whom was Pilima Talauva, the *mahadigar* or first minister. Himself of the old royal stock and overwhelmingly ambitious, the Adigar made little secret of the fact that his ultimate aim was to govern Kandy himself, and so bring back a Sinhalese dynasty in place of the Dravidian Malabars who had ruled the country since 1739. The precise steps by which he planned to do this are a matter for conjecture, as no reliable Sinhalese sources have yet been discovered to throw any light upon the background to his tortuous intrigues.

Power lay in the hands of the feudal ruling families, all of whom would have preferred to see a king of Sinhala stock on the throne. But mutual agreement upon a candidate from among themselves was impossible, with the result that the Nayakkar dynasty was maintained in power by the intense jealousy that divided the Kandyan oligarchy. The Tamil kings had also made themselves popular with the common people. They had been responsible for the glamorous Buddhist revival, and they had ruled the country with a light rein. Moreover, once a king was enthroned, he gained protection from the semi-divine attributes with which the Kandyans deliberately enhanced the status of

E

their rulers, and from the loyalty he commanded from the members of his immediate court circle. Once chosen, a King was, therefore, not easy to remove.

At the time the old king died, Pilima Talauva was too unsure of the support he commanded to gamble on seizing the throne himself. So he decided to install a puppet and chose an obscure and seemingly innocuous youth named Kannasamy, the eighteen-year-old son of the sister of one of the dead king's widows. Ostensibly the boy had nothing in his favour but a good figure,[9] but a stubborn tradition has persisted in Kandy that he was, in fact, Pilima Talauva's natural son.[10] Be that as it may, this apparent nonentity, who was to be the last of the Kandyan kings, was invested with the Sword of State as Sri Wikrama Raja Sinha, while Pilima Talauva consolidated his personal position by assassinating or executing a handful of his principal opponents, including the Second Adigar, a man described as being of an 'integrity rare in the court of Kandy'.[11]

North's letter to Sri Wikrama, in which he announced his arrival in Ceylon and professed the closest of friendship, was a model of traditional diplomatic obsequiousness and hyperbole.[12] However, the sentiments of the letter were quickly confirmed by the new Govenor's expulsion of three Kandyan refugees from Colombo and his rejection of the overtures of one of several pretenders to the new King's throne. As yet North was not thinking of territorial expansion. His policy at the time is revealed in his despatch to the Company of 26 November, advising them that it was pointless to conclude a treaty with Kandy. The aim, he suggested, should be to follow the example of the Dutch and keep in their hands the whole export and import commerce of Kandy, but to treat the country with more liberality than the Dutch, not encroaching on its territories.[13]

On 14 February, four months after he took office, North had his first meeting with Pilima Talauva. It was held at Sitawaka, by the banks of the Kelani Ganga, on the frontier between Kandy and the Maritime Provinces, the customary place for conferences between the Kandyans and whoever might be occupying the lowlands at the time. It was a magnificent occasion.[14] The Adigar was escorted by 5,000 followers, and although there is no record of the size of North's train, even when he was travelling on routine business he was in the habit of taking with him a company of soldiers, 160 palanquin bearers, 400 coolies and fifty servants, besides a string of elephants and horses. The Kandyan gifts to North included a gold chain, a ruby ring and elephants, but there is no record of what the Governor produced in return.[15]

North started the talks by making it clear that the provisions of the 1796 Treaty were null and void; it had not been ratified within the stipulated two-year period. After this opening, the discussions jogged along in a friendly manner to an inconclusive end, the Adigar complaining of the influence of the Malabars at court and hinting obscurely at some plan he had in his mind. The Adigar had, in fact, cast his first fly over North, but the fish had failed to rise to it.

The correspondence which the two men conducted during the next twelve months, supplemented by the overtures which various opponents of the Adigar made to North, gave the latter a much clearer picture of the internal affairs of Kandy than he had possessed when he met the Adigar at Sitawaka. The mountain kingdom, North came to realize, was inherently unstable. At any time her rulers might decide to foment or support unrest in the Maritime Provinces, and her existence impeded the free flow of trade about the island and prevented the construction of the much-needed roads between the east and the west coasts. In a pragmatic world there was little justification for such an annoying little state to retain its independence. British policy when dealing with such a neighbour was well defined by Henry Dundas, the Secretary of State for War (who was also responsible for the colonies), in a minute he appended to a civil servant's report on North's despatches:

'Our great care must be to do nothing by force or concussion of any kind, but if by conciliation and fair treaty we obtain a substantial right of interference in the Government of Candia, our great attention must be to improve the happiness of the people and the prosperity of the country. The sword must be exclusively ours and the civil government in all its branches must be virtually ours, but through the medium of its ancient native organs.'[17]

This minute was written nine months after North's next round of tortuous discussions with the Adigar, but it reflects the principles which, by now, were guiding the Governor.

When the two men met again in January, 1800, Pilima Talauva wasted no time in making his intentions clear. According to James Cordiner, the Colombo Garrison Chaplain and North's eulogist, at the very first meeting the Adigar suggested that North should help him to kill the King so that the British could become masters of the country—a proposal, Cordiner asserts, 'so horrible to the feelings of a virtuous mind,' that North indignantly rejected it.[18] There is some doubt as to whether the Adigar did express himself so bluntly (it was certainly not in his character to have done so), but during the subsequent eleven meetings he had with the British, he made no secret of his desire to remove his monarch by one means or another and so occupy the throne himself. The most likely explanation for the Adigar acting in this way was that he had now discovered that he had chosen the wrong man to be a puppet. Sri Wikrama had started to show unexpected strength and it was impossible to remove him except with British help. At the time of the previous round of talks, Pilima Talauva had probably suspected how matters were going but the events of the intervening year had confirmed him in his views.

So long as the decencies could be observed and the King's life preserved, North was quite ready to see him supplanted. To a blatant invasion of Kandy, North would not, however, acquiesce. By some means the King had himself to be persuaded to invite British troops into the country to afford him protection against his enemies. If this could be arranged and British troops established in the highlands, the King could then retain his titular trappings and live in safety in either Kandy or Colombo, while nominal authority would pass to the Adigar who would be supported by the British garrison. Dominated in this fashion, Kandy would have been on the same footing as the protected native states in India, a status that the Adigar may possibly have been prepared to accept. Perhaps, however, he was confident that, once he were in charge of the country, any British garrison could be dealt with in the manner of its Portuguese and Dutch forerunners.

There seems to have been something a little frenzied in the way Pilima Talauva strove to come to some sort of agreement with the British before the talks ended. At the time he was a very sick man, suffering from VD and fistulas, and the growing status of the youthful King must have been alarming to the ageing minister. He made no secret of the fact that his influence with his monarch was waning, and it is strange, in view of this, that North failed to realize that the Adigar lacked the power at the Kandyan court to persuade Sri Wikrama to jettison his independence by asking for foreign troops to protect himself. The discussions did, however, end with an agreement that the British should send an ambassador to Kandy with the task of negotiating a new treaty between the two countries. Approval was also obtained for the embassy to be escorted by 1,000 soldiers and six guns, a force, the British reasoned, capable of doing one of two things. While it was large enough to intimidate the King and the opponents of the Adigar, the show of strength could also persuade the King to ask for permanent protection if he happened to be alarmed for his own safety.[19]

The British military commander, Major-General Hay Macdowall (the same officer who seventeen years before had surrendered Trincomalee to Suffren) was chosen as the ambassador. North's instructions to him were in no way ambiguous. The essential point was to obtain the administration. The life and dignity of the King were to be preserved, but the General was given discretion to support whichever party might appear to be most favourably inclined towards the British, whether or not it happened to be the one centred upon Pilima Talauva. The Adigar was, in fact, expendable; if he were to find it advantageous to do so, Macdowall had permission to reveal the Minister's intrigues to the King. North had little liking for Pilima. His scruples of conscience extended to the master but not to the servant.

IV

Macdowall's embassy to Kandy is particularly well documented. In addition to the General's own despatches, and the account of his Brigade Major, Captain William Macpherson,[20] a subaltern in the 19th Foot, Robert Percival,[21] produced a vivid account of the expedition, as did Mr Jonville, a naturalist and scientist who went along as an interpreter.[22] This is not untypical. The paucity of Kandyan sources is matched by the profusion of British material. A dozen or so soldiers and officials produced narratives of their experiences of the early days of British rule in the island. Overshadowed though Ceylon was by the convulsions in Europe, the early nineteenth-century reading public was avid for accounts of the fascinating new corners of the world in which their sons and nephews were rummaging. In these specialized days, the breadth of knowledge of some of these authors is astonishing. Men like John Davy, the brother of Sir Humphrey Davy, who served as a doctor in Ceylon, were equally at home whether discussing botany or strategy, art or economics, politics or geology, literature or anthropology.

A salute of seventeen guns rumbled a farewell to the 1,164 soldiers of Macdowall's escort as they marched out of Colombo on 12 March, 1800. The 19th Foot, a Madras battalion of the Company Army, and a locally raised unit of Malays each provided five infantry companies. There were also four 6-pounders and two howitzers manned by Bengal artillerymen. In the administrative train were uniformed Madras pioneers, a large force of tent lascars and droves of transport coolies, carriage bullocks and wagons. As was the custom, His Excellency the Governor's letter to Sri Wikrama Raja Sinha was treated as a sacred object, wrapped in gold-tissue covered muslin, carried on a silver tray on the heads of young aristocrats, and protected from the elements by a canopy of white linen.

Macdowall took the traditional Portuguese invasion route to Kandy, past Sitawaka and Ruwanwella, then up the escarpment at Balane to Gannoruwa. Seven days after leaving Colombo, the embassy crossed into the King's territories at Sitawaka, the troops dragging the guns and supply wagons over the river, the banks of which were too steep for laden bullocks to climb. On the other side Pilima Talauva, accompanied by a cortège of seven elephants and nearly 1,000 soldiers, half of whom were armed with muskets, met Macdowall, the Minister's approach being heralded by the staccato crack of ceremonial whips, the drumming of tom-toms and the flare of a multitude of torches. The General now handed the Governor's letter to the Adigar, together with the usual lavish collection of gifts, packed in thirty-two separate cases. There was a dismantled stage-coach (a team of horses to draw it was also brought), gold and silver cloths, fine muslins and fifteen cases of Bengal sugar. For the Adigar himself there was a beautifully wrought gold betel box, part of the booty from Tippoo's palace, and for each lesser dignitary there was a lesser present.[23]

Macdowall found the Adigar in a difficult frame of mind. Complaint followed upon complaint. The pioneers must not be allowed to improve the execrable track; the General should not be displaying his flag; the artillery should not have been brought; and the guns, if they were to be taken further, must travel at the rear of the column and be covered with white cloths, the traditional token of peaceful intent. Pilima Talauva had to play his part. Important though it was to him to ensure that a strong British force reached Kandy, it was necessary to delude his rivals at court by making a pretext of obstruction.

The awkwardness of the Adigar was just one of Macdowall's worries. The climate was debilitating. Fiercely hot days alternated with wet nights, during which the camp sites were blanketed in thick, dank fog. The fact that the weary troops were intending to haul their baggage and guns up the muddy track to the capital seemed to be affording quiet amusement to the Kandyans. Macpherson, after making a reconnaissance of the route ahead, reported that no vehicle lighter than a 6-pounder gun could survive the surfaces. How to drag the guns through the mud was, of course, another matter. There was a further problem: much of the baggage was carried on the backs of porters—peasants who were carrying out their *rajakariya* (literally the 'king's work'), the labour payment they made in lieu of rent for their holdings. Their liability was limited to fifteen days' work each year, and it was natural for them to want to turn for home as soon as they had finished their stint—behaviour stigmatized by the British officers as desertion. The Adigar promised to replace the missing porters, but few men arrived. The villages were nearly deserted.

Women and children had been hidden from the troops in the safety of the jungle, and most of the men had been mobilized, as the British realized when they caught glimpses of armed parties of Kandyans. Hostility was in the air and the fear of ambush percolated the British column.

Macdowall's transport problems decided him to leave his guns and the greater part of his infantry at Ruwanwella, only eight miles beyond Sitawaka (and the last place to which supplies could be brought by water),[24] and to push on to Kandy with only a couple of hundred Malays and Sepoys. This decision, in its turn, brought protests from the Adigar, the presence of a large British force in Kandy being so vital to his plans. But Macdowall had no alternative. Without more porters he could not move his complete force to Kandy, and these the Adigar was unable to provide, or so it appeared.

So long as the troops stayed on the move, they remained reasonably healthy. Captain Kennedy, the senior officer of the detachment of the 19th Foot, went down with a disease that later killed him, and another British soldier succumbed to what was described as a 'coup de soleil'.[25] A soldier of the 19th Foot was drowned and another unfortunate man was taken by a crocodile, but otherwise the only casualties seem to have occurred among the men left behind at Ruwanwella. Here the chill of the night fogs contrasted with the sultry days, when the heat trapped within the enclosing hills seemed to smother the men. 'Dysentery, fluxes and liver complaints, became frequent; and the jungle fever, which often proves fatal when the person attacked has not had an opportunity of being immediately removed to the sea air, began to make its appearance.'[26] This jungle fever was malaria, the cause of which was to remain a mystery for many more years. Percival noticed that in this unpleasant climate, the Europeans stood exertion better than the natives, but that white and brown alike suffered from the malevolent leeches. '. . . most of the soldiers had their legs and different parts of their bodies streaming with blood. . . . The officers and men employed in clearing the jungles presented an appearance absolutely shocking, as they seemed to be completely covered with blood.'[27] It had been worse for the Portuguese, on whom the leeches had been able to enjoy their repast protected by the armour of their victims.

After Ruwanwella the road became progressively worse as it left the comparatively flat lowland country and started to mount into the foothills. The hill that climbed to Balane, the 'look-out' at the entrance to the Kandyan plateau, seemed to bar the way to the struggling column. The track, Jonville noticed, had been deliberately left in an unimproved state and was impassable either for laden horses or for palanquins.

'An almost perpendicular road, crowded with an innumerable company of Koolis carrying tents, palanquins and enormous cases; pioneers, lascars, soldiers, their wives and little girls of ten all carrying packages. The nobles of the Court dressed in cloth of gold, being pushed from behind to help them scale the rocks and roaring at those who allowed them to stumble; the cries of woe, the shouts of laughter from the greater number, the wailing of the babies at the breast, the finery of the costumes, in short the whole thing presented a whimsical mixture. . . .'[28]

It was fortunate that the British column was not trying to take the hill by assault.

Four weeks after he had left Colombo, Macdowall was received by Sri Wikrama in his palace. The tediously aggravating court ritual had hardly changed since Pybus suffered it, and an exhausted ambassador returned from his first reception after being fortified at 4 am on 'large balls of flour and honey, sweet cakes and fruit, with aqua pura'.[29] Macpherson, who witnessed the reception, described the King as 'a young man about twenty-one years of age, with an immense large head, and stupid vacant countenance',[30] a strange portrayal, utterly at variance with Sri Wikrama's real appearance. Percival, who probably described the scene at second hand, likened the monarch to Henry VIII, a far more accurate description.[31]

The talks came to nothing. With restrained good manners the Kandyan officials rejected Macdowall's proposal that a British garrison should be stationed in their country to protect their King. 'The Native soldiers of the Island,' one said, 'have at all times been his sufficient Guard. Should enemies to the Court of Candy arise the English will be the first to know it,' he pointed out. 'It is the duty of the English to defend the coasts from all enemies.'[32] The Kandyan trick of turning the talk back to the terms of the 1796 Treaty aggravated Macdowall just as much as the reasonable and conciliatory way they occasionally conceded minor and unimportant points. Nor did he enjoy the ever-present implication that the discussions were being held between equals. As interview followed upon interview, Macdowall became increasingly irritable and tried to bully the ministers, but neither argument nor bad temper managed to budge them. After a couple of fruitless weeks, the general left.

Although Macdowall had failed in his task of negotiating a treaty, he had learned a lot about Kandy and had some sound advice to offer to the Governor. The Adigar had always insisted that he was not all-powerful in Kandy, and Macdowall was now able to confirm that Pilima Talauva had told the truth. There were other parties at Court wielding considerable influence and Pilima Talauva was not prepared openly to oppose them. There was little or no sign of any immediate danger to the King, and even less indication that either Pilima Talauva or his advisers would contemplate admitting a British garrison to their hills. At the same time the Kandyans had given no indication of any wish to quarrel with their powerful neighbours on the coast.

From the military standpoint, the embassy had proved invaluable. The detailed reconnaissance of Kandy which Macdowall and his officers had been allowed to conduct was alone worth the £5,000 the expedition had cost. What is more, it had been in the nature of a dress rehearsal for any future invasion of the country that might prove necessary. Not only had Macdowall been allowed closely to inspect the Kandyan warrior and his equipment, but he had also gleaned first-hand knowledge of the Kandyan terrain—the climate, the disease and the deliberately unmade Kandyan tracks were all first hand experience. Above all the rehearsal had made it plain that the job could not be carried out without adequate transport.

Pilima Talauva also had been left with a great deal on his mind. The fact that Macdowall's force had returned to the coast had made it clear that the British were not prepared to appropriate the country without some sort of legalistic excuse. The Adigar had also been provided with further evidence of the growth of both the influence and the stature of his King. This knowledge must have increased his anxieties for his own safety, and his intrigues with the British continued undiminished. Now, however, he was dealing with a Governor on whom fruitless and wearying negotiations had left their mark. Plagued by overwork and ill-health, North's exasperation was leading him to arrogance. With his mind becoming increasingly attuned to the need for armed intervention in Kandyan politics, he was finding it less and less difficult to justify his actions. The liberal ideas he had brought to Ceylon were collapsing under the pressure of pragmatism.

In July, 1802, North's opportunity presented itself. The seizure by the Adigar's officials of the stock of areca nuts belonging to two parties of Moormen from the coast had led to a British demand for compensation. The Adigar proved dilatory, and North, after six months of unproductive correspondence, decided that the time for intervention had come. On 31 January, 1803, Macdowall again started for Kandy, but this time as an invader. Four days later, another column commanded by Colonel Barbut took the longer and less known route from Trincomalee for the same destination.

North either believed or persuaded himself into believing that Pilima Talauva had dragged him into the war. On the eve of the invasion, he reported to London upon the 'insidious designs of the Minister, who directs its notions, whose wish has (as I have frequently informed your Lordship) been, for some time past, to drive us into a war with his country, for the Purpose of overthrowing, by any means, the *****, whom he has exalted, and of raising his own Authority on the Ruins of his Throne'.[33] Perhaps North was right. Kandy was certainly anticipating war. Men were being mobilized from the villages, and a series of reports were received of parties of troops drilling in the interior. The seizure of the areca nuts was a pointless action, and the Adigar could well have made restitution for the loss if he had so wished. On the other hand, no one in Kandy had anything to gain from war except the Adigar and his supporters. Until then the King and his supporters had been consistently conciliatory in their dealings with the British, and it is hard to

75

understand how the Adigar, possessing only limited power, could have been able to provoke hostilities in so obvious a manner. Nevertheless there had been provocation, and North was given the opportunity he wanted. Perhaps Pilima Talauva was prepared to see the King expelled and accept the status of client-king. This was, in fact, a possibility envisaged by North, as his instructions to Macdowall reveal.[34] Pilima Talauva may have banked on the turmoil of war to provide him with the chance of establishing himself as his country's ruler when, in their turn, the British fell victims to the natural defences of the land. If so, he was either very confident or very desperate—possibly both.

CHAPTER 5
The First War: Invasion

I

MACDOWALL's small force cut a dash as it paraded in jaunty
fashion out of the gates of Colombo at the start of its march
towards Kandy. Impeccably smart, it seemed to an onlooker
'more like a pleasure party than an invading army'.[1] Another
spectator, the Rev Mr Cordiner, enthused about the way in
which 'the colours of the regiments were displayed'. 'The music
of the 51st's band,' he wrote, 'animated the march; and the
countenances of the soldiers, full of cheerfulness and joy, discovered all the spirit of chosen heroes rushing on to victory.'[2]

The first day's march on 31 January took the troops only a
little over four miles to the banks of the Kelani Ganga. Here
they halted to prepare for an evening inspection by H.E. The
Governor, whose arrival was greeted by the reverberations of a
nineteen-gun salute. After the parade, John Wilson, the Town
Major, entertained Mr North and the officers of the force to
dinner at the Cocoa-Nut Club, set on its small hill overlooking
the wide, palm-fringed river. By horse, curricle and palanquin
the leave-taking party then returned to Colombo, while Macdowall's officers, now themselves 'full of cheerfulness', made
towards their camp-beds by the side of the river.

Not counting the hordes of coolies, pioneers, gun-lascars,
servants and wagon-drivers, whom no one seems to have counted,
Macdowall's column contained some 1,900 fighting soldiers. The

understrength 51st Foot, mustering only 600 or so men, together with two companies of the 19th Foot, made up the European complement of the force. In addition there were two weak companies of Bengal Artillery, a company of Malays and the Ceylon Native Infantry, one thousand strong but nearly all recruits. Colonel Barbut's column, which set out from Trincomalee four days later, was about two-thirds of the strength of Macdowall's force. It included five companies of the 19th, in all about 400 men, the balance of the Malay Regiment, and a single company of Madras Artillery equipped with six brass 6-pounders, one $5\frac{1}{2}$-inch mortar and three coehorns;[3] thirty-seven elephants are recorded among the baggage animals.[4]

Macdowall was a capable soldier and he knew what he was doing when he signalled with ceremonial panache this leave-taking from Colombo. The 51st were not in good shape. During the Regiment's three-year stay in the island, reinforcements had been scanty and the rank and file were now, in the words of the senior medical officer, 'old men and boys.'[5] After three years of garrison duty in Colombo, the relief from tedium and the prospects of loot, excitement and prize-money were heartening, and a little parade-ground swagger to start the men along the road did no harm at all.

North had known this Regiment well in the past. It had served with him in Corsica, where it had been fortunate to be commanded by Lieutenant-Colonel John Moore, the prime trainer of fighting men of his generation. The professionalism this fine soldier had instilled into his officers was still apparent, and did much, in the months ahead, to compensate for the poor quality of their men.

The British Army in 1803 was, in fact, in the first stages of one of its periodic metamorphoses. The pattern is far from unfamiliar. During the years following the end of the American War of Independence, the commercial and political revival of Britain, which had been inspired by the young William Pitt, was coupled with the neglect for the armed forces customary at such times. As always, the protection provided by the Channel had lulled the nation into forgetting that foreign wars happen at all too regular intervals, with the result that the costly lessons of the past had been once again forgotten and the Army allowed to degenerate into supine ineffectiveness. In this state it faced the start of the French Revolutionary Wars.

The title 'Army' was all but a misnomer for the collection of very independent infantry and cavalry regiments that made up the land forces of the United Kingdom. Supporting and administrative services barely existed. The regiments themselves were, in effect, the private property of their colonels—rewards for personal and political services and usually a satisfactory source of pecuniary profit to their owners. But fortunately for the country, the bizarre system produced oddly effective results. These regiments were small, inward-looking communities that provided a background and a home for their soldiers, and to a lesser degree for their officers as well. Life in these communities fostered mutual confidence and intense loyalties, qualities which were reinforced by the rigid discipline suited to the needs of the slow-firing and short-ranged weapons of the time. As a consequence the British infantryman had, for a century past, regularly earned the respect of the armies of continental Europe.

Yet when war broke out in 1792, much of the basic quality of the British line regiments had been squandered. After being beaten by the American colonists (mostly ill-armed and badly-disciplined local levies), the Army faced the parsimony of peace, lacking even the satisfaction of having won the previous war. Morale suffered and the results were apparent in the badly-commanded, ill-officered and poor-quality troops who fought the disastrous campaigns in the Low Countries during the final decade of the century. Now, however, after ten years of war, an improvement was to be seen. In a large measure as a result of the vigour, competence and influence of the Commander-in-Chief, George III's second son, the Duke of York, the Army was being refashioned into the instrument Wellington would use to drive the French out of Spain.

The 19th Foot, the other British Regiment represented in Macdowall's column, had fought in the disastrous Flemish campaigns of 1794 and 1795. Since it arrived in Ceylon in 1796, a few months after Stuart had expelled the Dutch, losses from disease and battle had been light, despite the fact that the years had been not too uneventful. In 1799, two companies had fought under Colonel Arthur Wellesley in the Mysore War against Tippoo Sahib; and the following year the five companies which had formed part of Macdowall's abortive embassy had been despatched on active service to the Coromandel coast only three days after they had arrived back in Colombo. While these five companies were away, the other half of the unit was fully occupied in dealing with the 'joy-tax' riots, so called because they had been provoked by an ill-considered attempt by North to raise revenue by taxing such personal adornments as jewels, glass beads, and base and precious metal ornaments. This was the second time faulty administration had stung the placid people of the coastal provinces to violence, and again the details are sparse. Detachments of the 19th Foot had to subdue riots at places as far apart as Negombo, Matara and Manaar, so the trouble must have been widespread. In the course of these operations, two companies crossed the island on foot from Manaar to Trincomalee, the first British troops to do so:

'Though destitute of tents, and with a very small supply of provisions, they persevered, notwithstanding the rainy season had rendered the roads almost impassable. They, however, surmounted every difficulty, and suffered little from Fatigue.'[6]

Now, at the start of their march to Kandy, their medical officer was able to describe these soldiers as 'a remarkably fine body of middle-aged men, who have long been inured to a hot climate, and accustomed to active service in the field in different parts of India'.[7] This unit was to become even more accustomed to the climate. It was to serve in the island for seventeen more years with the result that the history of Ceylon during the early days of British rule in many ways mirrors the chronicle of this Regiment.

The headquarters and two companies of the 65th Regiment, the balance of the European infantry in the island, remained in Colombo to garrison the city. The detachment had landed in Ceylon the previous September; and, because of changes in the plans for the movement of the rest of the Regiment, it was to be held in the island until 1804. The make-up of the 65th was unusual. In an attempt to do something about the perennial recruiting problem, with five other regiments it had been brought up to strength in 1797 by filling it with boys between ten and sixteen years of age. The scheme could be said to have some merits: not only did it relieve the parishes of the expense of maintaining a proportion of their young paupers, but it also produced some fine young soldiers, as the record of the 65th in Ceylon was to show. Deplorable though the conditions were in which the soldiers of the time lived, most were inured to a harsh existence. One of these young recruits, John Shipp, who later achieved the unusual distinction of twice being commissioned from the ranks,[8] found that service in one of these units contrasted well with his previous life. Apprenticed as a nine-year-old parish orphan to a brutal Suffolk farmer and subject most days to a thrashing from his master, Shipp was little more than a slave-labourer before he was handed over to the army.

II

The cumbrous system of Dual Control had been abolished after the Peace of Amiens, and the home Government then assumed complete responsibility for the Maritime Provinces. One consequence of this change was that, by the start of 1803, all the units of the East India Company Army, except for the Bengal and the Madras artillery companies, had left the island. In their place now served the Malay Regiment and the Ceylon Native Infantry, who the following year were to change their names to the 1st and the 2nd Ceylon Regiments.

The Malay Regiment had evolved from the independent companies that had fought so well for the Dutch. After the capitulation they had transferred under their own Malay officers to the service of the Company, and North, when he arrived, found a corps about five hundred strong, a fifth of whom were used on revenue duty;[9] appreciating the value of these Malays, he doubled their strength, augmented the number of British officers from the two then serving with the unit, and placed them upon a more official footing. When the Regiment transferred from the Company into the King's service at the end of Dual Control, North marked the occasion on 31 May by presenting new colours before the Malays took their leave of Colombo, hitherto their station, and moved across the island to Trincomalee. The senior officer on parade that day, who replied to His Excellency's address, was a Scot named Major Adam Davie, of whom we shall soon hear more.

When North lent half of this Malay unit to the Madras Government in 1801 to fight the Polygars, they succeeded in distinguishing themselves.[10] Many of the soldiers were small rajas, whom the Dutch had exiled from Sumatra or Malacca to live in Ceylon as pensioners, or the descendants of these people. In the Dutch service they had earned a grim reputation for violence and robbery; Percival, who served alongside them for three and a half years in Trincomalee, knew them well and mentions the fear that would strike any Ceylonese who met one of them unexpectedly.[11] The infrequency of complaints about their behaviour after their transfer to British service suggests that the change benefited them. Percival praised their good discipline and admired the way they respected their officers, both British and Malay. The latter earned this respect automatically because of their princely rank, but the quality of some of their British officers was so poor that it is strange that they managed to earn it at all. Percival considered the Malays to be brave and ferocious troops, although probably less cruel and vindictive than their compatriots in Malacca, civilization having, in his opinion, mellowed them. Marshall respected them also; he noted that 'when passion for plunder, or vengeance, is raised, they engage on any enterprise with remarkable alacrity'.[12] In an apparent contradiction, Percival complained that although these Malays possessed 'comely countenances', in general 'their features strongly indicate their ferocious, treacherous and revengeful disposition';[13] the Malay women, on the other hand, he found alluring (as, it is said, did Governor North),[14] though he felt it necessary to warn his fellow countrymen of the dangers of rash dalliance. To provoke such proud and volatile men was to invite a kris between the ribs or powdered glass in the curry.

In the matter of uniform, one concession only was granted to the Malays. The men, but not the officers, were allowed to wear sandals instead of boots. In other respects they were compressed into the same tight clothes worn by their British comrades, to the detriment of both their comfort and their mobility. Only in their weapons was a difference permitted: they were allowed to retain their vicious krises.

Despite advice to the contrary received from his military officers, the success achieved by the low-country Sinhalese during the 1797 rebellion misled North into thinking that they might be made into tolerable soldiers.[15] As a result the Ceylon Native Infantry, manned by Sinhalese, was raised, but North soon discovered that he should have listened to the advice he had been given:

'A life of military discipline proved, in the highest degree, irksome and uncongenial to their habits. They deserted in great numbers, and examples intended to terrify only stimulated those who remained to abandon their service. At length a sufficient number of recruits was obtained from the coast of Coromondel, and the Corps of Singalese was disbanded. In those regiments which are now called Ceylon Native Infantry, there is scarcely to be found a native of the island.'[16]

It is an unpleasant picture—the unmilitary and gentle Sinhalese soldiery being stimulated to further desertions by the sight of their comrades ritually flogged on the parade ground. The experiment was not repeated, and the Ceylon Regiment was, in the future, to be manned by drafts recruited from Malacca, Java, India, and—as we shall see later—Africa.

III

In 1800 Macdowall had taken the classic Portuguese route to Kandy that passes close to the old fort at Balane—the line of the railway that now carves its way among the sheer rock faces up to Kandy. From Ruwanwella onwards most of the route was steep, rugged and wooded, while Ruwanwella itself, the natural place for a supply depot, had been found to be a very

sickly spot. Realizing that the prospects of forcing such a formidable approach against even slight Kandyan opposition would be
expensive, Macdowall now chose instead the more northerly
route running from Negombo by way of the Maha Oya. This
was the road taken in 1765 by the Dutch commander, Van Eck,
and the going was reasonably level for most of the way. Only
towards the end of the 100 mile march, when the Kandyan
escarpment leaps sheer out of the plain, did the problems become
really serious. A further advantage provided by this route was
that the force could be supplied by water from the time it left
Colombo until it reached the Kandyan border, thus easing the
intractable logistic difficulties of the campaign.[17]

This longer northern approach led inland through rice fields
and coconut groves, interspersed with clumps of dark green
jungle and steep forest-clad knolls. The days were hot and the
loads heavy; but much of each day's march could be completed
during the cool of the early morning. Anticipation was high, the
journey far from unpleasant, and the troops, when they reached
Kotadeniya, found a supply depot already stocked by the commissary. This post was now christened Fort Frederick, after the
Governor, and while the major part of the force halted for four
days to dig a redoubt for its protection, a small detachment
pushed across the border to reconnoitre the route ahead.

In 1800, Macdowall had found the Kandyan villages deserted.
Now there were throngs of seemingly friendly villagers everywhere, oblivious to the fact that their land was being invaded
and eager only to sell chickens, eggs, fruit and milk to the soldiers
(the last-named commodity the troops thought a great luxury).
The headmen told the British officers through their interpreters
that they were under orders from the King to behave in this way.
It is surprising that the villagers were prepared to obey the royal
instructions so literally, and the fact that they did so suggests
that they were confident that they had little to fear from this
particular breed of soldier; during its march to Kandy in 1800,
the army must have behaved well, something to which Asian
villagers (or civilians anywhere, for that matter) were not accustomed. The reason why the King issued such orders is obscure.
Possibly he was still hoping for a peaceful settlement, but it is

more likely that he was developing the traditional Kandyan tactic of tempting the enemy deep into the interior of the country before delivering the counter-stroke. On the other hand the orders may have emanated from Pilima Talauva, who had good reasons for smoothing the path of the British. Kandyan tradition has it that Macdowall's choice of route took the King by surprise.[18] If this is true, little time had been wasted in disseminating the instructions to the village headmen.

Leaving at Fort Frederick a garrison of 100 Sepoys, together with a dozen Europeans and an assistant surgeon to run the hospital, the main body of Macdowall's force set out on the next stage of its journey on 10 February. After a march of six miles, the troops forded the Maha Oya, following in the footsteps of the advanced guard into Kandyan territory. A further post to cover the crossing was built, another company of the Ceylon Native Infantry left to guard it, and the rest of the column pushed on the next day to Dambadeniya. There Macdowall was obliged to halt for four days; despite the sound logistic preparations he had made, the difficulties of carrying his supplies overland were now starting to slow him down. Most of the tents and much of the officers' baggage had already been dumped at Fort Frederick, but the pack bullocks were found to be untrained and the drivers of the baggage elephants were proving obstructive. As usual the mainstay of the baggage train was the muscles of the scarce and undependable porters, and these men were understandably averse to carrying loads like eight-gallon kegs of arrack (one of the staple articles of the British ration) across rough and possibly dangerous hills.

Macdowall had foreseen these difficulties. Only four days after he left Colombo, he had written to North[19] to warn him that the onset of the April rains, combined with this shortage of porters, would make it difficult for him to hold the capital for more than a few days. In any case, Macdowall emphasized, his forces were sufficient for only 'a rapid and transitory' campaign, and he suggested that the Governor should content himself with the capture of the Seven Korales, the rich province through which his intended route lay. He pointed out that it would be necessary to accumulate two months' supplies for 4,000 to 5,000 men at Fort Frederick, and he suggested that North should ask the Madras Government for reinforcements: two battalions of Sepoys, five hundred or so lascars and 2,000 to 3,000 'carriage cattle' were needed. Macdowall also took the opportunity to remind North of the disasters which had overtaken Van Eck in this self-same country.

Why did Macdowall write such a letter? Nothing had happened so far in the course of the easy and uneventful journey that could have changed his views on the course that he had visualized the campaign might take. Relations between the Governor and the General were cordial—even friendly[20]—and they had always worked in close harmony. Macdowall was not a fool, and the problems that now faced him must have been apparent for the past three years at least. A possible explanation for the letter is that Macdowall had so far failed to persuade North of the reality of the difficulties of the campaign, and that he now felt constrained to commit his doubts to paper so as to avoid being accused of lack of foresight in the event of a failure. Was he, in fact, clearing his yard-arm? Certainly North was very optimistic about the outcome of the expedition. On 30 January he had written to Madras to say that he did not expect to have to ask either for extra troops or for money unless a second campaign were to be forced upon him; for the present, he said, he needed only a thousand or two extra bullocks.[21] As he had previously complained on several occasions to London about the inadequacies of the garrison, and as Macdowall must have made his reservations known before he left for Kandy, North's letter to Madras was sanguine indeed.

A third rough fort was built on a knoll among the Dambadeniya paddy fields, and another small garrison was left to guard it. It was here that Macdowall had his first news from Barbut: the progress of the Trincomalee column had been quite as uneventful as Macdowall's, but vague reports had been received that the Kandyans were massing their men in the hills around their capital.

It was not until 17 January that Macdowall's column saw the first armed party of the enemy. The next day the first blood of the campaign was shed when the leading troops surprised a

Kandyan scouting party, wounding a Malay and taking a
Sinhalese soldier prisoner.

IV

The wounded Malay was probably a member of the King's
company of mercenaries, one of the many diverse units that
made up the Kandyan forces. The backbone of the army was
the conscript *levée en masse*,[22] raised either by the *dissawas* or
directly by the King's officers from the tenants of his royal
estates. At any one time only one third of the men of fighting
age might be called out, although the demand could well be
for a lesser number. A high proportion were armed with muskets
of varying degrees of decrepitude, some owned by the villagers
themselves and some kept in armouries by the *dissawas*; many
soldiers, however, particularly those from the eastern provinces,
carried only bows and arrows. A small cooking pot, a talipot
leaf for use as sun-shade or umbrella, together with fifteen days'
supply of food, consisting of a few cakes of *kurakkan*, a little
rice, and perhaps two or three coconuts, completed a man's
simple equipment. The fifteen days' food matched the fifteen-day
period he was obliged to serve at any one time; and he returned
to his village, at the most three days or so march away, when his
stint was finished, helping to carry back any sick or wounded,
to be relieved by a further levy. Such was the theory; in practice
the system was probably far less tidy. It was a cheap and simple
method of mobilization, admirably suited to provide the lightly-
armed and quickly moving troops needed to defend the Kandyan
hills and forests, but it did not produce men with the training
to defend or assault fortified positions. It also took time to call
the levies to the colours, and colours they had, the men from
each region carrying into battle the traditional flag of their
province.

As well as these conscript levies, there were various classes of
militia, manned by hereditary soldiers whose role was to act as
bodyguards either for the King or for their *dissawa*. The King's
troops were recruited from certain tenants of the royal lands,

some of them receiving pay, but many occupying crown lands as tenants-at-will in reward for their military service. Some were in constant attendance on the King, but others served in shifts. Some were used as a type of police, others served as artillerymen, but most of these men acted as guards upon their monarch, the two principle classes (sometimes called regiments) to whom this hereditary task fell being the *Atapattuwa* and the *Maduwa*. These regiments were uniformed: the *Maduwa* wore red jackets, and in 1810 a party of troops was seen to be drilling in high black caps, black jackets and white trousers. In Sri Wikrama's time the number of these militia troops was not large, probably no more than 400 to 800 being under arms at any one time.

The Nayakkar kings had come to depend less and less on the *Atapattuwa* and *Maduwa*, and to rely for their personal protection upon foreign mercenaries. There was nothing new about this. Knox found many foreigners, including large numbers of Europeans, among Raja Sinha's fighting men, while Marco Polo had been outspoken upon the same subject many years before:

'The inhabitants of Ceylon are not fighting men but paltry and mean-spirited creatures. If they have need of the services of soldiers, they hire them abroad, especially Saracens.'[23]

This is an unfair remark. The Sinhalese successes in open warfare against both the Portuguese and the Dutch contradict the Venetian's slur. Nevertheless a military life never held out much attraction for either highland or lowland Sinhalese; Marco Polo was not the only European to be disappointed that they never displayed that positive enjoyment of war which is so generally found among northern races. Primarily, however, the Kandyan kings looked abroad for their bodyguard because foreign mercenaries, lacking local ties, were more to be trusted to protect them against the powerful and intriguing Kandyan noblemen. The recruitment of Malabars for this purpose by Sri Wikrama's predecessor is said to have caused much discontent in his kingdom; and, by 1800, a unit of Malay mercenaries, mostly deserters from the Dutch, were also in attendance at the court. Some of the Malabars, like the Sinhalese militia, received grants of land; but the Malays seem to have served for pay alone, as did the

Kaffirs who, by 1803, had joined the force. When Jonville saw the bodyguard in 1800, the Malabars were smart, with red turbans and jackets with blue trousers, but the Malays were a tatterdemalion crew, dressed mainly in rags. The latter proved, however, to be the most dangerous of the Kandyan troops, cut-throats though most of them were.

Finally there were the *Appuhamis*, a cadet corps of the sons of chiefs, who provided a further personal bodyguard for the monarch, complementing the militia and the mercenaries. No Nayakkar king was ever murdered by his bodyguard. Perhaps in variety they had found the answer to *'quis custodiet ipsos custodes?'*.

V

Two days after Macdowall's first clash with the Kandyans a more serious skirmish occurred. The fifteen miles the troops had covered on the day previous to this had been tedious and tiring, and they were faced, when at last they arrived in camp, with the usual aggravating wait for the dawdling baggage coolies to arrive. Throughout the day's march they had observed the looming grey hills converging on both sides of them towards the apex of the triangular flat valley along which they were moving. Now, on 19 February, this formidable gateway to the Kandyan plateau had to be tackled.

The first obstacle was the granite hill of Galagedara, located 1,000 yards due north of the present village of the same name. The summit was topped by a stone redoubt, the ascent to which lay between perpendicular rocks and matted thickets, ground ideal for either a sustained defence or the delaying tactics at which the Kandyans were known to be adept. However, as the advanced guard of the 51st started to scale the steep rocks, Kandyans were seen to be running from the redoubt; and when the soldiers had clambered to the summit they found it empty but for three curious pieces of brass ordnance[24] and a large quantity of ammunition.

Leaving fifty Sepoys to hold Galagedara, Macdowall pushed on, only to find, a mile further up the track, another fort similar to the one they had already taken, frowning down upon them from Girihagama Hill. It was square in shape, with hewn stone walls and large gateways at front and rear, perched upon its granite hill, 500 feet above the track. An even more formidable obstacle than Galagedara, 'a few men,' Cordiner wrote, 'possessed of common resolution, might even repulse the assailants by a shower of stones.'[25] Climbing up the bed of a stream, in the face of heavy but inaccurate fire, the men of the Grenadier Company of the 19th Foot, commanded by Captain Honner, heaved themselves up the rocks, steeper even than those that had barred the way of the 51st, and burst panting across the ramparts of the fort. But as they clambered in, the defenders showed sound sense and decamped by the rear gateway, their line of retreat marked for several miles by the blood of the wounded they dragged along with them. Honner's only casualties were a soldier with a broken thigh and a sergeant with a bullet through the lungs; the former died soon after the action, but the sergeant in some miraculous way survived.

Just as the redcoats were seen to be climbing into Girihagama, the men below heard the sound of guns in the distance. It was Barbut's column bombarding Kandyan positions at Watapuluwa, just outside the capital, from across the Mahaweli Ganga. After starting on 4 February, Barbut's progress had been slow, although he had moved more quickly than Macdowall. His elephants had caused trouble, as had Macdowall's, and he had found it necessary to rest the gun-bullocks. Reaching Lake Minneriya, after a week's marching in the cooler early mornings and evenings, the Europeans were entranced by the beauty of this sole survivor of the vast artificial irrigation tanks of the east coast. Ajax Anderson related how they

'. . . all at once burst upon a most beautiful open country, with a fine lake in the centre; upon its banks, herds of wild buffaloes and deer were grazing, while acquatic birds, of all descriptions, were skimming along its surface. To add another feature to its beauty, this delightful landscape was bounded by a distant view of the Candyan mountains, rising in almost regular gradation over each other, at the extremity of the lake, till their summits were lost in the clouds; in short, forming together a combination of the sublime and beautiful, not often seen.'[26]

Captain Anderson, another officer of the 19th Foot, was an odd mixture. He loved Ceylon, but had a contempt for the Sinhalese, their culture, their character and their court. This he combined with a sympathetic understanding of their attitude towards the invasion of their country, and a measure of disgust for the British aggression. He also translated Sanskrit verse into English, an unusual accomplishment for a junior officer.

After leaving Lake Minneriya, the troops entered a thick and gloomy jungle. Here the going was so bad that it was often necessary to take out the bullocks and yoke the Europeans to the guns; but the country opened out, as they continued towards Kandy, and the trees increased in size. Short of Nalanda, on one side there were 'rocks, barren and perpendicular, on the other gently sloping hills, clothed with a most delightful verdure and interspersed with fine streams of water'.[27] They saw nothing of the enemy until they came to the final barrier to the Kandyan plateau, the pass known as Balakaduwa,[28] up which the main road from Trincomalee now runs. Here the track rose 700 feet from the river at the bottom to the escarpment; and, on the other side of the water, the Kandyans were waiting for them behind a strong breast-work. A few shells dispersed the defenders, and the dismantled guns were dragged up to the summit, again by the weary Europeans. As the men threw themselves down exhausted at the top, ten miles away they could see the town of Kandy burning.

The following day Barbut reached the river and opened accurate and effective artillery fire against the Kandyan positions at Watapuluwa, the firing that Macdowall's column heard in the distance. When the Trincomalee column ferried themselves over the river the next morning, not a single shot was fired against them. That day Macdowall's column also reached the river; and, as the columns sighted each other two miles away, the previously-agreed three-gun recognition signals were fired. Luck had played its part in the timing, but it had been no mean piece of staff planning. Barbut had marched 140 miles through rough and quite unknown country; Macdowall had covered forty miles less. The two columns had met on the outskirts of the capital.

To the annoyance of Barbut's men, Macdowall now halted them while he ferried across the river an advanced guard of the 19th Foot from his own column. Its commander, Major Evans, was instructed to push forward only a short distance, but after finding two deserted batteries, both complete with their guns, he probed forward until he found himself in the streets of Kandy. Except for a few pariah dogs, not a living creature was to be seen. As the men settled down for the night, uneasily ignorant of the whereabouts of their enemy, the burning buildings of the town, still alight after two days, roared and flickered around them. The King, his court, and all the inhabitants of the city had vanished towards the mountains of Uva, taking with them their religious relics, their treasure and their bitterness. In the fashion of the Buddhist Sinhalese, the exact time of the King's departure is said to have been fixed by the court astrologers.[29] There was little of intrinsic value to be looted, but North's presentation stage-coach, a memorial to Macdowall's previous visit, stood half-burned in the palace square.

Some of the buildings were still burning the next morning, 21 February, but reinforcements joined Evans to help extinguish the flames. The survival of many buildings suggests that the fires were inexpertly lit; and there is a tradition that the King's audience hall, with its superbly carved wooden pillars and the sacred *Dalada Mandapa*, the Temple of the Tooth, had been spared by Sri Wikrama's orders.[30] Kandy had changed little since John Pybus visited it. The lay-out, in fact, is much the same even today. There was the two-mile-long main street, wide enough to hold elephant fights, lined by houses that were little more than raised mud huts, although a few of the larger ones near the Palace were tiled and whitewashed. The lake had not yet been constructed, and the Palace buildings, of wood and stone, were set out in no regular pattern, but formed three sides of a square, each about 200 yards long. One observer likened it to Seringapatam, but it was nothing like so imposing. Compared to the ancient cities of Anuradhapura and Polonnaruwa, Kandy was no more than a village. Regular invasion and the consequent destruction of their capital had taught its inhabitants that it was futile to build for posterity. Although the lush beauty and fertility of the surrounding countryside was extravagant even for Ceylon, disappointment in the capital, combined with the lack of both action and prize-money (not to say loot), produced a sense of anti-climax among both officers and soldiers.[31]

CHAPTER 6
The First War: Deterioration

I

Two days before Macdowall started out from Colombo, North had written to Sri Wikrama proposing a settlement between them. His suggestions included the cession of the rich province of the Seven Korales to Britain, compensation for the traders whose property had been seized, the right of free access to the Kandyan kingdom for Europeans and Malays, and permission for the British to build a road between Colombo and Trincomalee. Included in the letter was a veiled threat to sponsor a rival claimant to the throne if Sri Wikrama did not accept the terms.[1] The King's polite and conciliatory reply to this ultimatum did not arrive in Colombo until the two British columns were closing in on Kandy. To North's rage, it ignored his specific proposals and did no more than suggest that the proper manner to discuss differences was by an annual exchange of embassies.

The arrival in Colombo of this final rebuff from the King coincided with a message from Colonel Barbut. After the death of Sri Wikrama's predecessor, Pilima Talauva had first imprisoned, but subsequently allowed to escape, a Malabar named Muttusamy, a brother of three of the late-King's wives and a strong candidate for the throne. Recognizing the latent value of Muttusamy, North granted him a small pension and placed him in the care of Barbut, who was then Collector of Jaffna. Now Barbut wrote to North to say that the inhabitants of the districts through which he was marching were asking that Muttusamy should be appointed as their King. Because of this, he had brought the Malabar forward to Lake Minneriya, where he would be more readily available if the need for his services were to arise.

As a captain, Barbut had distinguished himself in Stuart's operations against the Dutch, and subsequently he had acted with such success as the administrator of Jaffna that he had been allowed to retain the post even when enough of the new civil servants had arrived from England to replace the temporary military administrators. Barbut, even more than most of his contemporaries, had an eye to his own interests: the advantages of having his protégé on the Kandyan throne must have been manifest.

The letter from Barbut decided North. Without delay, he proclaimed Muttusamy as the rightful heir to the throne, and on 21 February Barbut started back down the Trincomalee track to collect the new monarch. With him on the long and tiring journey went the whole of the Malay Regiment, 300 men of the 19th Foot and two 3-pounder guns to escort the new ruler to his capital. On 7 March Muttusamy was installed in the Palace with considerable military pomp, and once he had him there Macdowall produced the terms upon which the Governor was prepared to allow him to occupy the throne. Kandy was to be stripped not only of the Seven Korales, but Sabaragamuva as well,[2] while the rump of the country was to be reduced to the status of a protected state. Muttusamy, who was a proud and quietly dignified man, jibbed at having to swear an oath of allegiance to George III; and he also refused to cede Sabaragamuva, his south-westerly province with the sacred footprint of Buddha at the summit of Adam's Peak. But his protests were of no consequence. His new subjects ignored him, and he sat in his charred Palace, a lonely figure attended only by a few domestics and the British troops upon whom his safety depended.

In the meantime, Pilima Talauva had kept up his correspondence with Macdowall, and the General now received a letter from him containing the surprising information that Sri Wikrama was lodged in his palace at Hanguranketa, about eighteen miles to the south-east of Kandy, and suggesting that the British should despatch two strong columns by two separate routes to converge upon the place and capture the King. The Adigar described the resistance that Macdowall might expect to encounter and promised that he would do everything possible to help catch the King. Macdowall reacted to the suggestion with some energy; and, on the morning of 13 March, two columns set out for Hanguranketa, one 500 and one 300 strong. No record of their routes has been preserved, but from the description of the countryside provided by Cordiner, it appears that one followed the Mahaweli Ganga as far as was possible, while the other took the rather shorter but rougher way that led in a direct line over the broken hills towards Hanguranketa.

A few miles outside Kandy, both columns came under heavy fire. Many men were hit, among them one of the two brigade-majors, who was killed. The Kandyans had sited their gingals, often called 'grasshopper guns',[3] to cover the narrow tracks, and their musketeers were so skilfully protected by the swamps and thickets that it was difficult to come to grips with them. Fortunately for the British, their enemies fired high in the manner of ill-trained troops, and they were easily brushed aside by disciplined musketry and the deft use of the light-weight coehorns. Steadily and methodically the two columns were able to push forward until, on the evening of the second day, they met outside Hanguranketa. Again the operation had been well co-ordinated, but again the bird had flown. The large red-roofed palace was empty. Hanguranketa, a pleasant little place in a basin of hills, looking a little like an English village, with its green in the centre, was set on fire, and the British then turned back towards Kandy. There was no alternative. The shortage of porters had limited the force to eight days' rations, but in any case there was nothing to be gained by pushing on into the wild, unknown, mountains.

By the evening of 16 March, the British force was once again back in the capital. It had forced its way through opposition similar to that encountered on the outward journey, the only difference being that, on the return path, the porters had suffered more casualties than the soldiers. The Kandyans, understanding the problems of logistics with which the British had to cope, now reverted to their well-tried habit of hitting at the baggage train rather than the fighting troops.[4] On the march up from the coast the coolies had suffered no losses and none had deserted. After this journey they seemed to evaporate. Another unpleasant portent was the desertion of a few native troops, one of whom, a Malay, aroused great indignation when he was seen several times to level his musket at Colonel Baillie, one of the two column commanders.

Pilima Talauva's motives for suggesting this foray to Macdowall are as obscure as most of his actions. Most commentators, starting from Cordiner, suggest that his plan was no more than a ruse to draw the British into a trap;[5] Turner, in his study of the Adigar, puts forward the theory that his opposition to the British was now genuine, the change of heart having resulted from North's sponsorship of Muttusamy which had destroyed his hopes of the British offering him the throne.[6] This is possible. On the other hand, Pilima Talauva may have really been trying to help Macdowall to seize the King. Not only would this further his designs but the foray into the jungle would inevitably weaken the British forces, thus making it easier for him to expel them from Kandy once he had been set upon the throne himself.

Certainly the rigours of the expedition, superimposed upon the fatigues and hardships which the troops had already undergone, did have a permanent effect on their health. From now on disease became endemic.

II

Circumstances being what they were, the performance of the British troops during the opening stages of this campaign was undoubtedly competent. Warfare in wet, hilly, tropical jungle was something of a novelty for the British Army. It was well acquainted with the heat and dust of Egypt and India; the Canadian and American forests had taught it much; only in the West Indies, however, had it experienced an environment so hostile and an enemy so elusive as it found in Ceylon. For this type of warfare, the British soldier was neither trained, equipped

G

97

nor clad. During the past few decades, modern armies have discovered how difficult it is to exist, let alone fight, in jungles such as Burma, New Guinea and Vietnam, even with the help of amenities such as air-drops, radio-communications, proper medicine, adequate food and sensibly-designed clothing. One can but marvel at what Macdowall's men accomplished.

In this high wet forest on the road to Hanguranketa, there were three levels of life.[7] High up among the foliage of the tall straight trees that had won in their fight to reach the sun, bees and moths thrived in the pure air, and squirrels and monkeys scuttled and jumped among the branches. Beneath this high canopy, gaily-coloured birds and butterflies fluttered in the open spaces among the lichen-covered trunks. Down below was the third level where countless seedlings thrust their way up from the damp, rotting vegetation towards the sunlight. Here in the thick matted undergrowth, any animal larger than a pig or a porcupine could move quickly only if it made use of the game trails. In this humid atmosphere, a variety of bright plants lent a dank gaiety to the scene, their brilliance emulated only by the white and red clad British or native soldier. Not that these uniforms could have stayed bright for long. Very soon the mud must have reduced them to the colour of the surrounding vegetation.

It is a pity that soldiers so seldom mentioned their clothes in their memoirs. Because they wrote for their contemporaries, not posterity, they assumed that their readers knew how they dressed and they rarely did more than make the odd casual reference to their garb.

Our knowledge of what the soldier wore in Ceylon is confined to a few sparse paragraphs in General Orders and Captain Arthur Johnston's bitter strictures on his men's unsuitable dress.[8] Largely we are dependent on the evidence we can cull from other theatres.

In 1803, the British Army was in the middle of one of its periodic reappraisals of its clothing that seem to occur every twenty-five years or so—and sometimes even more frequently. Although the changes were the product of the lessons learned during the past decade of near-continuous warfare, they were by no means all for the better. The long-skirted red coat, for instance, in which Stuart's men had landed at Trincomalee, afforded a measure of protection for the loins. Now this garment had been replaced by a simpler but tighter-fitting coatee, cut away at the waist into two shortish tails, and surmounted by a stiff upstanding collar supported by a wretchedly uncomfortable leather stock. The last-named often tended accidently to be lost on active service. The soldier's legs were still encased in black gaiters and the old-fashioned breeches; the gaiters were becoming shorter, but still took several minutes to fasten, even when dry; if the enemy were near it was rash to remove them but the result of keeping them on for several days at a time was unpleasant. The substitution of blue-grey trousers for these trappings in 1808 was as welcome as the battle-dress and gaiters that replaced the comparable putteed legs of 1939.

The British Army has always found it hard to standardize its millinery, even within the confines of a single regiment. This period was no exception. Improvised headgear was not uncommon in tropical stations, and even sensible wide-brimmed hats of the type shown in Plate 1 could be found. The upright felt shako, colloquially known as the 'stove-pipe' or 'sugar-loaf', was coming into use, and something like this must have been worn by Johnston's men, for he complains of the large brass plate in front, which grew hot in the sun; its other evil characteristics were the lack of a brim to deflect water from the back of the neck, and the glazed peak which reflected the sun into the wearer's eyes. An even worse version of this hat was introduced into the island in 1808; made of leather, difficult to clean, and so hot and heavy that it produced violent headaches, the soldier usually carried it in his hand whenever he was out of sight of his officers.[9]

Underneath his hat the soldier's hair was tortured and plastered into an uncouth pig-tail, the first sculpturing of which is described by John Shipp:

'A large piece of candle-grease was applied, first to the sides of my head, then to the hind long hair; after this, the same kind of operation was performed with nasty stinking soap—sometimes the man who was dressing me applying his knuckles, instead of the soap, to the delight of the surrounding boys, who were bursting their sides with laughter, to see the tears roll down my cheeks. When this operation was over,

I had to go through one of a more serious nature. A large pad, or bag filled with sand, was poked into the back of my head, round which the hair was gathered tight, and the whole tied round with a leather thong. When I was dressed for parade, I could scarcely get my eyelids to perform their office; the skin of my eyes and face was drawn so tight by the plug that was stuck in the back of my head, that I could not possibly open my eyes; add to this, an enormous high stock was poked under my chin; so that, altogether, I felt as stiff as if I had swallowed a ramrod, or a sergeant's halberd. Shortly after I was thus equipped, dinner was served; but my poor jaws refused to act on the offensive, and when I made an attempt to eat, my pad behind went up and down like a sledgehammer.'[10]

The matted hair incubated every type of scalp disease. The stench during a church parade could be appalling. When the Duke of York, with his eye for detail and the welfare of his men, abolished the pig-tail, it was one of his best services to the British soldier.

Although only small concessions to the tropical climate in the matter of dress were made officially, the need to buy articles locally did result in the employment of lighter-weight materials on occasion. The dress instructions for De Meuron's Regiment, written soon after it entered British service, indicate that white nankeen was used for waistcoats, trousers and gaiters, while cotton material was employed for shirts and the straps used to carry the rolled overcoats.[11] At times sensible officers might order their men to discard their red coats, and fight in these nankeen waistcoats—garments which were sometimes decorated at neck and wrist with facings in the regimental colour. Herbert Beaver, of the 19th Foot, who was the epitome of this type of officer, seems to have done so, as he mentions the Kandyans distinguishing the British by their white jackets.[12] But, by and large, soldiers were dressed with the object of inspiring dismay in their opponents and not to conceal themselves from observation, although Shipp's regiment, when serving at the Cape, did go so far as to wear green, and brown their pieces when operating against the 'Caffres'—the name by which Africans were then generally known.[13]

It is understandable that the soldier was often more communicative about what he carried than what he wore.[14] In his canvas knapsack, or pack, painted in his regimental colours and decorated with the badge on the back, would be two spare shirts, two pairs of stockings, perhaps a spare pair of breeches, spare shoes with a pair of soles and heels to repair them, as well as three days' rations. Above the pack was rolled either a greatcoat or a blanket, and strapped to the outside would probably be a camp-kettle. From one white cross-belt on his left side hung his bayonet, and from the other was suspended his cartridge-box, which rested on his right buttock and contained sixty rounds of ball ammunition.[15] There was also a canteen of water on his left side, and perhaps a haversack as well to hold the day's food and the little bits and pieces a soldier needs to have with him. All this could weigh as much as sixty pounds, not counting the 'Brown Bess' musket, a flint-lock weapon that added a further nine pounds to his load. It was, of course, far too much; but more often than not it is the lot of the infantryman to be burdened in this fashion. Medical opinion suggests that a man should not carry more than one-third of his body-weight. The horse, the mule or the camel is not expected to transport more than a quarter of his.

Although the musket's range was 300 yards, the combination of both good markmanship and a well-made weapon was required before a man could be sure of hitting his enemy at a third of this range. Each lead bullet came in a paper cartridge which had to be torn open by the firer's teeth; next a splash of powder was thrown into the pan to catch the spark ignited by the hammer striking the flint; and then the rest of the cartridge had to be driven down the barrel by the use of the iron ramrod. It was a slow process. There was also the danger from damp and wet. Even in Europe the risk of the rain penetrating the cartridge-box was acute; likewise a cartridge could be soaked during the operation of loading. In a Ceylon monsoon these dangers were even more serious, and a high standard of discipline was needed to ensure that weapons were at all times ready for use. If anything went wrong, the soldier was left only with his clubbed musket or his long, heavy bayonet to defend himself. The latter was an ineffective weapon in close country.

Seldom, in fact, has the soldier's dress and equipment at any time been less relevant to the conditions under which he had to fight.

III

As the weeks followed each other in Kandy, conditions progressively worsened. There was little rest for the men, whose health had started to deteriorate even before the expedition to Hanguranketa. Nearly every day Macdowall had been sending out patrols to scour the countryside around; and, shortly after the two columns returned from Hanguranketa, Barbut once again took a force down the Trincomalee road in an attempt to persuade some of the headmen to declare themselves for Muttusamy. But there was no sign of that enthusiasm which Barbut had proclaimed he had seen when he first marched up, and the expedition produced only further weariness and further casualties from snipers' bullets. Now the Kandyans were becoming that much bolder:

'Parties of banditti hovered continually round the out-posts. They concealed themselves in the woods and thickets, fired upon the guards and sentries and whenever any unfortunate stragglers fell into their hands, they put them to death in a most barbarous and shocking manner; but they never dared to emerge from their hiding places during the day, or to make their appearance at any post where they were six British soldiers.
'One European of the 19th, several Malays, sepoys and coolies, were found mangled in a most cruel manner. The wife of a Malay soldier met with a similar treatment.'[16]

The passage from Cordiner shows that the custom of using the pejorative 'bandit' to describe a guerrilla enemy has a long history, as is the complaint that this style of making warfare is in some way cowardly. His mention of the Malay wife reminds us that these troops were in the habit of bringing their womenfolk on active service, as they had done in the days they served the Dutch. The British regiments, however, had left their families in safety at the coast.

The slaughter of small parties of coolies carrying provisions up from Trincomalee soon severed that supply route; and the ambush of a squad of the Ceylon Native Infantry escorting mail near Dambadeniya resulted in the communications to Colombo being cut until a strong force of Sepoys was collected at Fort Frederick to force their way through to Kandy two weeks later. The temptation of a reward of ten rupees for a severed European head, or five for that of one of the native soldiers, spurred the Kandyans to greater activity. One fortunate Malay soldier was saved just in time when he was found by a party of his comrades, gagged and trussed, with a Kandyan knife poised at his neck. And it was, of course, easy to represent a coolie's head as that of a native soldier.

IV

The Kandyans started, at this juncture, to infiltrate large bodies of men into the British western and southern provinces. With the western forts stripped of troops this was serious: the garrison even of Colombo had been reduced to the two companies of the 65th Regiment and 300 Sepoys, but many of these men were now engaged in keeping the supply lines to Kandy open. The first threat was to Fort Frederick. A report received in Colombo on 13 March that 6,000 Kandyans were marching on the Fort resulted in Captain Bullock of the 65th being sent with fifty men of his Grenadier Company and the same number of the Ceylon Light Infantry to reinforce the post; a further twenty-five men from his Regiment joined Bullock as soon as he arrived (they had been patrolling in the neighbourhood). No Kandyans showed themselves, but as the post had proved to be signally unhealthy, Bullock was instructed to remove the stores by river and canal to Colombo[17] and then abandon it. Unhealthy it was. In turn every British soldier was evacuated to the coast sick with fever. After three weeks Bullock was the sole remaining European. One month after the party had set out from Colombo, one subaltern and two private soldiers were still alive. The rest, including Bullock, were dead of this fatal fever. The members of this Grenadier Company were picked men, all some six feet tall. Enlisted together as boys at Colchester, they were in the prime of life, and when they arrived at Colombo from the Cape not a single man had been on the sick list, possibly a unique occurrence after such a voyage.

A few days after Bullock had passed through Negombo on his way up-country, a further report arrived at the Fort with the news that 6,000 Kandyans had entrenched themselves at Mugurugampale,[18] five miles to the south-east of Fort Frederick and well inside British territory. Probably this report referred to the same party that had been threatening Fort Frederick. The Commandant at Negombo was Captain Herbert Beaver, a very forceful officer indeed. Wasting no time, he collected the only troops he could find—one sergeant and twelve soldiers of the 65th Regiment, the same number of Sepoys and a few lascarins, and marched immediately for the Kandyan encampment, twenty miles away. The story of the foray is related in another of Beaver's letters:

'About an hour after midnight we met with an obstacle; some pallisades with strong thorns opposed our progress, and the noise we unavoidably made in getting through alarmed a picquet, who instead of facing us, leaped around like so many wild hogs into the jungle, which enabled us to reach the fort very soon. The enemy immediately beat their tom-toms, and we expected them certainly to fight us. I did not, with only the twenty-six men who had kept up with me, think it prudent to wait for day-light, we therefore instantly advanced to the storm. The mountain in labour! We dashed up and over the parapet, where I was challenged by a sentry; this so alarmed all the Candians that they fled, and in one minute we became the possessors of a very strong fort, without the enemy firing a shot. Their force was really above 600, almost all armed with muskets, such as they were; they left a few behind them with some gunpowder, and the very tom-toms, that seemed to threaten us, which I now have for Herbert.'[19]

This was not untypical. In the manner of the heroes of G. A. Henty, small parties of British troops darted like gad-flies from one threatened point to another, outnumbered usually about twenty to one in actual numbers but nearer 200 to one in the inaccurate estimates they received about the strength of the enemy. Sometimes a column would be led by a civil servant. One of them, the energetic Hon Alexander Wood, reporting to Colombo that his dozen or so soldiers of the 65th were in perfect

health and spirits, added for Colonel Madison's benefit, that
they had

'. . . behaved themselves in the most exemplary manner, showing the
greatest kindness and attention to the black people, which is not always
to be met with in British soldiers, but is essentially necessary on such an
expedition as this.'[20]

They did not remain in their perfect health for long, but these
young unseasoned soldiers, only four months in the island, did
well before the fever killed them. Nearly everyone, including
Beaver, was racked with the disease, but there was no question
of anyone being able to spare himself, officer or soldier.

V

In Kandy too, disease was spreading with increasing momen-
tum. The onset of the rainy season, which turned the rough
tracks into quagmires, had further aggravated Macdowall's
already grave logistic problems, and a lack of food now further
debilitated the exhausted men. The same fever, which was causing
so much damage down-country and which in its symptoms
resembled the yellow-jack of the West Indies, was the worst
scourge of the British troops, although beri-beri (with its painful
dropsical effects) killed just about as many of them. Often a man
who had been weakened by beri-beri caught the fever and died.
The native troops were to some extent immune from the fever,
but beri-beri, dysentery and the ulcers caused by neglected
scratches took a heavy toll of them. The doctors correctly diag-
nosed the lack of fresh food, particularly vegetables, as the cause
of beri-beri, but they gave equal blame to the shortage of alcohol
and tobacco, then thought to be essential articles of diet. The
regimental surgeons noticed that units camping near rivers and
those that approached Kandy through the wetter country from
Colombo, rather than the drier east coast belt, suffered more
from fever than did men who had to carry out sentry duties in
the dark, but it never occurred to any of them that the common
factor might be the mosquito. Short of medical stores, the

provision of which from home had been shamefully neglected,[21] the doctors groped for a remedy for the fever, experimenting with every nostrum that occurred to them, the most popular of which were vicious purges and emetics. Mercury sometimes seemed to provide a measure of relief, but often it did no more than accelerate the symptoms.[22]

The greater part of North's effective fighting troops, including most of the Europeans, were now virtually trapped in Kandy, half-starved and diseased, with their communications to the coast all but severed. The political outlook was no less sombre. The Governor's mistake in sponsoring Muttusamy was becoming clear. Devoid of any influence among the Kandyan chiefs, not a single person of any importance had joined him. In any case, it appeared, he was debarred under Kandyan law from occupying the throne because he had, in the past, been convicted of fraud. Neither could North hope for succour from elsewhere. The news from Europe indicated that the resumption of the war with Napoleon was imminent; furthermore troops certainly could not be spared from India where Lord Wellesley was poised to crush the power of the Mahrattas. North may have failed to ask for help when Macdowall had seen that it would soon be needed, but now there was none to be had.

When, therefore, a letter from Pilima Talauva arrived in Colombo on 26 March suggesting yet again that North should help him to depose the King, the Governor grasped at the chance of extricating himself from his difficulties. In an attempt to cut his losses, he had, three days before, sent instructions to Macdowall to discard Muttusamy. Now he arranged for an encouraging reply to be sent to the Adigar's letter, but even before there was time for it to arrive, Migastenna, the Second Adigar, who was Pilima Talauva's nephew and close adherent, appeared in Kandy carrying a firelock wrapped in muslin, the traditional token of peaceful intentions.[23] Within three days Macdowall and Migastenna had arranged the terms of a truce and planned a further meeting between their superiors at which Pilima Talauva could elaborate upon his treasonable proposals. The change of circumstances had been startling. Suddenly North could see a way out of his troubles.

This truce could hardly have been concluded without the approval of the King. In any case, the one consistent thread in this tangled story is the apparent desire of the young ruler to live at peace with his powerful neighbours, however much he may have hated their presence in the island. Presumably he had his doubts about the loyalty of his two Ministers, but it is unlikely that he knew that they were planning to betray him. If he had known, he had adequate grounds for eliminating them, powerful though they were. The invasion of his country had done much to consolidate his position, and he now possessed a strong following among the Kandyan chiefs. Pilima Talauva, on the other hand, must have seen only too clearly that this growing power of the young ruler was part of a continuing process, and that soon it would be too late to contemplate supplanting him.

Earlier in March, before the Adigar's new approach to the Governor, North had decided with Macdowall to withdraw a large part of the garrison of Kandy to the coast. The decision was sound. Offensive operations were impossible during the rains, and the reduced force was adequate to hold the capital against an enemy incapable of assaulting a properly defended position. What is more, there would be fewer mouths to feed and fewer men to fall sick. There was no question of abandoning Kandy. Grim though the picture was, North was not yet ready to contemplate so humiliating a possibility. In any case, there were not enough porters to remove all the sick.

Had it not been for the truce, Macdowall would have found it hard to extricate his units through a hostile countryside. Now, assured of a peaceful march, he left Kandy on 1 April, taking the shorter route to Colombo by way of Balane. With him went the 51st Foot, the Ceylon Native Infantry, and some of the artillery; at the same time the flank companies[24] of the 19th Foot and part of the Malay Regiment set out in the opposite direction for Trincomalee. In Kandy, Barbut assumed command of the reduced garrison which now consisted only of 700 Malays and 300 Green Howards (the popular nickname for the 19th Foot), together with a large number of hospital patients whom it had been impossible to move.

Four hundred survivors of the 51st reached Colombo to receive a rapturous welcome from their wives and children. One hundred of their comrades had been left behind, either dead or gravely ill in Kandy. In the manner of soldiers in such circumstances, the officers celebrated their return by holding a party. The long colonnade, set apart for dances and music, in the grounds of the Governor's house in St Sebastian's Hill, was borrowed for the ball. The sides of the building were open to the night breezes, and under the roof of white cloth was suspended a fretwork of delicate moss, known as 'the jeweller's sorrow' from the inability of the craftsmen to imitate its delicate texture.[25] There was little further gaiety for this Regiment. Nearly every officer and soldier who returned to Colombo was admitted to hospital. Within three months only 100 of them were still alive. These unfortunate 'old men and boys' lacked the stamina to resist the medley of diseases that now attacked them.

'The deaths of both officers and men now occurred so frequently, that Colombo wore an aspect of great gloom and melancholy. Every street contained some persons sick of the jungle fever; and the funeral processions marched through the fort in silence, to conceal from those in confinement the mournful fate of their companions.'[26]

Neither the 51st nor the detachment of the 65th were any longer fighting units.

The gloom was not confined to Colombo. In Kandy the deteriorating morale of the garrison is reflected in the letters Ajax Anderson's friends wrote to him after he had been evacuated with some other sick to Trincomalee. On 12 April, one wrote:

'The men, I am sorry to say, are getting very unhealthy, principally of fevers, and that damned disease, the berryberry; we have forty-eight now in hospital, and have lost four men since you left us. I am convinced that nothing is so apt to bring on that plague, the berryberry, (for so it has literally proved to the 51st regiment) as low living, and exposure to heavy dews and the night air to which our men of late have been much subject. Tobacco, an article so absolutely essential to them, they cannot get here;'[27]

Eighteen days later there was a further letter from the same brother officer:

'. . . I am sorry, that if they keep us much longer in this hole, you will see very few of those fine fellows, you left behind, return. I have a long list of casualties this month, twenty-six or twenty-eight men, since your departure, and more than half our number sick, and indeed in a very bad way. They have every thing to fight against, though no man endeavours more to render them comfortable than Colonel Barbut. . . .'[28]

When Macdowall's column had marched down to Colombo through the Kadugannawas Pass, groups of Kandyans had gathered in a far from unfriendly manner to watch them pass, and some of them had even dared to approach quite close to the marching troops. Elsewhere, however, the hostile incursions into British teritory continued despite the truce, an indication that no one authority was in sole control of Kandyan affairs, neither King nor Adigar nor anyone else. The truce had allowed Macdowall to evacuate his men without molestation; and it also permitted some supplies to reach Kandy from Colombo, but with so few transport coolies available, the quantity could only be small.

VI

On 3 May, North and Pilima Talauva met at Dambadeniya. Migastenna was too ill to attend the meeting, and the First Adigar too was a very sick man. The current fever epidemic, which was causing such havoc among the British troops, was one of the most severe the country could remember; and the entire Kandyan court, with the exception of the King, is said to have fallen victim to it. But, as with the native troops, the disease did not attack the Kandyans in the same deadly manner as it did the Europeans. Certainly it affected neither the powers of decision nor the nerve of Pilima Talauva. The day following the initial meeting, he was ready to put his signature to North's proposals. These stipulated that the Adigar would arrange for the King to be handed over to the British, who would allow him to live in Colombo on an annual pension of 30,000 rix dollars,[29] the cash to be found by the Kandyans. Muttusamy was to have a similar amount, together with some empty authority in Jaffna. The Seven Korales and Fort Macdowall (established by the British below the Balakaduwa Pass, where Matale now stands) were to be ceded; and Pilima Talauva, in return, was to rule over the truncated kingdom with the title of *Utun Kumaraya* —the Grand Prince. Until the King could be netted, the truce was to continue in operation.

Barbut, with an escort of 300 Malays, had come down to the meeting, bringing with him an oddly optimistic account of the state of the garrison. Sickness, Barbut advised North, would soon diminish, and little was needed in Kandy but enough doolies to evacuate the invalids, with—of course—the coolies to carry them. This was Barbut's last contribution to the campaign. He now collapsed in his turn and was carried down to Colombo, where he died a few weeks later. Much has been made of a statement, the sole authority for which is Cordiner,[30] that only the unexpected arrival of Barbut's Malays prevented the Adigar from carrying out a premeditated plot to kidnap North at this meeting. On the face of it, the suggestion seems improbable. North never travelled without a sizeable escort—on this occasion it was commanded by Herbert Beaver, whom North had just appointed A.D.C. in recognition of his gallantry. It is hard to accept that the Adigar would have risked a direct personal confrontation with a body of regular troops. It is harder still to see what he could have gained from capturing North. Perhaps, however, he let it be known at court that he intended some such plan in order to provide an adequate justification for his attending the meeting.

The meeting poses many different questions. Was the Adigar acting in good faith towards the British or was his approach all part of some tortuous manœuvre to lull North into a sense of false security? If he was betraying the King, how did he explain the meeting, other than by producing the unlikely story that he was trying to kidnap North? To what extent did the meeting increase any doubts the King may already have held about his Adigar's loyalty? One can but conjecture. It is doubtful if the answers will ever be known.

Before the meeting broke up, Pilima Talauva had asked North to agree to Macdowall returning to Kandy to replace Barbut and so be available for further negotiations. To this North agreed, and the General, on 23 May, arrived back in the capital accompanied by two staff officers. To Macdowall's dismay he discovered that Barbut's account of the condition of the garrison bore no relation to the truth. Another of Anderson's brother officers provided a far more accurate description:

'. . . our mortality and sickness is every day increasing, such is the melancholy state of our detachment, that out of two hundred and thirty-four men, remaining of those you left behind, there are not above five fit for duty, and even their services are required to attend those who are in hospital. The number at present in the hospital is one hundred and twelve, mostly fevers, and fifty sick in barracks. The detachment at Fort Macdowall, have only eight men, out of fifty, fit for duty. Yesterday, on the arrival of Gen Macdowall, he ordered the whole of the convalescent sick to get ready to march for Trincomalee; but, dreadful to relate, when they came to be mustered, only twenty-three men out of the whole were found to be able to march.'[31]

On the last day of May, Quartermaster Brown, also of the 19th Foot, wrote:

'No news of these Adigaars yet. . . . The rains have been very heavy indeed for these three days past, it has hardly ever ceased a moment, and it is very cold at night . . . four of our men died last night, and how we are to get them buried, I know not, for there is scarcely a man able to walk, and not a scoundrel of a Candian will come near us.'[32]

On 10 June, Lieutenant Ormsby of the 51st Regiment, who was acting as Commissary of Provisions, despaired of the situation:

'What a melancholy catalogue could I give you of our departed friends. . . .
'God only knows what will become of us here, for if we are ordered to evacuate the place, there is scarce a single European that could walk a mile, and there are neither coolies or doolies. If we were to be attacked, we have only three artillerymen fit for duty. The Malay regiment have lost upwards of thirty men this month.'[33]

Once again the Kandyans were harrying the supply lines both to Colombo and Trincomalee. The loyalty of the Malays was also causing worry: sickness, semi-starvation, the lack of opium (as important to them as tobacco to the Europeans), and pay ten weeks in arrear were all doing their damage. Nevertheless, despite some desertions, most were still resisting the temptation to try to save themselves. In this respect, their Adjutant, Captain Nouradin, set them a sturdy example. Half-brother to Sangunglo, the commander of the King's Malay troops, he declined an invitation from his relative to turn his men against their British comrades.[34]

There was also little news of Pilima Talauva. In the sole letter Macdowall had received from him since he returned, the Adigar had said that the King would not allow him to come to Kandy, an excuse Macdowall described as perfidious.[35] It is probable, however, that it indicated no more than the Adigar's waning powers. His meeting with North must have deepened the suspicions the King held about him and strengthened the position of his opponents at court.

The inevitability of the disaster was becoming clear, and Macdowall decided once again to return to Colombo to persuade North that some means must be found to evacuate the survivors of the garrison. On 11 June, the General left Kandy, sick himself now, his bowels weakened by purges and his mouth badly infected by the large doses of mercury he had swallowed.[36]

To command in Kandy, Macdowall left the senior officer, Major Adam Davie, who had served in Ceylon for only a year, having transferred from the 75th Regiment to the Malays. His acquaintances afterwards remembered Davie as a well-disposed, inoffensive person, without any practical experience of war.[37] The contemplation of his new responsibilities overwhelmed the unfortunate officer. Anticipating the probable outcome of events with some accuracy, he asked permission to decline his new appointment on the grounds that it could bring him only discredit and blame.[38] His dejection is expressed in one of the last personal letters he wrote from Kandy:

'Henderson died on the 11th, and Bausset this morning; Rumley and Gonpil are also ill.
'The Lascars and Malays desert by dozens, and high rewards are offered to murder all the officers.—Batteries close on us.—Our bullocks carried off by force, and attempts even made to carry off the small mortars

from the park on the parade. A hopeful situation truly and a pretty time to succeed to such a command.

'Excuse this scrawl, it being the 19th letter I have written this day, and besides I am far from well. The General and his aide-de-camp left this on the 11th, both ill: I wish that they may reach Colombo safe.'[39]

Poor Davie! The finely drawn ascetic features shown in his portrait reveal little of a man of action. He was not cast in the heroic role and he had little cause for optimism.

On 25 June, North at last sent orders to Davie to evacuate Kandy.[40] It is difficult to see in North's action anything more than an ineffectual attempt to try to save something from the impending disaster. Small parties of reinforcements with doolies and some porters were now on their way from both Colombo and Trincomalee to help carry out the sick, but the account Macdowall had provided of the state of the garrison must have made it clear that Davie would require far more help than this if he were to hope to evacuate his hundreds of invalids.

CHAPTER 7

The First War: Massacre

In any case, North's orders to Major Davie to evacuate Kandy were despatched from Colombo too late. Two days beforehand the Kandyans had seized the posts at Girihagama and Galagedara, each of which was garrisoned by a havildar and a dozen Malay soldiers. Some had already deserted to the Kandyans and it was thought that those who remained surrendered without any attempt at resistance. Encouraged by this success, by the self-evident enfeebled state of the British garrison in the capital, and by the ever-growing number of their own levies gathering in the neighbourhood (estimates varied between 10,000 and 50,000 men), the Kandyans were ready to be convinced that the time had come for the kill.

On 23 June, the day following the fall of the twin forts, Davie received a letter from Pilima Talauva containing the news that the Kandyan attack was about to start. Ever since Macdowall had left, the two men had been in regular and open communication with each other, and one can but assume that the Adigar was still doing all he could to keep his options open. Davie heeded this warning and placed four 3-pounders in position to cover the main approaches to the King's Palace, within which he now concentrated his forces. It was a measure of the plight of the garrison that this had not been done before, for by now only twenty ailing European soldiers still retained enough strength to lift a gun and help man the defences.

Not that there were any defences in the true meaning of the word. The tangled mass of buildings which comprised the Palace was surrounded on three sides by a wall which was ornamental rather than military in concept. But the real weakness lay on the eastern flank. Here the Palace buildings were bounded by no more than a stockade, and rising acutely above them were the steep Udawatta Hills which tapered into a sheer escarpment at the south-easterly corner of the huddle of red-roofed and whitewashed dwelling-houses, temples and store-rooms. Against an attack in any way prolonged or determined, the 800-yard perimeter of the so-called fort was in no way defensible.

A fifth 3-pounder, with one of the mortars, had previously been emplaced on the flank of the hill which commanded the eastern end of the Palace. Now covered by thick forest, the siting of the battery here suggests that the hill was at the time clear of trees.[1] This post was held by only ten men—Sepoy gunners and Malay infantrymen; there had been a European in charge, a German artillery sergeant named Theon, but he was now in hospital recovering from an attack of beri-beri that would have proved fatal to anyone with a weaker constitution.

Before dawn on 24 June,[2] a party of Kandyan Malays crept out of the darkness and overran this hill-side battery, making prisoner the small garrison. Down below nothing was heard of this silent attack, and just before five o'clock, Quartermaster Brown of the 19th Foot was chatting with Ensign Barry under a verandah immediately below the battery, prior to going outside to shoot a few pigeons for the pot. Both men were quite unaware of the drama that had occurred in the darkness above their heads. Suddenly, in the dim light, they saw swinging round along the flank of the hill from the south-east a vast mob of the enemy, headed by the King's Malay mercenaries, at the head of whom was Sangunglo, their tall, stout, but nevertheless agile captain. Assistant-Surgeon Greeving estimated the enemy at 20,000 men but he usually exaggerated. In any case there was not enough room to deploy so many men against this short stretch of the perimeter.

Across the low stockade, which formed but a rudimentary obstacle, came a rush of men, led by Sangunglo. The Malay leaped upon Brown, pushing aside the Quartermaster's gun before he could pull the trigger (he was a corpulent officer and clearly less agile than his opponent), and stabbed him with his kris. As Brown fell dead, Barry bayoneted Sangunglo, and Major Davie, who had now arrived on the scene, finished him off with his sword. By now a few men of the 19th Foot had also appeared, together with Captain Humphreys, the artillery commander, who threw himself behind the 3-pounder. One round of grape-shot from this tore a gap in the massed ranks of the hesitant attackers, killing twenty-four of them and causing the rest to turn and run.

After this initial repulse, the Kandyans did not risk a further assault, but kept up a steady harassing fire with their muskets and gingals against the four sides of the perimeter. Soon they were able to turn the heavier weapons in the captured hill-side battery against the defenders. The fire seems to have caused few casualties, but the lack of enough fit men to hold the long perimeter allowed the Kandyans to infiltrate forward among the buildings during the course of the long morning. A spirited sally by a Malay lieutenant and twenty of his men relieved the pressure temporarily, but the handful of Europeans still on their feet were sick and exhausted. As for the native troops, the sight of some of their comrades, who had previously deserted, in the ranks of the attackers provided visible proof that they were unlikely to be ill-treated if they surrendered.

A grotesque performance now took place. Towards the end of the morning four British officers of the Malay Regiment came in a delegation to Davie and suggested to him that it was necessary to capitulate. When Davie refused to consider doing so, his subordinates, in a fit of hysteria, threw their swords to the ground, protesting that the Palace could not be held for more than another hour. This was more than their commander could stand. Seizing a pistol, he tried to shoot himself, but someone wrenched the weapon from him. This drama over, Greeving and Nouradin, the Malay adjutant, then intervened to point out that capitulation to the Kandyans was tantamount to another form of suicide. Their protest was in vain. Davie had, by now, decided to surrender; and, about mid-day, he went out to meet the Kandyan leaders, accompanied by Captain Nouradin and holding in his hand a stick to which a rag of white cloth had been tied.

Somewhere within the Palace were six officers of the 19th Foot, two of the 51st, and Humphreys of the Gunners. None of them are recorded as having been present during the incident described above, and none of them seem to have been consulted about the decision to surrender. There is little that can be said in defence of the British officers of the Malay Regiment. They still commanded 250 men who had shown that, given proper leadership, they were capable of putting up a sturdy resistance. Had these officers been of the calibre of some of their Malay colleagues, events in Kandy might have turned out very different, but they seem to have been a poorish lot. The year before, when Ensign Barry had been in trouble for encouraging one of his brother officers to challenge his senior to a duel, Macdowall had castigated them collectively and publicly, accusing them of 'insubordination and want of discipline', and condemning duelling as 'barbarous, unmilitary and immoral'.[3] Clearly their General thought little of them. Davie was, of course, their commanding officer, and he was hardly the man either to inspire confidence or exercise discipline. On the other hand, he was working with poor material. Only three months before it had been necessary to send a complaint to the Horse Guards pointing out the difficulty of obtaining officers for the Corps in view of the restricted service and the poor opportunities for promotion.[4]

Although there was no lack of sound officers in the British service, as the record of the three regiments of European troops which took part in this fighting demonstrate, the exercise of patronage through mistresses, creditors and clients managed to produce a not inconsiderable number of worthless ones. The methods used for raising troops at the start of the war against France accentuated every evil present in the normal system. Displaying masterly financial acumen, the Government created new units by selling commissions in them and using the receipts to pay the enlistment bounties offered to the recruits. An alternative scheme permitted newly appointed officers to be given rank in the raw companies and battalions in exchange for the recruits they could raise, the officers laying out their own money to pay the crimps who collected the recruits. Many of these people were quite unfit to hold the King's commission. Some were engaged merely in a complicated form of stock-jobbery to increase the monetary value of their commissions by a series of well-judged inter-regimental transfers. When such men could not avoid the obligation to join their regiments or when they found it advantageous to do so, the wretched troops suffered; but often they never joined at all. In Holland, many officers were drunk regularly on duty, obsessed by their own creature comforts, and quite ignorant of their professional duties, not unnaturally so as they never received any formal instruction on the subject. It was really not surprising that a proportion of these bad officers could find their way to newly-raised units in out-of-the-way places, of which the Malay Regiment was an example.

II

Surrender terms were agreed between Davie and Pilima Talauva, who was in command of the Kandyan army. Accompanied by Muttusamy and his suite of twenty-seven Malabars, the troops were to be allowed to march down unmolested to Trincomalee. The Kandyans were to care for the sick and wounded in hospital until arrangements could be made to evacuate them; and the artillery and ammunition were to be surrendered. According to Greeving, the Adigar also stipulated that the troops were to leave their ammunition behind; and an African named Joseph Fernando, who was still alive in Kandy in 1848 and who claimed to have been in command of the King's Caffre troops, said the same thing.[5] Neither the official account of the events nor any of the other narratives mention this vital point; and, on balance, it is hard to believe that Greeving's statement was true, inaccurate as his narrative was in so many other respects.

Events now moved quickly. Late that afternoon, as dusk was

falling, thirty-four Europeans, 250 Malays, a small party of Bengal gunners, 140 gun lascars, and a number of Malay and Indian wives, a few with small children, marched out of Kandy. With them was Muttusamy and his suite. It was a wet and stormy evening and all the way along the two-mile main street, a weird chorus of howling dogs accompanied the retreating column. Greeving relates that a horde of armed Kandyans beat and insulted the men as they marched, wrenching their firelocks from them, but no one else mentions this; and, once again, his account seems to be improbable. At 7 pm the marching men reached the banks of the Mahaweli Ganga at the Watapuluwa ferry near the village of Mawilmada, but there was no question of crossing. The river, usually fordable at this point, was in flood and there were neither boats nor rafts. Soaked, starving, sick and exhausted, the soldiers settled down for the night in the insistent rain.

Early the next morning, four officials arrived from the King with a demand that Muttusamy and his suite should be surrendered. This proposal Davie rejected, but some hours later a second delegation repeated the request, emphasizing that no harm was intended towards the Malabar and promising that boats would be provided for the troops to cross the river as soon as he had been handed over. Davie still refused to comply, but a third embassy that arrived an hour later was more preemptory: unless Muttusamy was surrendered forthwith, 50,000 Kandyans were ready to come and take him. After consulting his officers, Davie succumbed to this threat, tearfully protesting to Muttusamy that he lacked the power to protect him, and excusing himself on the grounds that the King had promised to treat his captive kindly. According to Cordiner, Muttusamy rejoined with the words: 'My God! Is it possible that the triumphant arms of England can be so humbled, as to fear the menaces of such cowards as the Kandyans?'[6], but one of Muttusamy's servants reported that his master told Davie that the troops should not be endangered on his account and that he was prepared to be delivered over to the Kandyan emissaries.[7]

Muttusamy, with three of his kinsmen and seven servants, were then led away and conducted into the presence of the

King about a mile to the east of Kandy. There, after a summary trial, the King condemned Muttusamy and his three relations to death. The four men were then taken outside, made to sit on the ground, and their heads were struck off with swords. Two of the servants were later hanged but the rest were released, after having had their noses and ears severed, and arrived in Trincomalee towards the end of the month.[8]

Davie did not have long to wait before discovering that his sacrifice of Muttusamy had, in every respect, been futile. At half past two, one of the sick Europeans who had been left behind in the hospital, dragged himself into the camp. He had a horrifying tale to tell.

III

A long narrow room in the Palace, previously used as a refectory for the *bhikkhus*, had been converted into a hospital for the European troops, and here, on the day of the surrender, were lying rows of soldiers, mostly members of the 19th Foot. Reduced to a diet of unhusked rice and arrack (supplies of the latter had now improved), it was not surprising that their death rate had recently mounted to a dozen or so daily. The news that the terms of the capitulation promised that the Kandyans were to provide medicines for them, and that they were to be evacuated to the coast as soon as possible, did little to reassure these helpless men; and the sound of Davie's drummers beating his force through the Palace gate was a signal for a few of the more mobile to make a desperate attempt to crawl out of the ward and try to overtake their comrades. Sergeant Theon described what followed:

'The garrison had hardly marched out of the front gate, when thousands of Kandians entered the palace at all sides, armed with swords, knives, clubs, old firelocks, etc, and rushed into the hospital, where I lay with about 149 other Europeans. I was at that time sitting upon a couch, being the only man in hospital, who could sit up, I had therefore a full view of the horrible scene that ensued.

'The Kandians had no sooner entered, than they began to butcher indiscriminately every one in the hospital, robbing them at the same time, cursing and reviling them, and spitting in their faces; they mostly knocked out the soldiers' brains with clubs, etc then pulled them out by the heels, the dead and the dying, threw many of them into a well, and numbers of the bodies were left in the streets and devoured by dogs, but none were buried. Some poor wretches got off their cots and tried to crawl away, but the Kandians murdered them before they could get out of the hospital, not many of the British soldiers cried out for mercy, but many called upon God, and some suffered death without saying a word.'[9]

The sole officer in the hospital, Lieutenant Plenderleath, the Adjutant of the 19th Foot, who had been severely wounded during the course of the dawn attack on the eastern perimeter, was savagely beaten before being thrown into a gutter to die. Except for the one man who escaped to bring the news to Davie at the river bank, Theon was the only survivor. Knocked unconscious, he awoke naked in the courtyard among the bodies of his comrades, the skin stripped from his stomach where a blister had been ripped off. As he crawled away on all fours, a party of Kandyans found him, tied a rope around his neck and strung him up on a convenient beam. Fortunately for Theon, they left him alone to die and the rope broke before he was strangled. When he came to for the second time, it was quite dark and he was able to crawl away to hide in an empty house. Here he existed on grass and rain-water for seven days before being discovered once again. By now the Kandyans were weary of killing, and Theon was imprisoned with Muttusamy's servants, some of whom he saw hanged and the rest mutilated. Then, in the company of the Malay and Lascar prisoners, he was carried before the King, who treated all of them with unexpected magnanimity, presenting them with money and clothes. Afterwards this very tough individual lived on in Kandy as a royal pensioner for twelve years, marrying a Muslim girl and raising a son by her.

In the south-eastern corner of the Palace was a separate hospital for the Asian soldiers. Greeving, who was in charge of them, states that twenty-three Malays and seventeen Moorish gunners were left behind, but there is no record of what happened to them. In the blood-lust of the moment, the Kandyans may have slaughtered them with their British comrades. Perhaps, however, they were spared. Another unresolved problem is the number of Europeans who died. Greeving put it as low as fifty-five or so, but Theon's figure of 148 is likely to be a more accurate estimate.

Dr Holloway of the 19th Foot was in charge of the European hospital. Theon mentions that he was 'very kind and tender to the sick . . . he remained with them night and day',[10] but he was not kind enough to stay behind and look after them. Neither did Greeving. Both the doctors left with Davie, abandoning their patients to the Kandyans.

IV

Throughout that first day by the river bank, the troops had been labouring to build rafts from the giant bamboos that grew in profusion near the water's edge, but the river was running so fast that no one had been able to carry a rope across to the other side. In accordance with their envoys' promise, a few Kandyans appeared after Muttusamy had been surrendered and seemed to be making some sort of preparations to help the troops in their work, but they soon disappeared, saying that they would return the next morning with boats.

The following day was a Sunday and the troops awoke, shivering in the dampness of dawn, to find themselves surrounded by hordes of Kandyans—Greeving put the number at 50,000. No boats appeared, but about ten o'clock Humphreys with his Bengal gunners managed to get a warp across the river. Their efforts were wasted. Hopelessly the troops watched some Kandyans on the far bank sever the rope. A direct result of this blow to morale was the start of a steady trickle of desertions by the Malays and gun lascars. In contrast, the Bengal gunners stood firm.

It is hardly surprising that the various accounts of what now happened differ in some detail. As far as can be gathered, a further collection of emissaries approached Davie with a demand that his men should surrender their weapons and march back to Kandy. To reinforce the ultimatum, a party of the enemy, consisting of some 200 Malays and Caffres, led by the brutal-looking Joseph Fernando, menaced the British troops from a distance of about a hundred yards. Davie then called his officers to a council of war, after which he ordered his men to lay down their weapons; but, before doing so, he refused a request by two or three old soldiers of the 19th Foot that they be allowed to hold a separate council among themselves. Davie's order provoked a few cries of protest from his men, but their hard discipline allied to their utter exhaustion seems to have prevented them from doing anything more than express this feeble dissent. But even now their commander lacked decision. He revoked the order so that he could destroy some papers. Then, for the second time he ordered his soldiers to ground their weapons, and they complied.

The Kandyans then approached and separated the Asian troops from the British. The former were marched off in the direction of the capital, while the European soldiers were in their turn separated from the officers and taken a short distance away. The Kandyans then robbed the men of their valuables and started to lead them pair by pair towards a hollow near the river bank which was hidden in a patch of thick bush. It was only after the first few men had been taken away in this manner that the rest realized what was happening to their comrades. As they reached the hollow, the Caffres were chopping them down with their large swords.

Meanwhile the officers were also being killed. One or two managed to shoot themselves with pistols they had concealed in their clothing; Barry killed himself with a musket he snatched from one of the executioners, and two officers of the 19th Foot threw themselves into the river to drown. Lieutenant Blakeney, who had been wounded in the chest and thigh during the battle and carried out of Kandy in a doolie, was dragged out of the conveyance and knocked on the head.[11] The last two officers to be led forward to die were Davie and his second-in-command, Captain Rumley; but, as the Caffres were about to kill them, Pilima Talauva arrived and forbade the executioners to slay them, issuing orders that they should be sent to the King.

Two other officers also managed to survive the massacre. Greeving seized Humphreys by the arm when no one was looking and succeeded in rolling down the hill-side with him unobserved. The two men reached a hole in the ground into which they crawled, and into it the Caffres then cast the bodies of their friends. After remaining concealed in this way for four days, they emerged and surrendered to a party of Malays they saw, among whom Greeving recognized an old acquaintance he had known when he was in the Dutch service. The King spared both men, as he did Theon. Like his illustrious predecessor, Raja Sinha II, Sri Wikrama had a fondness for keeping tame Europeans around his court. The following year, Greeving managed to escape to the coast, but after a short while Humphreys died in captivity.

The captured Asian troops were given the choice of entering the King's service. Some of the Bengal gunners and the Malays refused, protesting that they had already sworn an oath to a great King and that it was not possible for them to serve two governments. These the Kandyans killed, upon which the rest went over to the enemy, an understandable decision after the example some of their British officers had set them. A few afterwards escaped, including Milhanage Joannes and Mohamed Gani, Barry's Malay servant.

The only British soldier to survive was a Corporal Barnsley of the 19th Foot. Led down into the hollow, he had just enough time to see the scattered bodies of his comrades who had preceded him, before a blow from a sword in the back of the neck felled him to the ground. Unconscious for only a few minutes, he opened his eyes to see the Caffres working over the heaped bodies, beating both the dead and the still-groaning living over the head with the butts of their guns. Feigning dead, Barnsley received a further blow which laid him out once again.

It was nearly dark when the corporal next awoke. He first discovered that he had been stripped to his shirt, and that he could walk only if he supported his head with his left hand to prevent it falling forward on to his chest, the sword-blow had severed the tendons in his neck. Next he saw a crowd of Kandyans gathered around what he presumed to be an interesting spectacle because those on the outside were jumping in the air as if to get a better view of what was happening. The noise of pistol shots from this direction then made Barnsley suppose that the officers were shooting themselves.

When it grew light the next morning, Barnsley discovered that the Kandyans had gone. He made his way to the river, the level of which he found to have dropped despite the rain that had fallen throughout the night. Paddling with his right arm and holding his head above water with his left, he swam the river, nearly meeting with disaster when the strength of the current in mid-stream forced him to use both his arms to swim. When at last he gained the other side, Barnsley collapsed, his body still in the water. With an effort he summoned the determination to drag himself to the top of the bank, where he saw, to his horror, a Kandyan standing and watching him. Fortunately for Barnsley, the Kandyan was the more frightened of the two of them and was persuaded to give the Englishman a garment of sorts to wrap around himself. Thus equipped, the corporal set out to walk to Fort Macdowall, thirteen miles away across the hills, fighting against the pain of the wound that felt like a red-hot iron in the back of his neck and a racking headache caused by the blow from the Caffre's gun. That night he rested in an empty hut, nearly out of his mind with pain, but the next day he set out once again in the direction of Fort Macdowall, after binding up his wound with the remains of his shirt. Very soon he ran into a party of Kandyans. They treated him in a kindly manner, giving him a cake of meal to eat, which he found he could not swallow, and then led him to a village where some 5,000 armed Kandyans were resting. Their destination was the same as Barnsley's—the beleaguered Fort Macdowall, where they were going to reinforce the attackers. Again Barnsley was well treated and given food, this time rice and curry, some of which he managed to swallow with much trouble and pain. Then, taking the corporal with them, the Kandyans moved on towards their objective.

When they arrived in sight of their destination, the Kandyan chief, making use of the Malabar language, of which Barnsley understood a little, indicated that he wanted the corporal to take a message to the Commandant of the Fort suggesting (rather optimistically) that he and his troops should come out from behind the shelter of the walls and fight the Kandyans in the open. Two men then led Barnsley towards the hill upon which Fort Macdowall was perched, and left him at the bottom to make his own way up. As he approached the wall,

'. . . the sentinel was struck with terror at the emaciated figure and ghastly look; he was conducted to Captain Madge, commander of the Fortress at the time, who was thunderstruck by his appearance, and the melancholy tidings he bore. The first words he said, was "The Troops in Candy are all dished, your honour".'[12]

Stragglers habitually exaggerate ill-tidings. This one did not. Captain Madge made an immediate record of his melancholy news.[13]

The garrison of this small fort consisted of three officers, a surgeon, twenty-two Malays and thirty-two soldiers of the 19th Foot. Nineteen of these men were incapable of moving and the rest either sickly or convalescent. For three days past the Kandyans had been conducting a half-hearted siege, and Barnsley's news of the disaster in Kandy and the arrival of the enemy reinforcements decided Madge to evacuate the Fort, regardless of the fact that this would entail abandoning his invalids. Barnsley had told him what had happened to the patients in the hospital in Kandy so he could have been under no illusions about their probable fate.

At ten o'clock that night, when the moon had sunk behind the hills, Madge and his men crept quietly out of the Fort, leaving the lamps still burning to delude the Kandyans, and the sick men lying in their cots, waiting for their end.

For four days the Kandyans followed Madge, harassing his retreat. Then the garrison met a column of 150 Malay troops, an escort party for a convoy of 100 doolies and their carriers, moving up from Trincomalee to Kandy. The enlarged force was too powerful for the Kandyans to tackle, and the subsequent retreat to the coast was unopposed. The speed of march of the column was remarkable. Only seven days after leaving

Fort Macdowall, Madge's force arrived in Trincomalee, Barnsley still supporting his head with his left hand. Madge had conducted a masterly withdrawal and the subsequent praise he received was undoubtedly well-merited. As against this he had evacuated, without orders, a strong post which could have been held without difficulty against the irresolute type of attack which was all the Kandyans were capable of mounting. Reinforcements were on their way, with enough doolies to carry out the sick and wounded, and would have arrived within the week. Above all, Madge had abandoned nineteen sick men of his own Regiment to certain slaughter. For this he was neither censured by his superiors, nor—as far as one can gather—criticized by his fellows. Only in Marshall can one detect a shade of reproach:

'He must, however, have left the nineteen sick with great regret, being well aware that they would be forthwith put to death when they fell into the hands of the Kandyans.'[14]

It is gratifying to know that Barnsley survived. Shortly after recovering from his wounds, he was promoted to the rank of sergeant, but within a few months he had been reduced to the ranks for being found drunk on barrack guard. In 1805, he was invalided home, still a private soldier, and was last heard of serving as a member of a veteran corps in Fort George six years later. His comrades in his new unit probably thought him a formidable liar.

V

There is a postscript to the tragedy. Captain Nouradin and his brother, also an officer in the Malay Regiment, were not killed on the spot but brought before the King. As they came into the royal presence, they declined to prostrate themselves in the customary manner, but instead saluted the King respectfully, excusing themselves from performing the more formal abasement on the grounds that they themselves were of royal blood, their grandfather having been an independent ruler. This temerity failed to anger the King, and he repeated to them his previous offer to enter his service, inviting them now to take over the command of his Malay troops, vacant since the death of Sangunglo, their half-brother. Nouradin's reply was to protest that acceptance of the King's offer would disgrace them as they had both sworn allegiance to the King of England, and that they would live and die in his service. Their behaviour, contrasting as it did so vividly with that of their commanding officer, seems to have impressed Sri Wikrama. He held the two officers in prison until the middle of August, and then repeated his offer. Once again they rejected it. This time the King showed them no mercy. They were executed forthwith and their bodies dragged into the woods to be devoured by wild animals.

The fate of Rumley and Humphreys is uncertain. At first they were imprisoned at Hanguranketa, but Greeving reported that, at the end of August, they were in the company of the King. They seem to have died soon afterwards, but whether from disease or the King's executioners is not known.

For ten long years or so Davie clutched to his life. His death was often reported, first by Greeving who provided a graphic account of the manner in which he had attended the Major during his last illness and the way the Kandyans had disposed of the body. The King's treatment of Davie varied with his moods. At first he was half-starved and neglected, but later his captivity seems to have been as lenient as that of Knox. The King gave him money and valuable presents, provided him with servants and even appointed him to the titular rank of *Madige Dissawa*, or head of the bullock transport department of the kingdom.[15] Towards the end of his life, like Theon, he took a wife and had by her a son who survived him.

In 1805, it was being widely reported in Colombo that some Europeans had survived the massacre; and Sir Thomas Maitland, North's successor as Governor, sent a spy into the hills carrying a message hidden in a quill with the questions: 'How many of you? Your Name? Their Names? Circumstances?'[16] The messenger found Davie and returned with his reply, dated November, 1805, and a further letter which Davie had written the previous May, using for paper the back of a plan of Kandy in March,

10. *Major-General Hay Macdowall*

11. *Dr Henry Marshall*

12. *Sir Robert Brownrigg*

13. *The Hon Frederick North*

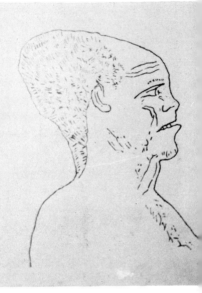

14. *Sri Wickrama Raja Singha, the last King of Ceylon*

15. *Joseph Fernando, the Executioner of Major Davies' Detachment*

16. *Gingals in the Kandy Museum*

1803, by Captain Vilant of the 19th Foot, a noted artist and draughtsman. Davie's reply read:

'None that I know of, but myself, Major Ad Davie, the rest all murdered, dead or starved to Death, am at Karaliada, about ten miles East of Kandi, north side of the river, without Meat or Clothes to cover me.

'Let not my friends know that I am alive, as I expect not to survive many days. I have done my duty to my Country, but it has not done so to me. After tamely allowing for two and a half years such cruel murders to pass unavenged, I can scarcely expect that my countrymen will ever come. But, if they should, I shall only say, 500 men are more than sufficient for the Subjugation of this Country. Touch not at Kandi, but to destroy it. One half of your Army ought to occupy the open ground around Dumboor, the other half clear of wood about a mile westward from Hangourankette, and send out Parties of fifty in every direction to burn or destroy. . . .

'Let not the least Confidence be placed in the Adigars, either 1st or 2nd. I am told, and have every Reason to believe, I am to be murdered on my Countrymen coming to Kandi. The Bearer could easily get me from this by moonlight, with a very few men. Reward the Bearer well, a pair of Shoes will be necessary.'[17]

The tenor of the other letter was similar: Davie did not hope to live much longer; he had done his duty, he expected revenge to be taken; to ravage the country would earn the support of the Kandyans; his Malay troops had basely and treacherously left the officers to be murdered.

Over the years the British authorities in Colombo carried on an intermittent correspondence with this melancholy personage, now a familiar figure in the Kandyan kingdom, wearing his faded scarlet coat, once white breeches, his feet bare and beard long and straggling. Quills and lumps of jaggery were used as hiding places for letters. Given a little energy, he might well have escaped, but he never tried. When he changed his abode to the capital, he is said to have walked each evening from the town down to the river bank, where forlornly he would sit, contemplating the obstacle that had prevented the escape of himself and his murdered men.[18] Continual sickness had sapped his strength and his will-power. Either in 1812 or 1813 he died of a dropsy, and it is a miracle that he managed to survive for so long. His last pathetic scribbled message to the outside world read:

'With everything they sent only omitted what I most opium [*sic*] without which I cannot exist & a phial laudenham & penknife. My health weak and my body weaker I cannot rise but for a short time ye Plan of ye Priest will not I fear much succeed I'll only say you know my Place of Abode & delay not ye Priest if he attempts anything at all will procrastinate my supplies of food are **** small & in arrears. For heaven sake send quickly laudenham & opium my torture is indurable [*sic*] you omitted a razor and penknife also a monthly Army list I wish to know my now rank that I may settle affairs.'[19]

Short of provoking a further war, Maitland and his successor did everything possible to effect Davie's release. A variety of schemes were concocted to help him to escape, all of which foundered, and every time negotiations were reopened between the two Governments, the British insisted that Davie's return was an essential prerequisite to any form of settlement, a condition which the King, in a seemingly perverse fashion, was adamant in rejecting.

To North's discredit, he tried to make Davie the scapegoat for the disaster; and it is possibly significant that, unlike his successors, he did not try either to contact the prisoner or to secure his release. His attempts to saddle Davie with the blame do not make pleasant reading. North's report to Lord Hobart, written on 8 July, queried the need for Davie to lay down his arms when he must have known that 'a corps of forty Europeans in good health, and of two hundred Malays, might cut their way through any army of Candians to any part of the island'. What North described (not very accurately) as 'the fort' was, he said, tenable against any force and was well supplied with provisions.[20] It bears repeating that North well knew the true state of the garrison and the defences.

As Dr Marshall makes plain, both Beaver and Cordiner were cautious in attributing blame to Davie.[21] The latter's subordinates —Greeving, Barnsley, Theon and the two natives who escaped— confined themselves to relating the facts as they saw them. If they did criticize Davie, their censure was suppressed. He found defenders. The anonymous author of *The War In Ceylon*, published in the 1804 volume of the *Asiatic Annual Review*, spoke out on his behalf, objecting to what he described as the official obloquy that had been cast upon the officer.[22]

Indecisive, pessimistic and hysterical, the faults of this weak and unhappy person are only too obvious. He should never have held the King's commission. Equally it can be said that such an officer should never have been left in command of the Malay Regiment when his inadequacies were already apparent to his superiors. At the time, however, it was not easy to remove an inefficient senior officer expeditiously. The Duke of York was in the process of reforming the management of the officer corps of the Army, but the effect of his changes had still to be felt in outposts as remote as Ceylon.

Disaster was probably inevitable. It is doubtful whether even a leader of the calibre of Beaver would have managed to extricate the garrison complete with their burden of sick men. Probably Davie trusted the Adigar to see that the men in hospital survived. He had adequate reasons for relying on the Minister's good faith. He knew that his seniors had been negotiating with the man for years; and he had himself been in continuous touch with him—the Adigar had even warned him that the Palace was about to be attacked. Knowing Pilima Talauva's disloyalty towards his King, Davie would have judged that it was in the Adigar's interests to ensure that the terms of the capitulation were carried out and the wounded protected.

But it is hard to justify Davie's behaviour on the river bank. There can be no excuse for his surrendering Muttusamy so tamely. Although some of the British officers of the Malay Regiment were useless, Nouradin and his fellows were staunch enough, and the Malays would probably have responded to some slight show of firmness by their leaders. Certainly the British troops were ready to fight it out, sick and exhausted though they were. Even after Davie had learned the fate of the men he had left in hospital, he was still prepared to order his men to lay down their weapons. Years later, a Kandyan chief commented that if the British had retained the sense to fire five shots, all his countrymen would have run away.[23] This may or may not have been so, but in Valentia's words:

'. . . it is incomprehensible that he should be induced to capitulate to so weak a foe as the King of Candy, and still more, that he should afterwards consent to surrender his arms, contrary to the terms of the capitulation. It is most of all extraordinary that he should deliver Mootoo Swamy to his implacable enemy, who immediately put him to death in the presence of those, who ought to have perished with arms in their hands, rather than have submitted to an act which has impressed an indelible stain on the British character. . . .'[24]

Who was responsible for the massacre? Dr Davy suggests that the blame lay with the King. After Muttusamy had been slain, he said:

'. . . the King again summoned the first Adigar and Malawa before him, and bid them follow the English and put them to death. The minister objected to the order, remarking, "It is highly improper for those who have submitted, to be put to death."—"What! (said the enraged King) are you siding with the English again?" The minister then left the royal presence, observing "Since he urges the measure, what can we do?" '[25]

Cordiner's account is similar. Possibly his narrative was Davy's source. When the King's officials brought Davie the demand to surrender Muttusamy they mentioned, according to Cordiner, that the King was greatly enraged with his Adigar for allowing the garrison to leave Kandy.[26] In his warning letter to Davie, Pilima Talauva had mentioned that he was in disgrace with the King.[27] This was probably true. He must have found it difficult to explain what had occurred during his meeting with North at Dambadeniya.

Unless he was making some sort of desperate attempt to prove his loyalty to the King, Pilima Talauva had little reason to perpetrate the massacre on his own initiative. Ever since North had jettisoned Muttusamy, the Adigar had sound cause to hope that he might still be able to conclude a satisfactory deal with the British, and he did, in fact, continue to try to negotiate with them long after the massacre took place. The killing was an irrational act, not in keeping with his character. On the other hand it could well have been inspired by the young and impetuous Sri Wikrama, angry at the invasion of his country and anxious to assert himself against a minister he both feared and distrusted. Against this, the King seems to have appreciated the value of European prisoners as a bargaining counter; and, on the whole, he showed clemency towards those survivors of the massacre who fell into his hands. Later in life, Sri Wikrama blamed his Minister,[28] and the latter in turn blamed the King.[29] Pilima Talauva also suggested that the chief to whom Muttusamy surrendered was responsible; he himself, he protested, had arrived on the river bank just in time to save the lives of some of the officers,[30] an account of the incident which is supported by Greeving's story.[31]

The British allocated equal blame to the King and to the Adigar, but the weight of evidence does suggest that Pilima Talauva may not necessarily have been responsible.

CHAPTER 8

The First War:
Kandyan Incursions

I

MADGE's abrupt departure for the coast left the British with only a single remaining foothold in Kandyan territory.[1] This was Dambadeniya, in the Seven Korales, where North and Pilima Talauva had held their final meeting. Lying just across the border, the small fort was the first staging post on the supply route from Negombo to the Kandyan capital. Looking out across the paddy fields which surrounded it, from behind the slight redoubt of fascines and earth, the garrison of fourteen convalescents of the 19th Foot and twenty-two invalid Malays awaited the Kandyan attack.

It soon came. As Pilima Talauva was assaulting Davie's men in the Palace, a mob of several thousand men, commanded by Migastenna, surrounded the fort. The ensign in charge of it was a young man called Grant who had been the main protaganist in the Malay Regiment's duelling scandal the previous year in Colombo. Himself so sick that he could barely walk, he issued orders for the feeble defences to be strengthened with stacked bags of rice, and all day his handful of men lay out in the sun behind this rough breastwork, sheltering from the incessant musketry and gingal fire and taking the occasional shot at any Kandyan bold enough to approach their perimeter. One quick rush and the Kandyans could have flooded across the wall, but that was not the way they fought. Each morning Migastenna

sent a delegation under a flag of truce to tempt Grant to surrender with promises of a safe conduct and coolies to carry the
sick, but the young commander was of a different calibre from
Davie or Madge. Refusing to capitulate, he hung on to his
post. Then, on 26 June (the fourth day of the siege) a small
party of men which had been making its way from Colombo
to Kandy fought its way into the fort. These reinforcements
gave Grant the strength he needed to hold out. In the meantime,
news of his predicament had reached the coast; and, on 5 July,
Captain Robert Blackall of the 51st, with fifty men of his own
Regiment and fifty Sepoys succeeded in raising the siege. Blackall
had been ordered to bring the garrison back to the coast, and
he wasted no time in doing so. The same night as he arrived,
he not only destroyed the large stocks of provisions and stores
held in the fort, but made an attempt under cover of darkness
to trap Migastenna. The ruse failed because the Kandyans heard
the British patrol approaching, but it had the result of persuading
the Adigar and all his people to take to their heels. With a sottish
despair not uncommon in exhausted soldiers, some of Blackall's
men drank themselves stupid while they were in the process of
destroying the fort arrack store. This resulted in a British soldier
and some Sepoys falling behind as the column marched out of
the fort. They were never heard of again. But for these stupid
wretches Blackall lost only one man during the entire relief
operation. His report reflects a certain arrogance:

'That Britons should brave all dangers and fatigues when employed in
their country's cause is neither new nor extraordinary but when I see
not one but many of the native troops vying with us in braving fatigue
as well as equally daring in the field, I confess, Sir, I am struck with
admiration and applause.'[2]

II

Just ten days after Davie had been attacked, the last British
soldier had been expelled from Kandyan territory. It was a
disaster of a type only rarely experienced by the British in the
East Indies, and one for which the small European community

of Colombo seems to have been quite unprepared, even though it was common knowledge that Davie's force was in the most perilous straits. As the news of the massacre filtered through, a bitter demand for revenge was heard:

'Revenge! Revenge! their ashes cry
On that blood-thirsty crew;
Ye human fiends! the hour is nigh
To stern-ey'd Vengeance due!

And when the sword with blood is dy'd,
In that tremendous hour,
The mercy once to us denied,
'Tis fruitless to implore!'[3]

Impatience for vengeance was tempered by the realization that worse things might be in store. Cordiner, who was there at the time, remembered that 'when the news first reached the garrison, it produced universal consternation: it was like a clap of thunder, which had been for some time portended by a dark and gloomy sky; and was followed by an awful and overpowering calm'[4]. This calm possibly saved the British. It was due to the Kandyans breaking off hostilities in order to celebrate their *Perahera*, the great religious festival of the year, and the excuse, on this occasion, for even more than the usual rejoicing.

At the start of the year, the British garrison had amounted to nearly 5,000 men. Now, at the end of June, some 2,000 of them were either dead or prisoner.[5] In Colombo, 'the hospitals were crowded with sick and dying; and the barracks occupied only by a small number of invalids and convalescents'.[6] Both the 51st Foot and the detachment of the 65th Foot had nearly ceased to exist, and the defence of the southern and western settlements depended largely upon the Ceylon Native Infantry, a Regiment composed predominantly of untried recruits,[7] and a number of newly raised and hastily trained independent companies of Malays. In Trincomalee and Batticaloa there were altogether some 300 survivors of the Malay Regiment, and about 500 men of the 19th Foot, the tougher 'middle-aged' men of this Regiment having survived the rigours of the campaign better than their comrades in the two other English regiments. Nevertheless 338 of 843 Green Howards were to be in their graves by the close of the year, and few of them, or of the Malays, were now fit for duty.[8] On the face of it the situation was hopeless. At any moment tens of thousands of Kandyans could erupt from their hills and overwhelm the scanty garrisons strung out along the scattered coastal forts. To this danger a new dimension was added when in mid-August the tidings arrived that Britain had been, since May, once more at war with France. The hope of help from overseas now seemed remote indeed—help for which North had pleaded as soon as news of the massacre reached Colombo:

'But I am doing all that I can with safety to secure Resistance against any Invasion which that cruel and dastardly People may make into any Part of our Territories. In the meantime I have most earnestly solicited the Continental Presidencies to send me Succours; and altho I know that their troops are all employed, I hope that the Importance of this Island and the Atrocity of the Act which has prevented Tranquillity in its Interior, will induce Them to strain every Nerve to afford me One Thousand Men. From Europe, when this letter reaches your Lordship, I look for greater reinforcements. . . .'[9]

No wonder that Arthur Wellesley, preoccupied as he was with the Mahrattas, fumed to his brother, the Governor General, at the 'disgraceful issue of the folly in Ceylon'.[10]

As soon as *Perahera* was over, the expected happened. Hordes of armed Kandyans swarmed out of the hills across the coastal provinces to surge around the walls of the little forts, without, however, actually trying to assault them. Everywhere the lowland Sinhalese rose in sympathy. Even Manaar and Jaffna in the north were invaded, but the danger extended right down the east coast, around Trincomalee and Batticaloa, as well as in the strongly Buddhist south and the narrow strips around Chilaw and Puttalam where Kandyan influence most easily made itself felt.

Macdowall had made good use of the breathing space provided by *Perahera* to strengthen as best he could the garrisons of Negombo, Chilaw, Puttalam and Matara. It was against the last-named that the Kandyans first struck. Here, as Captain Beaver complained, 'the Commandant, lying unaccountably buried in his fort, without ever making a single sortie, the country was soon overrun by the enemy.'[11] What was worse, this Commandant evacuated Tangalla, twenty-two miles to the east, and withdrew its garrison into Matara. North's reaction to this news was to send the ubiquitous and energetic Beaver, now his A.D.C., to replace the Commandant. Beaver, only four days up from his sick-bed after yet another bout of fever (which he was now learning to cure with local remedies), set off for his new command at three hours' notice. On the morning of 22 August, he arrived in Matara, having taken sixty hours to cover the 103 miles, the final twelve of which he did by sea, travelling in a minute fishing boat, because the road between Point de Galle and his destination had been cut by the enemy. That same evening, and again on the next two nights, he sallied out from his fort to chase the Kandyans away. Then on 26 August, a few reinforcements having arrived, he fought his way along the coast to Tangalla, drove out the Kandyans, replaced the garrison and was back in Matara all in three days. There he heard that Hambantota was closely besieged. Off Beaver rushed once again, but the garrison of sixty invalid Malays needed no help. Under the cover of the guns of the brig *Snow Minerva*, they sallied out of the fort and put the Kandyans to flight.

In a couple of weeks Beaver pacified the south of the island and expelled the invading Kandyans from the British settlements. It was an extraordinary feat of arms for a sick man in his fortieth year, who with hardly a break had for months been campaigning in the jungle. His energy was such that in the intervals of marching and fighting he could find the time to keep up with his private correspondence, as well as prepare the long official despatches expected by his seniors. His letters provide a vivid picture of the campaign. One extract reads:

'The Cingalese lie concealed till you come close upon them, then they give one regular fire, and fly; this is the general case, and I suppose I was about six yards from their grasshoppers, the balls of which are about an inch in diameter, when they let them off. We were attacked from three points at once, but immediately carried them all; took both their masked and their open batteries, and burnt every house in the country. My opponents are a mixture of Cingalese rebels and Candians;

they pick off at least one European or two, from me, at each encounter, as we are obliged to be in advance, and consequently it is only now and then that a Sepoy or Malay is killed.

'I have two cohorns, and whenever I know the exact situation of the enemy, we are sure to rout them out by a few shells, and thereby save our men. I cannot give you an idea of the country; the jungle is so thick, and the fastnesses so strong, that we are not a moment sure but what we may be destroyed by a masked battery. My whole force now consists of only 60 Europeans, 140 Sepoys and 170 Malays.'[12]

As Beaver was hastening down the coast towards Matara, Colombo itself was in the gravest peril. On the night of 20 August, a large force of Kandyans captured the little fort of Hanwella, overlooking the smooth waters of the Kelani Ganga and only twenty miles from the city. The next day the Kandyans advanced a further five miles. Except for the newly raised 500 strong militia, in which North himself had enlisted as a private soldier so as to discourage disputes among the Burghers concerning rank,[13] Colombo was all but denuded of effective troops. Alarming though the situation was, there seems to have been little panic. Cordiner mentions that many of the European families took refuge in the Fort; clearly some of them did not. By quietly remaining in his country house and taking no precaution for his safety other than to increase his Sepoy guard with a dozen Europeans, the Governor set an excellent example of imperturbability.[14]

By now Macdowall had the measure of his opponents. All he could scrape together was a single subaltern, Lt Mercer of the 51st, with thirty Europeans, seventy-five Sepoys and about the same number of armed lascars. These he despatched the next morning to meet the invading column. Mercer chased the Kandyans back through Hanwella and across the border beyond Avissawella, slaughtering a quantity of them and capturing forty prisoners and some guns. For the time being Colombo was safe.

As Mercer was retaking Hanwella, simultaneous threats were developing against Chilaw, Puttulam and Negombo. Here also the British used their few troops to the best effect. Instead of sitting behind their fortifications and waiting to be attacked, they went out to meet their opponents, parties of between twenty and one hundred Malays or Sepoys, stiffened whenever possible by a few survivors from the British regiments, making vigorous and successful sallies against the Kandyan columns. Considering the rawness of the Asian troops, the unsuitability of their equipment for this type of warfare, and the state of health of most of the British officers and soldiers, the speed of movement, mobility and endurance of these parties were little less than phenomenal. Their success was such that only once were the Kandyans able actually to lay siege to one of the coastal forts. This was at Chilaw, only twelve miles from the frontier. The fort was a petty affair, 100 yards square and surrounded by a three foot deep ditch with a ten foot high sloping rampart of earth, topped by a row of stakes. Inside was a single stone building and a few palmyra-leaf huts to house the troops. Two young civil servants with sixty native troops held the place against 3,000 Kandyans. Reduced to firing copper *pice* from their guns after their grape shot was exhausted, one of the havildars suggested to his commander that he was wasting money: 'Put in powder enough and the noise will be sufficient to keep them off.' It was. Although they brought their batteries to within hailing distance of the garrison, again the Kandyans could not nerve themselves to assault the position. After four days the siege was raised when small parties converged to their aid from Negombo, Colombo and the newly recaptured Hanwella.[15]

III

Early in September, the danger to Colombo once again became acute. Well aware of the garrison's parlous state, the King decided to lead his Malays and Malabar guards, together with 12,000 Kandyans, against the city. In his path lay Hanwella, commanded since its recapture by Mercer. The fort was now in such a ruined state that Mercer had moved his men to the stone house belonging to the local *mudaliyar*. Sheltered by the slight wall surrounding this building, Mercer repelled attacks by the Kandyan leading troops on both 3 September and the following day. By the second evening many of the defenders had been wounded and Mercer himself was nearly incapacitated through sickness. However, a handful of reinforcements were rushed up from Colombo on 5 September, and that evening Captain William Pollock rode up to the fort alone in the dark to take over command. Arriving at 10 pm, he found himself in charge of less than 100 men, all convalescents and all said to be suffering from a weakness in the knees, the normal aftermath of an attack of the fever.

Pollock's arrival coincided with that of the King with the main part of his army. Covered by the fire of 3- and 6-pounder guns, served by lascars of the Bengal and Madras artillery who had been taken at Kandy, early the next morning the King's men advanced on the improvised fortress. Fortunately for the defenders, the Kandyan guns failed to do the slightest damage. Not only were they loaded with grape instead of ball, but they were laid too high (deliberately so, it was later determined) and the shot flew harmlessly overhead. The reverberations of the guns, however, combined with the throbbing of the drums and the clamour of their cries, encouraged the massed horde of men to move forward until they were no more than 200 yards away from the feeble defences. Here they halted, apparently daunted by the sight of the pointed muzzles of the British guns, as yet quite silent, and the sight of the red-coated shoulders of the defenders drawn up behind the wall.

The Kandyan army was now packed into an open space bounded on the left by a thick belt of jungle and the right by a stretch of scrub running down to the river. Suddenly from the trees on their left a volley of musketry tore into the flank of the Kandyans. The fire came from Mercer, whom Pollock had despatched with half the garrison by way of a hidden path to lie in ambush for the Kandyans before the assault started. The crash of Mercer's salvo was the signal for the defenders' guns to pour their grape into the massed ranks confronting them, whereupon Pollock led the rest of his infantry out from behind the wall towards the attackers. Halting short of the struggling Kandyans, packed so tightly that they could hardly move, Pollock poured volley after volley into them, each detonation duplicated by the crash of the salvoes from Mercer's men. It was two hours before the Kandyans could struggle free to escape and during this time only a few of the King's Malay mercenaries managed to close with the British. It was more of a massacre than a battle: the next day the British buried 270 Kandyans, and all the roads about Hanwella were found to be covered with the bodies of the mortally wounded who had died as they fled. The cost to the British was two wounded. Eighty Kandyan prisoners, the royal standard, and a large range of weapons and ammunition were captured. Just outside Hanwella, a richly ornamented bungalow, built for the King's reception, was destroyed; in front of the building were planted two stakes on which it had been the intention to impale the captured British.

The greatest prize, however, was the recovery of twenty-six Malays and 150 Indian gun lascars. The sincerity of their delight at being recaptured was confirmed by the manner in which they had laid their guns during the battle. A British renegade named Benson, still dressed in his artillery uniform decorated with a gold chain and a silver sword, both presents of the King, was mortally wounded during the fighting.[16] Also in the King's train were Captains Rumley and Humphreys who failed to escape and who both were soon to die. A further forty British Malays, who were about the King, had planned to capture the ruler as the British approached, but Pollock's sickly men were far too exhausted to pursue the flying Kandyans, otherwise the King might well have been taken. As it was, he managed to find the time to vent his anger upon the commander of the leading troops, Levuke Rala, the *dissawa* of Uva. The King knew that Levuke, who was a rival of Pilima Talauva, had been intriguing with the British on his own account, so the failure of the attack provided the excuse for the removal of the *dissawa*'s head. The men of Uva were later punished by being put to work opening up a 2,000 acre paddy field, a task for which they were informed they were better suited than for fighting.[17]

The debility of Pollock's troops did not delay their commander for long. Three days after the battle, he pushed on after the Kandyans, his force strengthened by the arrival of a further thirty-five Europeans from Colombo. These were the last soldiers left in the city still capable of marching. Other than invalids and pensioners, Colombo had now been denuded of every man. The sole combatant officer was the Town Major and one-legged men were often to be seen mounting guard.

Brushing aside small delaying parties of Kandyans, Pollock once again passed Avissawella and crossed the river at Sitawaka into Kandyan territory. Here he halted for one day to allow a small detachment under Captain Buchan, which had come up from Negombo, to overtake him. The two small columns then pushed on, level with one another but separated by the river, until Pollock observed Ruwanwella ahead upon the opposite bank. He could see that it was defended, not only by well-sited batteries, but by the entire Kandyan army he had defeated at Hanwella, reinforced by the troops of the Second Adigar. Very soon the British found a ford and pushed an assault party across to the far bank under the usual intense but inaccurate hail of round shot, grape and musketry. The capture of one of the batteries and the death of its twenty-six defenders were enough to persuade the rest of the vast Kandyan host to decamp once again. Buchan's column arrived just too late to trap the retreating Kandyans, but it was the end of their offensive.

By 15 September, the British troops were back in Colombo with the unbelievable news of their victory. Only ten days before the prospect had been nearly hopeless. Now Cordiner could reflect:

'The season of anxious suspense, at Colombo, was now over: the horizon brightened: and lamentation and mourning were, for a time, succeeded by thanksgiving and rejoicing.'[18]

The pattern was much the same around the entire coastal belt. Small parties of half-trained or invalid Malays or Sepoys, sometimes stiffened by a few sick and tired Europeans, but led by energetic and aggressive junior officers or civil servants, darted from one point to another to send the Kandyans scurrying back to their hills. Although there is certainly some justification for Maitland's accusation that North's despatches exaggerated the scale of the fighting,[19] it was an astonishing feat. In little more than a month the local rebellions had collapsed, and the Kandyan invaders had been cleared from most of the littoral. Only in the emptier country of the north and east, where the distances were greater, was resistance protracted until the end of October. Although there was a sensible reluctance among the Kandyan levies to come to grips with the disciplined British troops, their superiority in numbers was vast and they were operating in their own country. A lot has been learned in recent years on the subject of the problems of countering guerrilla forces. Unskilled though the Kandyans may have been, both in more formal warfare and the art of guerrilla fighting, by any reputable standards Macdowall's men did very well indeed.

IV

Ruwanwella was the supply base for the King's offensive against Colombo, and it was consequently packed with stores and magazines of various kinds. These Pollock destroyed before he withdrew, setting fire at the same time to over 1,000 houses. From now on this type of terrorism became commonplace, as small parties of troops started to raid deep into Kandyan territory, burning and despoiling as they went. Far more serious to the villagers was the systematic destruction of crops, food-stocks and fruit trees.

The extent of the atrocities committed by the British during these operations is far from easy to establish. There is no lack of evidence of the way they ravaged both the Kandyan country-side and the coastal areas which had risen in sympathy with their compatriots, but any details of actual brutality towards the local villagers are sparse. Two specific incidents are often quoted. The first was the flogging of local leaders during the suppression of the rebellion around Matara and Galle. Each of these men was sentenced to receive 1,000 lashes, a barbarous punishment in Sinhalese eyes, but one to which the British were in the habit of subjecting their own soldiers and sailors. There is no mention of similar punishments being inflicted elsewhere in the island.

More frequently quoted are the details of a raid made into the Seven Korales by a party led by Captain Robert Blackall.

17. *Sir John D'Oyly in conference with Ehelepola, and two chieftains,
probably Kapuvatta and Molligoda, in March, 1815. A mohottala
(standing on the right) keeps a record. This is the only known
portrait of D'Oyly*

18. *Pilima Talauva and General Macdowall meet on the border in 1810*

British Officer
75th Regiment of Foot

FAC-SIMILE OF MEDAL STRUCK BY CEYLON
GOVT TO REWARD ACTS OF GALLANTRY DURING
THE CANDIAN REBELLION OF 1818 & AWARDED

TO L:CE CORP: R.McLOUGHLIN P:TS J. WILSON
C. SHEPPARD AND W: CARTER 73:RD REG: WHO ALL
DIED OF FEVER,ERE THE DECORATION WAS ISSUED

19. *A British Officer of the 73rd Regiment of Foot*

20. *Facsimile of the only medal struck during the Kandyan Wars*

21. *The King's Palace at Kandy. It shows a Perahera in progress*

The officer's official report, which can be seen in the Public Record Office,[20] describes the ruthless manner in which the rich countryside was despoiled. His conclusion reads:

'. . . brought in all safe and sound and in high spirits back to Negembo after having for seven days traversed where we pleased the Enemy Country without a man sick or wounded and after having burned 93 villages and 80,000 upwards Parahs of Paddy[21] besides everywhere dispersing at once their armed parties having shot six of their Warriors and made prisoners as many more.'

The six prisoners, the report reveals, were unarmed peasants. Of the six men shot (one, in fact, was hanged), four were taken with weapons in their hands and the other two were killed during the fighting. Blackall's report was seen by the Duke of York himself and brought down the rebuke that the officer's actions were 'extremely disgraceful to His Majesty's arms'.

Writing a few years after the events described had taken place, Marshall was outspoken in his criticism:

'It must be admitted that the incursions of our troops into Kandyan territory, during the years 1803 and 1804, were calculated to fill the population with the most unfavourable opinion of our justice and humanity, and to confirm the worst prejudices against the European race.'[22]

But Marshall is complaining only about the devastation of the country. The recital of the destruction of houses, stores and gardens disgusted him; in his view, a plea of vengeance gave no sanction for such enormities. The sacrilegious looting of a Buddhist temple (the Malay soldiers refused to assist their British comrades in the work) particularly enraged him. Nowhere does he hint at British atrocities against the population, and he is hardly the man to have shrunk from mentioning such matters if he had known about them. Perhaps even more pertinent is Sri Wikrama's protest about the behaviour of the British: he complains about the burning of houses and similar acts, but makes no direct accusation of brutal behaviour.[23] Certainly the British dealt harshly with the villages. On the other hand they did as much damage in Portugal when they laid waste their ally's country as they retreated to the lines of Torres Vedras, and no more than the Russians did in their own country as they withdrew before the French in 1812.

Illogical though it may be, it is more reprehensible to bayonet a child than to starve it to death. Although the despoliation of a countryside can result in uncounted deaths, the brutal treatment of a handful of persons arouses far more opprobrium. The five men flogged at Galle more likely than not died under the lash, but the fifty fishing boats burned at the same time probably caused many more deaths. Thousands of Kandyans may have died from hunger and disease because their foodstocks and shelter were destroyed, but the accusation of deliberate British brutality rests on very little evidence. P. E. Pieris mentions 'shocking atrocities, perhaps unrivalled since the days of Jeronyme de Azavedo . . .' but supports his accusations only by quoting Blackall's misbehaviour.[24] He could, of course, have been right. When men are opposed by an enemy too elusive to catch, when they are embittered by cruelties perpetrated against their comrades, and when they are worn down by fatigue and disease, atrocities are often the unhappy concomitant to such a campaign.

V

Neither the authorities in India nor the British Government could contemplate the possibility of an undefended Trincomalee falling into the hands of the French. Difficult though it was, somehow or other reinforcements for Ceylon were scraped together. From India, two companies of the 34th Foot were despatched to Trincomalee, 300 men from the 10th Foot were drafted to fill some of the gaps in the 19th Foot and the 51st, while a couple of weak battalions of Sepoys were found, one of which, recently returned from the Eastern Islands, was only 300 strong. The satisfaction felt by North that these troops arrived only after he had regained control of the coastal settlements with the shattered remnants of the original garrison[25] was tempered by the bleak rebuke which arrived the following year from Lord Hobart. Writing in March (the news of the disaster had been slow in arriving) to say that the 66th Foot, augmented to 800 men, had sailed with a fair wind a few days previously, and that a 'Black Regiment' from the West Indies would arrive in Colombo in October,[26] Hobart complained:

'I was much disappointed at finding you unexpectedly engaged on a War, which altho' unquestionable as to the Justice of the principle upon which it has been undertaken, I have observed with deep concern has been attended with consequences of the most disastrous nature. . . .'[27]

He suggested that further hostilities should be confined to the vicinity of the British settlements. What is more, they should be terminated as speedily as possible.

North and Macdowall also saw to the strengthening of their local forces. A further infantry battalion was needed and to man it they sent to Bombay and Goa for African slaves. The introduction of this fresh element into an already cosmopolitan little army (British, Malays, Sinhalese, Bengalis and Madrasis were all represented) seems to have been inspired by the hope of finding troops better able to withstand tropical disease, and not (as has been suggested) in order to terrorize the Kandyan peasantry.[28] The Africans were also easier to administer. They lacked the dietary and religious problems of the Asian soldiers, and they did not have to be accompanied at all times by a horde of camp-followers. There was nothing new about this use of African slaves as mercenaries. The Portuguese had long employed them, as had many Indian rulers,[29] and Sri Wikrama had, of course, a number in his army. Regardless of the reasons for raising these Caffre troops (as they were always called), they certainly very soon became known for their brutality. Maitland reported that negroes possessed the peculiar advantage that their very name struck terror into the minds of the inhabitants,[30] while, in 1815, Major-General John Wilson in extolling their virtues to Whitehall was ingenuously frank on the subject:

'Both the natives of India and the Candians have a greater dread in encountering the Caffres than even Europeans—from the latter, they expect Mercy, if conquered, from the former they look for nothing but Cruelty and Death.'[31]

147

The initial purchase of Africans was made in Goa from slaves who had been taken there in prizes captured transporting them from Mozambique to the French islands. This batch of 176 men averaged at £37 per head: 32,513 rupees purchase money; 1,552 for provisions on the voyage to Ceylon; 13,600 for demurrage and freight, with the addition of an agent's fee of 10%. Later consignments, brought one of 500 individuals bought direct from Mozambique, including youths (to join a recruit company of boys) and women. The last-named had to fill the specification of being between fifteen and twenty-five years of age, sturdy and well-built.

This new unit was at first called the Caffre Corps, but it changed its name to the 3rd Ceylon Regiment in 1805 when the Governor decided to provide the three locally raised units with more formal titles.[32] Promotions from other regiments produced most of the officers, and it is noteworthy that the first three ensigns all came from the ranks.[33] Losses among the early drafts were sadly high. The customary ill-treatment during the Mozambique passage caused many deaths, particularly from beri-beri, and about one quarter of the first 600 recruits died during their first year in Colombo. The survivors flourished and, once they had settled down, made good soldiers: 'Fine, hardy, stout, good-humoured fellows, and excellent road-makers.'[34]

Twenty-nine years earlier, slavery had been declared illegal in the United Kingdom; in only another three years a start was to be made in suppressing the trade itself. For a humane individual such as North to raise recruits in this manner might well be said to reveal an odd ambivalence in his character. The purchases in Goa and Bombay were not difficult to justify: the captured slaves could not be turned loose to starve and to turn them into soldiers did, in theory at least, make them free men. On the other hand, there is no way of excusing the purchases in Mozambique. This involved a direct participation in the slave trade. The best that can be said is that the Africans gained their freedom at the end of their service and that their mode of existence was no worse than that of their British, Malay and Indian comrades, all of whom were volunteers.

Other measures taken to strengthen the local forces included the forming of a small force of cavalry, the lack of which had been conspicuous during the Kandyan incursions into the lowlands. Initially it consisted only of twelve Europeans and the same number of Indians, mounted on horses bought in India, but later the force was increased in size to 100 sabres. Two companies of gun lascars were raised to support the two recently arrived Royal Artillery companies, a measure quaintly justified by North on the grounds that it was essential to save Europeans from dangerous exertion in hot weather.[35] Finally, to remedy the shortage of intelligence, a force of twenty-four Sinhalese guides was raised. At a monthly cost of only 208 rix dollars,[36] this was an amazingly cheap corps but probably they also received a bonus on the results they produced.

VI

The appointment, in May 1803, of an officer of the King's Service to succeed Major-General Macdowall as commander of the military forces in the island severed the final link between Ceylon and the East India Company. The new commander was Major-General David Douglas Wemyss, an experienced officer only forty-four years of age who had seen much active service in America, the West Indies, Flanders and Italy. His paper qualifications seemed to fit him for the job.

The change-over did not take place until March, 1804, ten months after the appointment had been made. In many ways, Macdowall's departure was a loss to the island. He had known Ceylon for more than twenty years and he understood the problems of campaigning there. He is often criticized for the disaster at Kandy but it is not easy to see how he erred. His plans for the invasion were soundly laid to make the best use of his limited resources; he understood the administrative difficulties and the danger that sickness could well aggravate them; he could hardly have anticipated the severity of the pestilences that were to beset his force. He can be blamed for failing to dissuade North from undertaking the campaign, but he did at least avoid destroying the unusually sound working relationship that existed between the Governor and himself. Without this close co-operation and the consequent absence of friction between military and civil, it is hard to see how the defence of the settlements against the Kandyan incursions could have been conducted so capably. Certainly any earlier mistakes Macdowall may have made were expunged by the masterly manner in which he fought this part of the campaign. The aggressive, mobile operations were boldly planned and brilliantly executed.

The custom of dealing ruthlessly with unsuccessful generals— even though the fault may not be theirs—is by no means unsound. Macdowall was fortunate to avoid such a fate. He survived the disaster and was eventually promoted to be Commander-in-Chief in Madras. Paradoxically, he then quarrelled with his Governor and so was dismissed from his command. On the voyage home in 1809, he died in a shipwreck.

By contrast with Macdowall, Wemyss was the archetype of a contentious military man. The fact that the relative powers of the Governor and his senior soldier had been insufficiently defined had mattered little in the past because of the close harmony existing between North and Macdowall. Perhaps it was premonition that persuaded the Duke of York to insert the following sentence in Wemyss's instructions:

'The first object I recommend to you is to give every assistance in your power in support of His Majesty's Civil Government, and that you will endeavour to cultivate a cordial relationship and good understanding with His Excellency the Governor as the best means of insuring the good of His Majesty's Service.'[37]

The Duke was personally acquainted with most of his senior officers. He could well have known that a warning was necessary. An industrious and competent soldier, who had been professionally trained in the Prussian Army, his time at the Horse Guards since he was appointed Commander-in-Chief of the Army in 1795 had taught him much about the need for establishing sound relations between the military and the civil authorities. After two rather chequered years commanding in Flanders during 1793 and 1794, the authority of his royal background and the understanding he had gained of the men who had served under him were to serve him well in his formidable task of re-creating the British Army.

Until the end of the nineteenth century the Army was to suffer from a divided system of command, with the Commander-in-Chief in charge at the Horse Guards and the Secretary of State running matters from the War Office. The machinery with which the Duke had to cope was far more convoluted. The authority of the Commander-in-Chief was far less than the title implied, as he exercised only limited control over the regular infantry and cavalry regiments alone. The artillery and the engineers were the responsibility of the Master General of the Ordnance, who was also in charge of fortifications, maps and the supply of weapons and ammunition. The supply of rations and the control of land transport were in the hands of a civilian functionary, known as the Commissary-General, but the movement of troops overseas was ill-managed by a Committee of five naval captains who sat as the Board of Transport. Both the Commissary-General and the Board of Transport were responsible to the Prime Minister, as was the Barrack-Master-General, who was in charge of living accommodation for the troops. Recruiting policy and strategical planning were in the hands of the Secretary of State for War and the Colonies (not to be confused with the Secretary at War, a different official who held the purse strings). The Foreign Secretary was also very interested in the planning of campaigns, and he was usually forceful enough to make his voice heard. If this were not enough, the Home Secretary was in charge of the Militia, and later the Volunteers and the Yeomanry when these forces were raised. There was small chance of such a bevy of conflicting organizations being able to act with speed and decision, even if the will to do so had existed. Working within such a system, the Duke was well qualified to advise the newly-appointed Wemyss.

The advice was not taken. Wemyss's tour began in an inauspicious fashion with a dispute with the Governor on the subject of his field allowances, a dissension that was to rumble on throughout his tour in the island. Very soon after he arrived, his ignorance of Asian troops led him into ordering the Muslim Sepoys of the Bengal Volunteers to attend divine service, an act

151

that nearly provoked a mutiny and provoked the Marquis of Wellesley to threaten to bring the unit back to India.[38] Then, in September, Wemyss started a long quarrel with the Judges of the Supreme Court which was to continue until he left. The dispute started over the use of a piece of ground in Colombo Fort, allocated to the military as a parade ground but used by the Court, which held its sittings in the Fort, as a convenient place for the administration of corporal punishment. The row progressed from one Gilbertian climax to another with Colonel Baillie, now the Commandant at Colombo, and Wemyss himself both being summoned before the Court and bound over to keep the peace. There followed challenges to duels, public insults and a letter from Wemyss described by North as a 'flower of vituperative eloquence' and a 'gross slander on the proceedings of the Court'.[39] At one stage matters became so impossible that North reported to the Government that he had laid plans for his A.D.C., Herbert Beaver, to place the General under arrest if the need arose.[40] Poor North was sandwiched between two equally culpable parties—a foolish General and absurdly conceited Judges—neither of whom he had the power to control. In such circumstances it was not easy to govern a country and wage a war at the same time; and much of the Governor's time was spent on temporising between the disputants and writing his recurrent and prolix reports. So shaming did he find the business, that he felt constrained to excuse himself to Lord Camden, Hobart's successor at the Colonial Office, with the following apology:

'The many confidential Letters with which I have lately tormented you, on the very disagreeable subject of our internal Broils, will naturally make you dread the sight of a private one from me. . . .'[41]

These time wasting squabbles all but brought the work of government to a halt, but nearly as serious was Wemyss's conduct of the war. To North's understandable chagrin, his General consistently refused to discuss with him the details of any military matters. North's sole tool for controlling Wemyss was tightening the purse strings, a course of action hard to maintain in the middle of a war, with each demand for money made under the plea of dire military necessity. Wemyss did, in fact, waste money as he pleased, much of the unnecessary expenditure harming rather than improving the efficiency of the forces. Of ideas to end the war, he was all but devoid. Other than to continue the raids into Kandyan territory during the more healthy time of the year in order to terrorize and destroy, Wemyss's sole operational innovation during 1804 and 1805 was an ill-conceived blockade to prevent salt and other articles entering Kandy. To initiate this, Wemyss had to split his troops into small parties living in outlying places, often noted for their insalubrity. With a frontier 700 miles long to be watched, the plan had little hope of success.

CHAPTER 9

The First War:
Johnston's March

I

As Hobart's despatch to North, expressing his cold displeasure at the latter's ill-conceived military adventures and suggesting the limitation of further hostilities to the vicinity of the British settlements,[1] was starting on its lengthy journey to Ceylon, the Governor was himself addressing the Secretary of State with ambitious plans for a further offensive against the Kandyan capital. Heartened by the ease with which he had repulsed the Kandyan incursions, North was now insisting that the King must be deposed in punishment for the massacre and that retribution must also be exacted from Pilima Talauva:

'Till these ends are accomplished, I should consider myself as betraying the Honour of my Country if I proposed or accepted any Terms of Peace. That they may be accomplished in a campaign of Three Months, with a Strong Army well appointed and divided into a great number of Small Detachments, not exceeding Three or Four Hundred Fighting Men each, I think extremely Possible, and, to accomplish it, I shall deem it my Duty to set in Motion every Engine of Violence and Policy which Circumstance may present to me and Morality allow. . . . If it be accomplished it would be my Advice to occupy and retain the whole Country, as H.M.'s right by conquest.'[2]

North had a particular distaste for Pilima Talauva. His rancour was not surprising. In the years during which the two men had been intriguing with each other, on the whole the initiative had

stemmed from the Kandyan. To North, quite unable to penetrate his opponent's Asian mind and understand his motives, the
Adigar seemed utterly unscrupulous and untrustworthy. Moreover, Pilima Talauva had shown himself to be by far the shrewder
man of the two.

The brash audacity displayed by the Adigar was, at times,
amazing. The very day after the massacre, he sent an oral message
to the British in which he tried to exculpate himself; included
was an accurate forecast of the King's operational plans, a
warning that the defences of Dambadeniya should be strengthened, and a rather optimistic request that all his previous correspondence should be destroyed.[3] By February of the following
year, he was once again in regular communication with Macdowall: more information about the King's intentions was
forthcoming; North was advised to threaten a further attack
against Kandy, and a suggestion was floated that the British
should entice the King's other ministers to a discussion on peace
proposals during the course of which they should be abducted.[4]

North was determined to reject any peace proposals, whatever
their origin, so long as the King remained upon his throne and
the perpetrators of the massacre were unpunished. Not only
did he reject Pilima Talauva's unwelcome approaches, but others,
originating from Migastenna, met with the same fate, even though
the Second Adigar was a more acceptable intermediary as he
had been absent from the capital at the time of the massacre.
But the Kandyans were no more anxious for peace than the
British. Well aware that their enemies were fully committed
against the Mahrattas and the French, they had everything to
gain by awaiting the outcome of events. If the French had succeeded in invading Ceylon, one might well speculate whether the
Kandyans would have repeated their historic error and once
again allied themselves with the newcomer in order to rid themselves of their current affliction.

In the meantime, North was planning a fresh offensive. The
arrival of fresh troops from India during the latter months of
1803, coupled with the hope that further help might be on its
way from the United Kingdom, provided him with the justification for hoping for success. His strategy was based upon the use

of small columns of troops of the type he had described to the Secretary of State, none larger than 600 fighting men. This plan had several advantages. Recent experience had demonstrated how quickly these more handy divisions could move in comparison with the unwieldy bodies of troops which had snaked their way along miles of jungle tracks in 1800 and 1803. It was also thought that the effect on the Kandyans would be to disconcert them. Threatened from every direction by quickly moving and converging columns, it would be difficult for them to seek refuge by withdrawing from one area to another as their enemies approached.

In any case, the problem of assembling in one place the hordes of porters needed to carry the supplies for a large force made it impossible for the British to operate in any other fashion. Four coolies were needed to maintain each fighting man for a period of fifteen days, so to operate 2,000 men entailed putting five times that number into the field. Companies of semi-disciplined gun lascars and porters had been raised during the past twelve months, but most of the human carriers had still to be collected on the spot. At any time porters were difficult enough to find, but the experiences of the villagers in 1803, when half their number either died of disease or were slaughtered, had made them doubly determined to avoid this hazardous toil. There was no question of recruiting a large number of men from any one area; but, with a variety of starting points, there were better prospects that each column could tap its own hinterland with some hope of success. This strategy of small converging columns had been conceived before Macdowall left Ceylon in February, but it was left to Wemyss to work out the detailed plans. If the Kandyans had been a more aggressive enemy, such a strategy might well have proved hazardous to the British as they could have been defeated in detail. As it was, the fighting of the previous year had shown that small columns had little to fear so long as the troops stayed fit and could be provided with food.

A further lesson which had been learned once again in 1803 was the near impossibility of campaigning during the months of the monsoon. Rivers normally fordable were then in spate; rudimentary tracks were at their worst; and disease tended to reach endemic proportions. Because the north-east monsoon was due to end in March, and the south-westerly would start shortly afterwards, it was therefore necessary to postpone the beginning of the campaign until August or September, when the worst of the bad weather should be over.

II

In August, General Wemyss started a tour of the coastal forts with the object of inspecting his troops, furthering his knowledge of the topography of the island, and explaining his operational plans to his subordinates who would have to carry them out.[5] At Batticaloa, then a pleasant little harbour, overlooked only by the Dutch-built fort and a few houses set among their coconut plantations, Wemyss met Captain Arthur Johnston, the local garrison commandant. Johnston, who had been commissioned at the not abnormally early age of fifteen, had arrived in Ceylon with the 19th Foot in 1796. By 1804, his knowledge of both the country and the Kandyan methods of warfare were extensive. He had been promoted at the start of the war to command an independent company of Malays, and had experienced a lot of skirmishing work while escorting the supply columns that toiled up and down the jungle tracks from the coast into the interior. Later he had, for a time, been seconded to the civil government to administer the provinces which Muttusamy had notionally ceded to the British, and was lucky enough to be evacuated as a sick man from Kandy before disaster overtook the garrison.

After outlining his plans to Johnston, Wemyss left for Trincomalee. Shortly afterwards Johnston received written confirmatory orders which read as follows:

'MOST SECRET

Trincomalé, Sept 3, 1804.

Sir,

In the event of your not having marched towards Arriagam, you are directed to have a strong detachment in perfect readiness, as soon as possible, to march to Candy, by the route of Ouva. To enable you to equip a strong force, a detachment of Europeans and natives will march from this as soon as the weather clears; and, when joined by it, you will proceed towards the enemy's country, arranging so as to be within eight days' march of the town of Candy on the 20th instant, which is the day fixed for the commencement of general co-operations. You will then proceed direct upon Candy, not doing any injury to the country or people, unless opposed; and as different detachments are ordered to march precisely on the 20th for general co-operation for the destruction of the enemy's capital, the various columns will be put in motion from Columbo, Hambingtotte, Trincomalé, Negumbo, Chilou, and Pouttalim, the whole to be within eight days' march of Candy on the 20th instant; and, on the 28th or 29th, the Commander of the forces fully expects a general junction on the heights of Candy.

The General fully relies on the execution of these instructions; and, from your well-known zeal and activity, he has no doubt of a perfect completion of his wishes.

I have the honour to be,
Sir,
Your obedient servant,
R. MOWBRAY,
Act. D. Adj.-Gen.'[6]

Hard on the heels of this instruction came a further letter, signed also by Mowbray and dated five days later. It read:

'The Commander of the Forces directs you will, on the receipt of this, reduce your division to 300 men, as you will then be enabled to have a sufficiency of Coolies for the purpose of entering the enemy's dominions. As some unforseen obstacles have prevented the various columns forming the intended junction, about the 28th or 29th instant, on the heights of Candy, agreeably to the instructions transmitted to you on the 3rd instant, you are directed to march on the 20th of this month, bending your course towards the province of Ouva, and form junction at the entrance of that part with the detachment ordered from Hambangtotte, which will march the same day, the 20th instant, by the route of Catragame, on the great road leading to Candy, which is frequented by the King, for visiting the temple.

'You will, in junction with the other detachments, concert such measures as will best tend to effect the greatest devastation and injury to the enemy's country.

'All persons found in arms to be immediately made examples of, and the peaceful and defenceless peasant to be spared.

'You will note in writing all observations relative to the country, as our future operations will be guided by them in that part, and transmit your journal to me, for the General's information.'[7]

The slovenly imprecision of the first instruction was matched by the vagueness of the second. The latter Johnston read as merely a modification of the original routes and timings, but even if he had been doubtful about its interpretation, there was no time for him to check his commander's intentions. So he made his final preparations, sent a message to Lt-Col Maddison at Hambantota with details of a proposed rendezvous, and on the evening of 20 September embarked his stores and his European troops—two officers and seventy men of the 19th and a sergeant and six gunners of the Royal Artillery—by river for Sorikalmunai, twenty-seven miles upstream. The next day they were joined there by fifty-three Malays and 175 Sepoys belonging to the Bengal Volunteers. In all there were seven British and five native officers with the column. Only 550 pioneers and coolies could be found, half the number needed, and to move the balance of his supplies Johnston had been obliged to collect a number of carriage bullocks,[8] whose unsuitability for the task was soon to be demonstrated. The shortage of transport was such that the gunners were able to take only a single light 1-pounder gun and one small coehorn.

III

In his march across the fifteen-mile-wide coastal belt that led towards the frontier-chain of hills, Johnston passed through a district recently stricken by a small-pox epidemic and consequently deserted by its inhabitants, who had fled into the woods to avoid infection—a factor that had further increased the difficulties he had experienced in recruiting his coolies. Then, as soon as it entered the Kandyan country, the column plunged into a wild, hilly region, utterly empty; during the first sixty miles of the march, the troops saw not a house nor a human being. Threading their way along faint jungle tracks that twisted round the base of hills, some tree-covered and some eroded into fantastic shapes, the men soon started to suffer from the effects of the sultry and sticky days in the forest, and the contrasting cold and foggy nights. The weight of their cumbersome kit, three days' rations, and eighty rounds of ball ammunition, took a heavy toll of their physical resources, so much so that when the column reached the first village, a week after it had left Batticaloa, Johnston found it necessary to send back to the coast twenty-two sick Sepoys and two Malays.

The next day signs of cultivation increased. Not only the valleys, through which the troops were marching, but much of the lower slopes of the hills above them had been cleared of vegetation. The villages were quite deserted, but high on the terraced hill-sides numerous parties of Kandyans started to make an appearance, observing the column as it passed. Then at three o'clock that afternoon, as the troops were descending into a steep valley close to Kieratavelly, the village chosen by Johnston as his rendezvous with Maddison, the Kandyans discharged their first ineffectual shots at the British. The latter returned a more accurate fire and a wounded Kandyan soldier was captured. He provided the disconcerting information that nothing had been heard of any other British column invading the country.

Kieratavelly was described by Johnston as being on the borders of Uva, and it probably occupied the site of the present village of Bibile,[9] on the road running between Badulla and Batticaloa. The column had already been on the road for nine days, and had covered, Johnston calculated, 124 miles of difficult country. The capital still lay on the other side of the wild and unknown Uva mountains; and, in a countryside stripped by its inhabitants of all provisions there could be no question of lingering to wait for Maddison to arrive. Johnston had no alternative but to press on, and this he did, burning the house of the *dissawa* as a sign to the other column that he had passed through.

During the night they spent in the village, the troops could see a circle of fires flickering on the hills around them; and, when they set off at daybreak, large numbers of Kandyans clung to their flanks, but did no more than exchange a few shots with the advanced and the rear guards. A sixteen-mile march brought them to the village of Pangaragama, on the banks of the Mahaweli Ganga, which from here winds a circuitous course to Kandy through forests and gorges even today untraversed by any road. Swollen by rain, the river was 150 yards broad, and rafts had to be built to make the crossing. Towards nightfall, the troops observed some Kandyans on the opposite bank, and there was every indication that the crossing was likely to be disputed, but the next morning the level of the water was found to have fallen. A party of volunteers waded across, and the Kandyans fired a few rounds at them before disappearing.

While the stores were being ferried across the river on the rafts, Johnston sent Lieutenant Virgo, the company commander of the Malays, with his men to destroy the royal palace of Alutnuwara, seven miles downstream, which he had heard housed a depot of weapons and other military stores. Virgo carried out his task, but Johnston does not mention what the palace was found to contain.

For the next two days, the path of the column lay along the north bank of the great river, a wearying route that involved skirting precipitous gorges and clambering in and out of a succession of steep ravines. Then the troops once again had to ford the river so as to strike towards Hanguranketa, and the parched and exhausted men struggled up the pass towards the royal city on the afternoon of 3 October, the rays of the near-vertical sun reflecting cruelly upon them from the jagged rocks. Possibly heartened by the obvious fatigue of the soldiers, the Kandyans were now starting to become a little bolder: that morning Johnston had suffered his first casualties—a soldier of the 19th Foot killed, and several followers wounded.

The next day's march northwards from Hanguranketa was even more exhausting. The route lay now along a steep ridge, in many places nearly perpendicular and so narrow that stretches had been improved by artificial footways built on stakes driven horizontally into the rocks. Although the small baggage bullocks were accustomed to the mountain trails, many of them crashed headlong down the slopes, carrying their valuable loads with them. Late that evening, the column regained the river, and that night they camped under the lee of a steep hill which Johnston picqueted with a company of Sepoys. It was a wise precaution. A hail of musketry and gingal fire woke the troops at first light, but most of it passed over their heads because they were sleeping in a slight hollow. Covered by this fire, a party of Kandyans actually assaulted the hill-picquet, but they were repulsed with heavy casualties. This fighting cost the British two dead and a number wounded (including some coolies). When, therefore, the column resumed its march, it was encumbered by a further number of injured men who had to be carried.

The troops were now following the more northerly of the paths taken by the British during their abortive operation against Hanguranketa the previous year. Confined on their right hand side by the unfordable river, and on their left by the steep hills, it was a hazardous route. Concealed among the rocks and the trees of the opposite bank, the Kandyans were able to move parallel with the column and direct a galling fire into its flank. The crackle of musketry echoing backwards and forwards across the water proved too much for the bullocks. Many, wild and unmanageable, broke away from their drivers and shed their loads.

After three miles of this unpleasant confusion, Johnston found his way barred by a large house, loop-holed for defence, and covered by a battery of guns on the far side of the river. As his sole light gun was being brought into action against the house, the axle-tree smashed, and it was fortunate for the British that the Kandyans fled as the leading troops rushed the house. Johnston camped here after an unsatisfactory day, during which slight progress had been made. There was little rest to be had. The night was enlivened by thousands of Kandyans, fitfully illuminated by a galaxy of torches, hurling imprecations at the invaders from the adjoining hills. It was a manœuvre, Johnston thought, calculated to terrify his native troops and so encourage them to desert. The Kandyans managed also to divert a stream which ran close to the house, so depriving the troops of their much-needed water; in return, Johnston could do no more than bombard them with his single coehorn—ineffectively, however, as nineteen of the twenty-three shells discharged proved to be dud rounds.

When they woke the next morning, the troops heard the heartening sound of distant firing from the direction of Kandy, but Johnston was faced with the problem of dealing with the Kandyan battery that threatened him from across the river before he could resume his march and bring his long and vulnerable column of porters and bullocks forward. A raft they had laboriously constructed during the night sank, but two sturdy soldiers of the 19th Foot, Simon Gleason and Daniel Quin, swam the river covered by their comrades' fire and snatched a boat from the far bank. Using this, Lt Vincent, their company commander, crossed with about twenty men and marched down the river bank to take the battery in the flank. This was enough to cause the massed Kandyan defenders to fly into the woods, all at the cost of two of Vincent's men wounded.

Two hundred yards away was the beautiful royal palace of Kundasale, richly ornamented with treasures given to the Kandyan kings by their several European enemies. Johnston, on finding that it contained large stocks of munitions, fired it in accordance with his orders, reluctant though he was to do so.

The capture of the battery opened the road to Kandy and Johnston now pressed forward. During the previous night he had made out his reports ready to present to the officer commanding the town, confident as he was from the sound of the firing that his countrymen had already arrived. He soon discovered his mistake. A volley of musketry from the hill above the palace greeted his advanced guard, and the sight of the enemy flying through the streets confirmed that no one had reached Kandy before him. On 6 October, after 180 exhausting miles, the small British column was alone in the capital, deserted except for a single woman and a small boy. Sergeant Theon, who had been held in the town, had been marched off into the the Dumbara hills with his fellow captives as his comrades approached.[10]

IV

His weary troops established in the royal palace and the vital hill commanding it safely picqueted by a party of sepoys, a worried Johnston 'looked with great anxiety for the arrival of the other detachments',[11] but it was not until the following evening that the peril facing the force became explicit. A Malay officer and some of his soldiers, captured with Davie, escaped from Dumbara and brought the news that six British columns were said to have entered Kandyan territory two weeks earlier. Five columns were reputed to have been repulsed and the Kandyans were now biding their time for disease and fatigue to prepare Johnston's men for the fate that had overtaken the previous intruders into the capital.

The next morning, a party of escaped Sepoys confirmed the report of the Malays. Robustly maintaining an outwardly cheerful demeanour, Johnston was now a desperately anxious man. He knew the Malay officer to be reliable; what is more, the report of the six divisions corresponded with the facts. It was hardly possible that the Kandyans could have repulsed all the other columns, but what else could have happened? The routes from Trincomalee and Colombo were both shorter and easier than the path his column had taken, and, by now, one of the others should have arrived. His ammunition and supplies were running low, and already he was encumbered by a number of sick and wounded. The north-east monsoon seemed to be setting in early and Johnston well understood the problem of crossing rivers in spate. If he stayed on in Kandy and no one else arrived, a repetition of the disaster of 1803 seemed inevitable. To retreat would imperil the safety of any other column that might then be approaching the city and would result in Johnston's personal disgrace.

By Johnston's admission, his troops, both Asian and European, were disturbed. Many of the latter had been in Kandy with the 19th Foot the previous year. They were now billeted in the very buildings in which their comrades had been butchered:

'They saw displayed in savage triumph in several of the apartments of the Palace, the hats, shoes, canteens and accoutrements of their murdered comrades, most of them still marked with the names of their ill-fated owners.'[12]

Bombardier Alexander Alexander, who must have met survivors of the expedition, paints a lurid canvas with a looting of an arrack store, a broad hint of rape, and a mob of hysterically unnerved soldiers rallied by Johnston with vulgar and uncharacteristic rhetoric. There is certainly much exaggeration here. Except when describing his personal emotions, Johnston's description of the expedition is dispassionately factual. He had, it goes without saying, every reason for putting a good gloss on his story, but from the start to the finish his account of the events has the feeling of authenticity. In no way does he present an uncritical eulogy of his soldiers. On the other hand Alexander's readable but high-coloured account is full of errors. He was, unfortunately, a man with a grudge against his fellow-men. He never says a good word for any of his comrades in the ranks; a snob who despised his fellow-soldiers as much as they seem to have disliked him, he had an unhappy capacity for laying bare a rather mean little soul on nearly every page of his book and displaying himself as an ingratiating and envious whiner. Rather unwisely, too many people have uncritically accepted his account of events.

Opinion among Johnston's officers as to whether the force should stay or retreat was divided. Because of this, he declined to follow the usual procedure of calling a council of war to discuss what had to be done, realizing that to do so would give expression to what might well be unpleasant differences of opinion. Loth as he was to disobey his orders, he decided that his primary duty was to ensure as best he could the safety of his troops. So, as a precautionary step, he decided to move them to the left bank of the Mahaweli Ganga, where they would be better placed to retreat either to Trincomalee or Colombo if he received no tidings of the other columns. To return to Batticaloa by the way they had come was unthinkable: not only was the route too long and difficult, but Johnston had heard that the Kandyans were engaged in blocking the passes around Hanguranketa.

V

At dawn on 9 October, after only fifty-six hours in the capital, Johnston's men marched out, leaving an undamaged city behind them. On the outskirts they saw a number of skeletons hanging from trees, the remains of Davie's slaughtered officers, and they found the bones of his soldiers littering the ground near the ferry. Here they halted at a spot now known as Lewella—the Shore of Blood—to build rafts to cross the unfordable river. On the opposite bank, the Kandyans (of whom little had been seen for the past two days) started to assemble in vast numbers and scream insults at their enemies, combined with invitations to the Asian troops to desert. Not one of them, either then or subsequently, succumbed to the temptation; and, what is more, not a single coolie had as yet decamped.

That same afternoon, two small rafts were built and punted laboriously across the river by a small party, which then proceeded to disperse the Kandyans opposing them at bayonet point and seize a small bridge-head. That night the sick and wounded men were ferried over to the far bank, but a sudden spate of water carried one raft away and made the other unmanageable, thus delaying the completion of the crossing until the next afternoon. Even then the tents had to be abandoned on the Kandyan side of the river.

The difficulties he had experienced in crossing the Mahaweli Ganga convinced Johnston that it was unwise to linger. Nothing had been heard of any of the other columns, and the constant skirmishing of the past twenty-four hours had made serious inroads into his already scarce ammunition. Some of the men had expended every round they were carrying and the reserve stock had been reduced to two barrels, each containing 800 rounds. Acting with his usual decision, he decided to head for Trincomalee rather than Colombo, thus avoiding the twin hill forts of Galagedara and Girihagama which guarded the Colombo road. He gave orders for each man to be issued with a six-day ration of rice, the rest of the stores to be destroyed, and the surviving bullocks, which would have slowed down the marching men, to be slaughtered. An alarming incident occurred as the stores were being burned when the artillery ammunition exploded, killing and wounding a number of porters and wounding the Royal Artillery sergeant seriously in 'his breech'; taking advantage of the consequent confusion, the Kandyans attacked the party but were quickly driven off with only slight loss.

Johnston did not allow this sort of thing to delay him. By

five o'clock that afternoon, the column was on its way, the porters struggling under the burden of their doolies, laden with sick and wounded men. After fighting their way up the slippery track through the Dumbara Hills, everyone at last threw themselves down on to the soaking ground to spend what was left of the night just short of the summit of the Atgalle Pass, near the present village of Wattegama. Tired, wet and ravenous, they lay awake listening to the sound of crashing trees being felled by the Kandyans to obstruct the next stage of their march. At dawn on 11 October, the column was faced with the task of capturing the strongly defended summit, and then pushing down the winding track that dropped for 1,000 feet on the far side. The Kandyans resisted in a far more determined manner, and the day's fighting, during which a succession of breastworks and barricades of felled trees had to be surmounted, cost Johnston thirteen soldiers and thirty followers killed and wounded; among them was Vincent, who was badly hit in the groin. That evening the exhausted troops staggered past the ruins of Fort Macdowall, burdened by their increased tally of wounded, to halt only when darkness and rain prevented them from seeing where they were putting their feet.

It was much the same for the next two days as they made their way through the jungles of Matale. As the troops grew weaker, the Kandyans became bolder, now cutting in to stab and slash in hand-to-hand fighting. As usual their primary targets were the terrified coolies, who rid themselves of their burden of sick and wounded men, either diving for cover in the jungle or throwing the marching troops into disorder as they tried to find safety among them.

The company of the 19th Foot led the way, with the Malays acting as rearguard and the Sepoys protecting as best they could the burdened porters. In a column of this type, strung out in double or single file along winding jungle tracks, movement is never smooth, and delays and bunching inevitably occur at every obstacle, however small. As a result the men in the front outdistance those in the rear. Gaps occur, and, if discipline tends to flag, it is hard to persuade the leaders to wait for those behind to catch them up. Not only was Johnston faced with this problem, but he also found it difficult to distinguish the pathway from the elephant tracks, so that it was not surprising that, on 14 October, he found that he had lost all contact with the British company, both of whose officers had now become casualties and were being carried in doolies.

That night Johnston found shelter for what was left of his force in an abandoned village. To the delight of everyone, it was found to contain a quantity of rice, already boiled. It was the first proper meal the men had eaten, and the first time they had found shelter from the rain in five days.

The next day the pursuit at last slackened, possibly because the weather was too much even for the Kandyans, clad as they were only in their loin cloths. But even without human opposition, the troops still had to battle against the evils of their environment. Each day from dawn till early afternoon, they sweltered in the humid forest; then the rain sheeted down to drench them for the remaining hours of daylight and throughout the shivering night. Cases of malaria and dysentery multiplied, and with no more than a little raw salt beef and mouldy uncooked rice to eat, the men became progressively weaker. Wounds could not be dressed because the coolie who carried the medical stores had deserted, and gangrene started its deadly work. Because of the lack of coolies, the doolies had to be discarded, and the sick and wounded were either carried in cloths slung from poles or supported by their slightly stronger comrades. In the confusion the wounded were sometimes abandoned, and more than once these men were recaptured, trussed and slung on poles, ready for removal to some dreadful death. Vincent travelled with an open knife in his hand, ready to kill himself if capture seemed to be inevitable. Probably he had to use it. When Johnston halted for the night of 16 October, just short of Lake Minneriya, he came upon his missing British troops. With them was Lt Virgo, whom he had despatched two days earlier with orders to find them and bring them back to the main column. Without guides, the British troops had found their way to this spot by sheer chance. Virgo had managed to overtake them, but the exhausted men were unwilling to obey an order from an officer of another regiment to retrace their footsteps along the terrible miles they had travelled, understandably so as their hopes of meeting the rest of the column would have been remote. The coolies who had been carrying the wounded had all deserted; and, with their strength gone, the soldiers had been forced to abandon their comrades. Vincent, another officer and two other men were left in this way, and nothing was ever heard of them again. It is typical of Johnston that he tried neither to disguise the facts of this pitiful story nor to apportion blame for what had happened.

The next day the reunited column faltered onwards towards Trincomalee. By now Johnston himself was so weak from dysentery that he was forced to allow his men to carry him in his cloak; tortured as he was by doubts as to whether he had made the correct decision in leaving Kandy, his mental suffering matched his physical misery. It was not until 19 October, just outside Trincomalee, that his mind was put at rest. Some officers from the garrison met the column, news of its approach having been received in the fort only that morning, and from them Johnston learned that his second instruction from Wemyss had been intended as a cancellation of the first. He should not have marched to Kandy at all. Wemyss had countermanded the operation, primarily because he had formed the opinion that the shortage of coolies made it impracticable; instead he had substituted a plan for the several columns to do no more than enter Kandyan territory, and carry out the greatest possible devastation—one point, at least, upon which he had been specific. Marshall's stricture is apposite:

'The object of this inroad into the Kandyan territory was thus officially avowed to be for the purpose of indulging, to the uttermost, the spirit of vengeance and devastation at the expense of the inhabitants. Whatever the public authorities may intend on occasions of this kind, it is seldom that they so grossly commit themselves, by specifically commanding the perpetration of acts of savage barbarity.'[13]

The other columns had completed their ravaging missions, and all had long been back at the coast. Hope for Johnston's return had been abandoned when news was received through some border-Sinhalese that his detachment had penetrated to the capital.

Johnston's chagrin at the news that he should not have marched to Kandy was acerbated when he learned that he was thought to have disobeyed his orders deliberately; but at the subsequent court of inquiry he was cleared of all blame. Afterwards he received the praise he so amply deserved for the skill and courage with which he had held his force together and extricated it with the loss of only thirty-eight officers and soldiers killed and missing. Of the coolies, seventy-six were known to have become casualties, but many more were missing, either killed by the enemy or having deserted during the final stages of the march. Several years later, a Kandyan chief who had helped to harry the retreat insisted that Johnston must have possessed supernatural powers: only this could explain the extraordinary quality of his judgement and energy, and his escape while passing through a continual ambush.[14]

Two individuals were court-martialled. Virgo, an elderly promoted ranker, who had started life as a bandsman, had acquitted himself well and had lost an eye in the fighting. Nevertheless his failure to persuade the advanced guard to return cost him a six-month suspension from rank and pay. For allowing the four wounded members of his Regiment to be abandoned, Sergeant Henry Craven of the 19th Foot was sentenced to be transported for life, but he died eighteen months later, still awaiting shipment to Botany Bay.

It would have been easier for the survivors if they had not managed to drag themselves back:

'And thus they at length reached Trincomalee, cold, wet, dirty and lousy; almost naked, many barefoot and maimed; officers and all alike starved and shrivelled, their countenances haggard, forming an assemblage of the most miserable looking men it is possible to conceive. All had to go to hospital on their arrival; their strength appeared only to have endured to this point, then to have utterly deserted them. Indeed this retreat was as fatal to the men as the massacre had been, for almost all died in the hospital; few, very few, survived.'[15]

Alexander was stationed in Trincomalee at the time. This description is so vivid that he must himself have seen the arrival of the column.

Johnston survived, and he continued to serve in Ceylon for a further six years. His military service is commemorated on a tablet in the parish church at Shalden in Hampshire:

'Sacred to the memory of Lieut-Col. Arthur Johnston, of Clare in the County of Tyrone, Ireland, formerly of the 19th Regiment of Foot and 2nd Ceylon Battalion, late of His Majesty's Royal Corsican Rangers, and Assistant Command. of the Royal Military College at Farnham. 'His services in Ceylon (where he signalized himself on many occasions, but particularly in Command of an Expedition to Candy in the year 1804, which place he captured under difficulties the most appalling), laid the foundations of a disease which, after many years of severe suffering, terminated his life on the 6th June, 1824. He was born on the 7th July, 1776, and married Martha (daughter of Thomas Smith Esq.) by whom this tribute of affection is erected to his memory.'[16]

There were no children by this marriage, but he had previously married a Burgher girl in 1808, by whom he had a daughter who lived in Ceylon until 1897.[17]

When Johnston reached England, he entered the Senior Division of the Royal Military College as a student. The Duke of York was responsible for the existence of this institution, which he had set up at High Wycombe in 1799 in an attempt to remedy the lack of any form of officer training for the infantry and the cavalry. In charge was General Jarry, a French emigré who had been head of the Berlin *École Militaire* under Frederick the Great. Thirty officers were admitted annually, each recommended by the Commander-in-Chief and having a basic knowledge of his profession, together with some facility in French and geometry; to save money, officers had to pay for their own tuition. Jarry's college became the Senior Wing of the Royal Military College in 1802, when Colonel le Marchant took charge of it, and a Junior Wing was established at Great Marlow for the training of gentlemen cadets. Of the first hundred boys selected, thirty were the sons of officers who had died on active service and whose education was free. Twenty more, also the sons of officers, paid forty pounds annually, while the rest paid the full fee of ninety pounds. Four years after entering at the age of thirteen, these young men received free commissions in the cavalry or infantry. Until then the sole educational establishment had been the Royal Military Academy at Woolwich for the training of officers of the Ordnance; Britain had been the only major European power without a system of military education.

Johnston's age and experience were such that when the new Commandant, Sir Henry Douglass, was seconded to serve on Moore's staff in Spain, he was put temporarily in charge of this embryo Staff College and supervised its removal to new premises in High Wycombe. His suitability for the post is apparent from the suggestions he made at the end of his book[18] for the better conduct of future campaigns in tropical forest country, recommendations that could well have been made compulsory reading for later generations of officers in many European armies, including his own. Johnston's strictures on the clothing of his men have already been mentioned: he complained that white pantaloons made their wearers conspicuous, and that the position of the troops was revealed by the sun's reflection on their glistening weapons and the brass plates of their hats; he recommended a green or grey uniform and a light carbine for warfare in the jungle. Johnston also insisted that it was necessary for officers to learn something of the local language, not only so that they could interrogate prisoners and obtain information from villagers, but also to talk to their own troops without having to use interpreters; what is more it would enable them to converse with educated Asians and so better their understanding of the country in which they were living. His criticism of those Europeans who were contemptuous of the local languages contrasts with Percival's advice, written just before the outbreak of the war:

'The Ceylonese language is so harsh and disagreeable to the European that few or none ever attempt to speak it; nor, indeed is it at all necessary.'[19]

Johnston also expressed sound views on the need to organize and supervise transport on methodical lines. Elephants he found to be slow, vulnerable and easily fatigued. Bullocks could live on the land, as opposed to coolies who ate up their own loads; except in fast moving operations, the former were, therefore, to be preferred, but he emphasized the need for proper animal management, disciplined drivers and adequate supervision. As far as the coolies were concerned, he suggested that not only did humanity require that they be treated with kindness, but that it was also politic to ensure that they were properly fed, sheltered and paid.

Perhaps Johnston's most perspicacious comment was to suggest that as each British soldier had cost the taxpayer at least £100 by the time he arrived in the East, the objects of the campaign, even from a financial standpoint, might have been better secured by applying a smaller sum of money to bribing the right people at the Kandyan court.

VI

The story of the other divisions is soon told. Blackall, starting from Negombo with ninety Europeans and a hundred and ten Asians, was joined by two smaller detachments from Chilaw and Puttalam. He then proceeded once again to lay waste to the Seven Korales, burning and destroying everything he saw to within a day's march of Kandy, and driving off a great quantity of cattle. To help in the work of spreading terror in the country-side there was the newly raised cavalry unit, now operational.

Because coolies were easier to come by in the neighbourhood of Colombo, Beaver was able to collect 3,400 followers to carry the stores and supplies for his 600 fighting men. Although the column was far too ungainly, this able officer managed to manœuvre it swiftly across wild and unknown country in the direction of Matara in an abortive attempt to capture Pilima Talauva. Maddison, who had left Hambantota before Johnston's message arrived, tried to penetrate into Sabaragamuva, but was forced southwards because of the drought and joined forces with Beaver.

On the other side of the island, Horner's column devastated the hinterland of Trincomalee. It was indeed, in the words of North's despatch, '. . . a year undistinguished by any brilliant or important Advantages'.[20]

Repeating their error of 1803, the Kandyans broke out once again into the British provinces in the February of the following year. It was a gesture as incomprehensible as it was profitless. Cordiner ascribed their boldness to the withdrawal of the two Bengal battalions to their own country,[21] but after their previous experiences they could hardly have hoped for any success from such tactics. Again minute parties of British troops were able to repulse and disperse the half-hearted incursions. Johnston, now in command at Hambantota, again distinguished himself.[22] The usual pattern of devastating counter-raids by the British followed, falling upon a countryside now both starving and ravaged by small-pox. The war was, however, faltering towards its indecisive conclusion and the arrival of a new governor was to herald the end of the fighting.

CHAPTER 10

Between the Wars

I

By the year 1805, North was no longer able to cope with his duties. He was a spent man. Ever since the disasters of 1803, he had been striving to rid himself of his burdensome responsibilities; and, in the October of that year he had been forced to admit that he felt incapable of carrying on for much longer the complicated business of office in a satisfactory manner.[1] During the long months it took for his despatches to reach London, for the over-burdened members of the Government to find the time to deal with them, and for his replacement to be chosen, North's health deteriorated, and with it his self-confidence. In February, 1805, his repeated requests to be recalled culminated in the despairing cry, 'I must repeat to your Lordships that nerves, shattered and unstrung as mine are, are not formed to encounter the Fatigues and Disgusts of such a Government as this.'[2] The progressive deterioration of his handwriting, as revealed in his letters in the files of the Public Record Office, mirrors this physical and mental breakdown, as does his pathetic confession, 'I hope I have not done wrong, but I am not certain whether I have acted like a good politician or a great nincompoop.'[3] Frederick North had much in common with his famous brother, who towards the end of his long public career could, in similar fashion, write, 'I am perfectly miserable, and tremble at the vexations and troubles that are hanging over me.'[4]

At last, on 17 July, 1805, Major-General Sir Thomas Maitland, the Earl of Lauderdale's brother, arrived in Colombo to take North's place. In a letter to the Secretary of State, written a week earlier, North had admitted with perfect candour that his relief

'. . . cannot take place too early for the Advantage of the Country and the Interest of Government. As I trust, from the High Military Rank of the General that both the Civil and the Military Power will be vested in Him, He will be able to carry on his administration with a firm Hand; to reform the Abuses and curtail the Expenses of his Government, on a Steady and Deliberate Plan, in the Exercise of his Authority. . . .'[5]

Because Maitland was a soldier, it was simple to vest both the military and the civil power in him; and Lord Camden, the new Secretary of State, was not slow to seize the chance of curtailing General Wemyss's appointment as military commander in the island. This ill-humoured officer was still conducting his acrimonious and protracted squabble with North about his allowances, and Camden now settled the matter once and for all in terms by no means ungenerous. His letter to the General on the subject was, however, couched in the bleakest of phrases, and it concluded with the information that Maitland's appointment made it incompatible with the regulations of the Service that Wemyss should remain as Lieutenant-Governor of the island. It was well-merited retribution for eighteen months of perverse conduct, and Camden did not temper the blow by the courtesy of an expression of even formal thanks for his services.[6]

With all his faults, North was a sympathetic person. His subordinates were attracted to him, and because of this he was able to retain their loyalty. His relationship with Macdowall was exemplary; it could well have been otherwise, with consequences which would undoubtedly have been truly disastrous. Although the ultimate future of the Provinces was in doubt during the greater part of the seven years of his tour in office, he substituted a sound and relatively honest government for the chaos of the rule of the East India Company. He was the founder of the Ceylon Civil Service, second only in reputation to its

Indian counterpart, and he established the judiciary and the fiscal system of the island upon sound lines. With no support from Whitehall, he extended as best he could the chain of schools bequeathed to the country by the Dutch (possibly it is not wholly irrelevant that Ceylon's literacy rate today is the highest in Asia). The success of his Medical Department in introducing small-pox vaccination for the time being virtually eliminated the disease, so much so that the four hospitals used for its treatment could be closed. He established a rudimentary system of poor relief, opened orphanages, and introduced a regular postal service, both internal and external.

Unfortunately North's vision was not matched by a corresponding ability to carry his reforms through to fruition. Often he tried to do too much too fast. The changes he made in land tenure, involving the abolition of *rajakariya* were premature and had to be reversed by Maitland. Forced labour was anathema to North's liberal principles, but cash wages were an insufficiently attractive bait to tempt the Sinhalese to labour on public works. Despite the manner in which it hindered the commercial progress of the country, the oppressive powers which it gave to the chiefs, and the British dislike of something so akin to serfdom, *rajakariya* was not abolished until 1832, and elements of the custom continued to linger on for a further forty years.

Even when the country was at peace, North found it hard to produce the cash and the administrative energy to complete his many imaginative projects. In the chaos of war, much of what he had started collapsed. The war itself was the product of his visionary ambition to control the interior of the island, and to this design was linked a petulance provoked by the failure of his diplomatic overtures to the Kandyans. After the disasters of 1803, this petulance grew into a revengeful obsession, and the Governor's liberal principles foundered under the strain. A man who had, at one time, been too scrupulous to encourage Pilima Talauva in his plots to dethrone the King was capable of jettisoning Muttusamy, conniving at the ravaging of Kandyan villages, and neglecting to try to secure Major Davie's release after making him the scapegoat of his errors. Impulsive and unstable, North was an idealist who stumbled into an unnecessary and disastrous war, and then became corrupted by its stresses.

II

Maitland was the antithesis of his predecessor.[7] Both men belonged to aristocratic families, but there any similarity ended. On the male side Thomas Maitland belonged to a famous clan of Lowland Scots that for generations had bred tough border marauders. His mother was the daughter of a wealthy Norwich weaver, and his character was an amalgam of the two strains. Lacking any formal education, he had little use for abstract principles and no interests other than his work. Energetic, arrogant and ruthless, his officials respected him because he was both able and fair. Although he was as relentless in pursuit of his ambitions as he was of his enemies, regardless of all else he was guided by the need to uphold 'The honour of his Majesty's service', a phrase often heard in his broad Scots tones (the lairds had not yet learned to speak with the clipped accents of the English public schools). From his mother Maitland inherited the shrewd financial acumen which he brought to every aspect of government. Although he was a soldier by profession, he had made his reputation in politics and public administration. The twelve years he had spent as a junior officer, mainly in India, had given him an understanding of the fundamentals of his profession and a lifelong interest in colonial affairs. When he entered Parliament on the Whig benches, his radical outlook brought him into prominence: as an opponent of the war against Tippoo Sahib, an attacker of Warren Hastings, and a continual critic of British military failures in the Low Countries, he developed into a vexatious nuisance to the Government. Then, in 1797, after a short period back in uniform as a brigadier, he was entrusted with the command of the British forces in San Domingo, still nominally a French island but controlled effectively by the negro nationalist, Toussaint L'Ouverture. Whether the appointment was made in an effort to buy Maitland's silence is not known. Perhaps the object was to get him out of the way where his voice could no longer be heard. Whatever the reason may have been, from now on Maitland did become a loyal supporter of the Government, possibly because the rise to power of Napoleon suggested to him, as it did to many others, that stable government and strong defences had to take priority over liberal reforms.

San Domingo provided Maitland with his opportunity. On his own responsibility, and ignoring the advice of his seniors, he arranged for the British forces to be evacuated from the island, thus rescuing the Government from a potentially disastrous situation. His talents both as an administrator and a shrewd negotiator had been disclosed. Command of an expedition to Quiberon Bay followed, but this was cancelled, and Maitland returned to Westminster as a supporter of the Ministry, a member of the Board of Control for India, and a Privy Councillor.

When he was appointed as successor to North in 1805, the confidence of the Government in his judgement was revealed by the fact that he was asked to define the main lines of his policies for Ceylon before his instructions were drafted. These instructions, when they were issued, contained a vital sentence, which not only indicated the Government's disgust and annoyance at North's territorial adventures, but gave Maitland his charter for the future:

Abstracted from every principle of Justice, there does not appear any principle of Policy which ought to induce Great Britain to wish the entire subjugation of that Island, as the advantages derivable from such a Possession could not be commensurate to the Expense of maintaining it; but when the Principles of Justice are combined with those of Policy (and on all occasions they ought to be inseparable), I feel satisfied that there is no ground for our desiring greatly to extend the territory we acquired by just Rights from the Dutch. . . .'[8]

In an eleven-page despatch written in Colombo on the day after he had relieved North of his burdens, the new Governor set down his initial impression of the problems which confronted him.[9] He expressed confidence that he could restore tranquillity to Ceylon; while, in the course of sympathizing with North on his lack of power to control Wemyss, ungrammatically but precisely he condemned the extravagance and absurdity of this erratic officer:

'There have I much fear been but few instances in the annals of British government, of a conduct more reprehensible or less calculated to forward the views of His Majesty's Government than this officer. In adding enormously to the military expense of the Establishment, he has contributed little or nothing to the efficient military force of the island.'[10]

Maitland asked North, who had not yet sailed, to comment on the contents of this despatch, an indication that an agreeable working relationship existed between the two men. This harmony is reflected in another of Maitland's letters:

'. . . I do not believe that there exists a more honourable Man or one who has the Interests of his Country more at heart: indeed in the only Department he has immediately under him, the Civil, little is required to be done as far as I can see immediately, and I do not at all feel disposed to alter any of his arrangements.'[11]

Three months later, after he had made a comprehensive inspection of his new estate, Maitland's conclusions had shifted somewhat. Laudatory references to North still preface his latest despatch, but he goes on to say that although the Government of the island presented a surface appearance of uniformity and efficiency, what was a sound system had, in fact, been weakly operated. Regulations were not enforced; many had become blank letters. Inactive and indolent civil servants had been allowed the scope to give way to their failings, and many of the regulations were inapplicable to large parts of the territory.[12]

Maitland set himself three tasks: to stop the war; to reduce the extravagantly inflated military establishment; and to bring order to the chaotic finances. In accomplishing this he had a virtually free hand. Engaged in a world-wide struggle for the very existence of their country, the members of the British Government had little or no time for the problems of Ceylon. Unpalatable though it must have been to Mr John D'Oyly, Maitland's Chief Translator, his brother spoke the truth when he wrote to say: 'You must be aware that no great interest exists in the public mind concerning so remote and so little important a settlement as Ceylon.'[13] That Maitland had to wait two and a half years for a reply to his first despatch is some indication of the priority Whitehall was able to afford to the island's business. Ignorant as they were of the local problems, the ever-changing Secretaries of State were only too willing to accept the judgements of a man they knew to be reliable, so long as they received no requests either for financial or for military help. Luckily for them, no man was more willing to accept responsibility than 'King Tom', as Maitland was nicknamed. He wielded powers, subject only to the law, that were close to being absolute, and these he exercised for the public good, as he understood the meaning of the term.

Maitland managed to cut the size of the army without in any way reducing its efficiency. He organized his forces to defend the provinces, not against a Kandyan incursion but a French attack upon Trincomalee. As he had no intention of invading Kandy himself, he was able to economize in both the independent companies of local troops and the swollen bands of pioneers, most of whom rotted in idleness in the long intervals between the infrequent punitive expeditions. In two months, Maitland reduced the 10,827 men under arms by one third, but in doing so he increased the strength of nearly every combatant unit.[14] He had little confidence in either the Malays or the Sepoys, but he much admired the African troops,[15] so much so that towards the end of his tour he raised a second battalion of them, the 4th Ceylon Regiment.

Two years of plundering the Kandyan countryside had done severe harm to the morale and the discipline of the troops. Maitland reported that 'my attention has been principally employed in collecting the Regiments, improving their discipline, and relieving them from the total disorganization in which I found them'.[16] The judicious court-martialling of some insubordinate officers helped in this process.[17] To the benefit of both finance and efficiency the multitude of independent and well-paid appointments held by regimental officers was abolished, and the wide financial powers that even subalterns had the opportunity of abusing in the field were curtailed. His success in restoring the effectiveness of his forces was such that when, on 3 August, 1806, he received a plea from the Madras Government for help in quelling the mutiny that had just erupted at Vellore, he was able to arrange for the 400-strong 19th Foot to embark from Colombo at just two hours' notice, a sure indication that the troops were once again on a sound footing. Maitland provided this help with noteworthy ill grace, using the opportunity to catechize Lord Minto, the Governor General, in thirty-six interminable foolscap pages, not only on the Company's relationship with native princes, but also upon the entire civil and military administration of India.[18] When the British officers of the Madras Army mutinied in 1809, Ceylon was able to provide help on an even larger scale. Maitland in person welcomed the returning troops at Trincomalee, and entertained them to a public dinner which was preceded by racing, wrestling and pig hunts.[19]

As soon as he found out what was wrong with the civil administration of his Provinces, Maitland set to work to put it right. North had tried to compensate for the low salaries of the civil servants by creating a multitude of sinecures held in plurality, and by allowing his men to engage in private trade. Corruption was still common, and one of the first things Maitland did was to order an investigation into the affairs of the Collectorship of Jaffnapatam, held by the young Lusignan, now promoted to what was one of the senior posts in the island. Lusignan, who knew no Tamil despite his proficiency in European languages, was held to have been the victim of his underlings, and Maitland showed sound sense by doing no more than ordering him to pay the deficit and posting him to a subordinate appointment more suitable to his years, thus retaining a promising man in the Service.

Maitland abolished the sinecures, combined other posts, and forbade private trade. To offset this, salaries were increased, and in 1808 Maitland was able to introduce detailed regulations for the classification, pay, promotion and conduct of his administrators. Promotion was dependent on their serving a fixed period in each rank, and proficiency in Sinhalese or Portuguese earned a junior a credit of one year's service. Maitland failed only in persuading Whitehall to raise the minimum age of entry to the

Service. Fifteen-year-old boys continued to be shipped out to him, their ambitions centred on a pension ten years later, just at the age they were becoming physically and mentally attuned to their work. For most officials, service in the colonies was looked upon as a period of dangerous drudgery during which they might gather the competence needed to enjoy a pleasant retirement in Surrey or Cheltenham, provided that they were fortunate enough to survive. A few individuals saw it otherwise: their work was an end in itself. One of these was John D'Oyly, who died in Kandy after an unbroken stay of twenty-three years on the island.

Maitland reduced paper-work and insisted that his officials should use the time so saved in making frequent and regular circuits of their districts. Many of North's innovations he retained and improved; others he abolished, including the new system of land-tenure. Distasteful though *rajakariya* might be, it had to be brought back in order to ensure financial solvency.

If anyone dared to oppose him, Maitland quickly showed how ruthless he could be. Lushington, the Chief Justice, who had squabbled with Wemyss, had the temerity to challenge the Governor's authority. Maitland quietly waited until Lushington had provided him with sufficient rope; and, when the opportunity afforded, the Chief Justice departed. This was Maitland's habit. He never forgave an affront. Although he was quarrelsome himself, he would not suffer his subordinates to behave in the same way, and anyone who failed to work smoothly with his colleagues soon felt his wrath. But ruthless autocrat though Maitland was, without human understanding he could never have moved as quickly as he did. His programme of retrenchment needed the loyalty and co-operation of his soldiers and civil servants to be effective, and this they gave him. He was a hard taskmaster, but like many of his kind, his men liked to work for him.

Because no financial statements were attached to North's despatches, it is hard to make an estimate of the fiscal difficulties which Maitland faced. From 1798 onwards, the revenue had increased each year, and North might possibly have met the estimated expenditure for 1803 which amounted to £331,000. The war prevented this happening. No figures can be found for 1803, but the deficit for the following year reached £240,000. During the first half of 1805, the military expenditure alone had risen to £474,000, and the success of Maitland's financial measures is demonstrated by the fact that in 1808 he had cut this figure by more than half; what is more, he had balanced the budget for the first time. He was a capable housekeeper.[20]

Maitland's vital but most simple task was to stop the war. Unless Kandy and the British Provinces could co-exist, little else was possible, and his despatch of 19 October summarized his intended policy:

'I shall not enter into any foolish expeditions; I will not throw away the Lives of His Majesty's Subjects by Disease in burning and destroying the defenceless Huts of the innocent Natives.'[21]

His policy was successful. He left the Kandyans in peace, and the war, by tacit agreement, faded to its conclusion.

Maitland considered that a formal peace treaty was of little value, as tranquillity was only likely to be maintained so long as the British kept an adequate garrison in their settlements. Nevertheless, he did all he could to negotiate such a treaty. Within two months of his arrival, he had approached Moratota, the *Maha Nayaka Unanse* (or head of the priesthood), a man respected both by the King and by Pilima Talauva, and one whom North had used previously as an intermediary. D'Oyly, the Chief Translator, who was in effect the head of intelligence, acted as the Governor's mouthpiece in this and in subsequent approaches.

As a preliminary to any treaty, Maitland insisted on the surrender of the Kandyan-held captives, including Davie, but his opponents stood out for the completion of the treaty before they surrendered the captives. In the end they released about 300 Malays and Sepoys, but their attitude then hardened, and they reverted to the clauses of the still-born 1796 negotiations which contained the provision for the grant of an outlet to the sea. Nothing was ever agreed, nor was Davie released, but Ceylon did at least have ten years of peace.

III

While most of the officers of the British Army were recruited from the landed classes, all but a handful of the men came from the opposite end of the social spectrum. It was not easy to persuade a man to enlist when to be posted to many tropical stations was the equivalent of a sentence of death. Fortescue estimated that 40,000 British soldiers died or were killed in the West Indies between 1793 and 1796; regularly every two years, regiments would lose their entire strength.[22] To make good such losses, to replace the casualties suffered by units in the Low Countries, and to fill the proliferating newly raised regiments, it was not surprising that during the last decade of the century the refuse of the jails, together with a fair proportion of children and the aged, had to be persuaded, cajoled or cheated into the Service. Pay was derisory; the food was bad. Even for a brutal age, the discipline was savage. For all but minor offences, the punishment was flogging, administered in instalments if the attendant surgeon feared for the victim's life. Unless a man were in trouble with the law, or had perhaps put the wrong girl in the family way, he had to be very hungry, bored or drunk to accept the King's shilling.

The trouble was that although the British were prepared to use the press-gang to man the fleet, the idea of levying soldiers by direct conscription was unpalatable. However, as the threat from France increased, a suitable compromise was found in the shape of the County Militia. This force was raised by selective ballot for local defence, and although the monied were able to buy themselves substitutes, the standard of men serving in the ranks was relatively high. With the transfer of militiamen to regular regiments, the back of the recruiting problem was broken. More than half the regular army recruits were obtained in this way, and by and large these men were of a much sounder type than those who had joined direct from civilian life. There were many potent reasons for transferring: large bounties were offered —usually £10, but at times quadruple the figure; garrison life in England was dull and men wanted to see the world; there was also the robust philosophy that if a man had to wear the King's uniform, he might as well see a little fighting in it.

With the spread of literacy among working people towards the latter half of the eighteenth century, a few better-taught men were finding their way into the ranks, and some were starting to record their experiences. Two of these, both of whom were fortunate enough to survive, served in Ceylon at this time, and both portrayed the peacetime existence of soldiers manning the coastal forts. The first, Bombardier Alexander Alexander, upon whose character we have already touched,[23] landed in Ceylon in June, 1803, with one of the companies of Royal Artillery, and was invalided home seven years later. The second author, George Calladine of the 19th Foot, covered a rather later period, as he arrived in January, 1815, and left as a corporal in 1820, when his Regiment at long last returned home. Alexander, the natural son of a wealthy Glasgow merchant, had been brought up in an Ayrshire labourer's family, and had received his education at the hands of a brutal village pedagogue. Calladine, on the other hand, was of a humbler, but nevertheless respectable background. The son of a widowed Leicester gardener, he had been bound apprentice to a framework knitter. Trade was so good that even as an apprentice Calladine could earn four shillings daily, enough to allow him to idle away a day or two at the start of each week. The combination of boredom and the lure of travel tempted him to enlist in the militia, and later transfer to the Regular Army, an action he never admits to having regretted, despite the contrast between the squalor of life in the barrack-room and the affluence of a Nottingham tradesman's house. Calladine enjoyed the good times, weathered the bad, and viewed his Regiment with not uncritical affection, censuring those officers who lacked professional ability and contemptuous of others who, as he put it, avoided service in the West Indies because they 'were rather afraid of becoming food for land crabs'.[24]

During their time in Trincomalee, both men experienced the effects of tropical disease on soldiers who had been debilitated by service up-country or who lacked resistance because they were not acclimatized to the tropics. Alexander watched one or two of his comrades being buried each day: the largest and stoutest died first, and the women and children perished with their men-folk; everyone was sick and it was hard to find men with strength enough to bury the dead. During his seven years in Ceylon, Alexander was rarely well, and it is remarkable that he managed to survive. Calladine contracted dysentery six months after he arrived, and he describes how four or five of his comrades died in hospital each day. Three years later, during the 1818 campaign, he went through the same experience once again.

Calladine noted that the officers survived better than the men, and he attributed this to their bungalows at Trincomalee being built on low ground and so escaping the noxious vapours that blew around the barracks on the hill-tops overlooking the sea. Writing about the epidemic of 1804, Dr Cordiner made a more accurate diagnosis. The fever, which was not contagious, was caused by

'. . . a vitiated atmosphere, want of accommodation, bad living and intemperence. Even in the seasons when Trincomalee was best provided with fresh provisions, the garrison subsisted five days of the week on salt meat, with the addition of any other vegetable but rice.'[25]

The accommodation was so bad that the houses even of the officers were a danger to health. During the rains, it was impossible to find a dry spot in any room, and camp cots were provided with painted canvas covers to protect the occupants from the rain pouring through the leaking roofs.[26]

Alexander understood that the foul food was the greatest danger to the men's health, although he thought, like many of his contemporaries, that hard physical work in the heat was a contributory cause. The meat given to the soldiers was carrion, old and diseased, soft and flabby with a rank odour, heavy and loathsome, offensive both to sight and smell. The rice was small, of bad quality, full of dirt and dust. It was boiled under the filthiest of conditions and flavoured with curry. This was the mid-day meal. For supper a small rice-flour cake was served, and breakfast was the same with a little fish or bullock's liver added. A quart of arrack was issued daily to each five men.[27]

Calladine complained less about the food, and it is likely that he had less reason to do so. At times he was even complimentary. At Batticaloa in 1816:

'After our company had been here awhile and got a little acquainted with the inhabitants, we were very fond of the place. In the first place, all kinds of provisions were very reasonable, duty easy, liquor cheap and good, and we had all the indulgence that soldiers could expect. Although Captain Jones was a very strict man, yet to a man that conducted himself with propriety he would give any reasonable liberties. . . .'[28]

This raising of standards is likely to have been a dim reflection of the improvements to the living conditions of the soldiers brought about by the Duke of York's energy and ability, some of the effects of which had even penetrated to Ceylon.

Not unnaturally, every account of life in Ceylon is overlaid with the grim problem of fending off the ever-present threat of disease. Everyone, both doctor and layman, had his personal theories as to cause and cure. Some, as we have seen, came near to the truth; others were more fanciful. Percival, for instance, attributed the good health of his troops, all of whom were mature men living under peaceful conditions at the coast, to the fact that:

'drinking plenty of arrack and smoking tobacco, counteract the bad effects of the atmosphere and the water; while the natives on the other hand live so abstemiously, few or none of them eating flesh, or drinking anything but water, that once they are seized with these exhausting distempers, their constitutions want strength to resist them, and they usually fall victims.'[29]

Percival's troops also drank tea, found by them growing wild around Trincomalee:

'They cut the branches and twigs, and hang them in the sun to dry; they then take off the leaves and put them into a vessel or kettle to boil, to extract the juice that has all the properties of the China tea leaf. . . .'[30]

It was forty years before tea was first grown commercially in Assam, and three-quarters of a century before it replaced the blighted coffee as the main plantation crop of the highlands of

Ceylon. Although it was provided as a hospital comfort, this is the sole contemporary reference to tea-drinking in their barracks by British troops, and it can only be assumed that, for the time being, they lost the taste for the brew.

Like nearly every European, both Alexander and Calladine drank to excess, the former in gloomy disgust at his enforced existence among men for whom he had nothing but contempt. Only the dread of the halberts or the gun-wheel exercised any restraint upon him. Calladine drank in a more companionable fashion, but he, like Alexander, was conscious of the threat of the lash and successful in avoiding it. At times he was even abstemious, selling his daily arrack ration for its market price of 7d, but this was not always possible as an officer was supposed to check that every man drank his portion as it was issued. Although he was aware of the connection between ill-health and excessive drinking, his account of the way he spent a free day indicates that he did not take the dangers very seriously:

'We had a very pleasant toddy drinking party at Batticaloa. Having leave for the day, a few pounds of joggery (sugar), a few dozen eggs, two or three bottles of rack, we would make the best of our way to the topes (groves of trees), and being snugly seated under the spreading branches of the trees, secured from the burning sun, we would get a large chatty on the fire, with six or eight quarts of toddy, and after mixing the rack, sugar and eggs, seat ourselves around, each having a cocoanut shell, dip into the flowing bowl, and pass along the day in the greatest of pleasure, good company and hilarity.'[31]

Like their betters, their main solace and recreation was drink, and many, as Dr Marshall complained, became perfect sots. 'It is much to be feared,' he wrote, 'that the regular issue of spirit rations tends to excite a desire for the immoderate use of arrack.'[32] The trouble was that there were few amusements other than drink. A singing company existed in Calladine's unit which performed in church each Sunday; Calladine himself took part although he was far from being a religious man; he also tried his hand at plaiting straw hats, and at hunting alligators and monkeys. During Alexander's time at Trincomalee, the troops were playing tennis in the roofless church; and by 1822, quoits, cricket, handball and football were all being played.[33] Private Wheeler, a similar type of man to Calladine, writing about the 51st Foot, after they returned home from Waterloo, describes

'. . . two play days a week, viz. Wednesdays and Saturdays. These days were passed as follows. After the morning parade, every one is busy employed in cleaning appointments. This done the day is devoted to athletic exercises, boxing, wrestling, running, picking up a hundred stones, some times on foot and others on horseback, cricket, football, running in sacks and any other amusements we might fancy. This produces an excellent feeling between officers and men, for the officers always take part in their diversions.'[34]

Nevertheless, the 51st Foot were ahead of their time. Sport was still far from being a common part of a soldier's life.

One way of escaping from the barrack-room was to form a liaison with a local woman, and this both Alexander and Calladine arranged. The former said he did so because he wanted to improve his diet, and so cure the continual flux that threatened to kill him. He managed to find an attractive Sinhalese, who cooked his food properly, but whose nature matched that of her husband; she bore him a fine son who delighted his father by his habit of enjoying cigars while still in the stage of taking nourishment from his mother. Calladine's reason for setting up house was equally hard-headed: living out of barracks helped him to resist the temptations of drink.

In contrast to the privations of the soldiers, the officers and their colleagues in the civil service lived in a manner (to use the current usage) both genteel and refined. In Cordiner's time half of this privileged *élite* still lived within the fort walls, but the rest had moved out to build themselves houses in the new suburbs of Slave Island, Colpetty and Mutwal. Visitors to Colombo habitually commented on the charm of the society they found there, limited though it was in size. Every member of the small community knew everyone else intimately, and relations between the civil and the military were usually excellent. 'The urbanity of manners,' as Cordiner put it, 'which distinguishes the soldier is universally known, and in this respect the garrison of Colombo has been singularly fortunate.'[35]

190

Some men drove themselves hard (the length of their despatches bear witness to this), but many spent the greater part of each day in well-organized idleness. James Campbell recounted how officers filled their time in 1820, and what he had to say tallied closely with Cordiner's experiences ten years before:

'We get out of bed at gun-fire, or soon after five o'clock; and should there be a parade we, military, go to it; if not the morning is devoted to some sort of gentle exercise, such as riding a few miles, until about eight o'clock, when the heat begins to be somewhat oppressive. . . .
'If we take a morning's walk, which is seldom, it is usually in the botanical gardens, which have lately been much improved by Mr Moon, the superintendent, under the auspices of Lady Brownrigg and now contains many rare and beautiful trees, flowers and shrubs. . . .
'After the morning's exercise, we bathe, dress and sit down about nine to a substantial breakfast; something in the Scotch style, in point of variety of eatables. From breakfast until about two, the hour of tiffin, is usually given up by a few to reading, writing, some interesting study, or indoor occupation; and by too many to downright indolence. From eleven to two is the period of the day alloted to paying visits, when we use our palanquins, or bandies, as gigs are called; for it is then considered too hot for riding or walking. . . . Some make a complete dinner at the hour of tiffen; and others, I consider them the most prudent in every sense of the word, are satisfied with fruits of every kind, which are in great abundance and bought for a mere trifle. From tiffen until about four o'clock is usually spent in chat or gossip; our horses are then brought to the door, as all the world soon after turns out for rides or drives, usually upon the Galle face, until sun-set. We all, however, get home about half past six, then dress and sit down to dinner at seven. Most people, from eating too much at tiffen, or rather as much as they are able, only go through the form of dining; and may perhaps, condescend to taste some Yorkshire ham, coast mutton— that is mutton from the continent—hot curry and English cheese. About nine o'clock, unless we have company, we usually rise from the table, and by ten most people are in bed. Thus, from the way in which they begin, Europeans in general acquire habits of indolence, which they probably never get rid of as long as they live. A military man is occasionally roused from what may be properly called a state of apathy, by way, or preparations for war; but a civilian is allowed to enjoy permanent, undisturbed, nabob-like repose.'[36]

The cocoon-like British social clubs date from the earliest days of the occupation. The first was the Cocoa-Nut, perched above the Kelani River, where Major Wilson dined Macdowall's officers the evening before they marched for Kandy. It provided whist and good food, the twelve members taking it in turn to entertain the others to dinner after an afternoon at cards. The meal was served at four o'clock, and the hosts competed with each other in the lavishness of their hospitality. The next club to be founded was the Quoit, at Bambalapitiya, on the opposite side of Colombo, between the Cinnamon Gardens and the sea. In the early days of its existence, the members played their game before breakfast, dressed in comfortable white jackets with a silver quoit, about the size of a crown, dangling from their necks; but in 1804 the time of play was switched to the evening when it became fashionable to dine at a later hour. Except when special entertainments were arranged, ladies were admitted to neither club, nor, needless to say, were either Dutch or Sinhalese. The Hollanders mixed little with their conquerors, although a few fathers of marriageable girls did entertain bachelor British officers with some notable successes. North worked hard to improve relations between the two communities which had been marred by some unfortunate remarks Percival had made about the charm of the Dutch women[37]—unjustly so, it seems, because when the Governor visited Jaffnapatam, twenty Dutch girls attended a ball given by Colonel and Mrs Barbut in his honour, and they earned Cordiner's praise for their beauty, vivacity and good manners. Mrs Barbut was famous as a hostess; and, after her husband's death, she waited for five years before remarrying, thus avoiding the unseemly haste in which most of her counterparts took another spouse. Six months was the usual period of waiting, but Mrs Barbut was fortunate; North had been able to secure her a pension of £300.[38]

The Dutch could hardly afford the pace set by the British. Except for a few, the nine hundred strong community, mainly officer prisoners-of-war and the families of deceased officials, were living in much reduced circumstances, but they still managed to 'maintain an appearance, in the eyes of the world', as Cordiner put it, 'sometimes affluent and gay, always decent and respectable.'[39] Often they managed to exist only by renting their houses to British officers and officials.

To social intercourse with the Sinhalese, but one reference

exists, and that relates to the early days of the occupation, in which Percival admits to the arrogance of his countrymen:

'The young Cingalese ladies of high rank dress by no means inelegantly, and neither their appearance nor manners are disagreeable. They are frequently met at the parties of the Dutch, who are much more partial to their company than the English. For the naturally distant and haughty temper of our countrymen, and their unacquaintance with the native language, they never dream of associating with the Cingalese, or receiving them at their parties.'[40]

The soldiers were less inhibited. Campbell wrote:

'Many of them [the soldiers] having in their walks become acquainted with the Kandyans, they appear to be on the best possible terms with each other; yet, I am something uneasy, lest the ladies may occasion misunderstandings; for the soldiers are very obliging, both to them and the men; even assisting them—as many of the latter as are absent roadmaking—in the cultivation of their fields. It amuses me greatly, as it does the Kandyans, to see how admirably some of the men work with the buffaloes and oxen, in the rice fields, and also afterwards, in treading out the grain.'[41]

The cost of living was ruinous at the standard the British set themselves: a taste for English ham, cheese, pickles and preserves; contempt for local produce, such as oranges and pineapples; Madeira at forty shillings the dozen, and claret at double the price, not to mention English ale. Such imported luxuries, deemed to be essentials, made life expensive enough. To this had to be added overheads, such as the £200 needed annually to pay the thirteen bearers of a palanquin. No bachelor could live in what was judged to be comfort on less than £800 a year, and a subaltern who drew £300, even with the benefits of his mess, had to practice rigid economy to avoid running into debt. It cost £50 to maintain a horse, £10 more than in the last days of the Indian Raj, when a subaltern's emoluments had hardly changed, although far less was expected of him. In both 1803 and 1933 a servant's wages were much the same: Macdowall's palanquin bearers earned eleven pence daily; 130 years later, a *syce* was paid twopence less. It was not surprising that the officers, who had paid hard cash for their commissions, looked forward so much to the prospects of active service and prize-money. When the 51st Foot narrowly missed the storming of Seringapatam, Lt Samuel Rice regretted that his Regiment 'were not fortunate enough to share the honours with the conquerors of Mysore and divide with them the immense treasure of the tyrant in his capital. It is at least two thousand pounds out of my pocket, besides the chance of plunder. . . .'[42]

The contrast between the living conditions of officer and soldier, wide though it might be, was no worse than that to be seen in cottage and mansion in any English county, but it was small wonder that the officers survived the rigours of the climate better than their men, despite their claret and gluttony. In 1804, when the neighbouring line regiment had to help the Gunners to bury their dead, Alexander noted that not a single officer perished, and he attributed their survival to their better diet and their avoiding exposure to fatigue and the elements. But even he did not grudge them their infinitely better lot. It was in the natural order of things. Possibly all that can be said is that those officers who cared for the well-being of their men (and they seem to have been in the majority) did what they could within the limits of the system to make the lot of their soldiers a little less unendurable.

IV

During the decade that began with Maitland's arrival in Ceylon, the transformation of Sri Wikrama Rajasinha from the puppet-like tool of his minister to a ruthless and all-powerful autocrat was brought to its conclusion.[43] It was the struggle of a single man of alien race against the powerful oligarchy of native aristocrats through whom he had to rule. Despite the well-justified suspicion and ill-favour with which the King viewed him, Pilima Talauva continued to head the strongest faction among the chiefs. After the events of 1803, the King banished him to his *dissawa*, but two years later the Adigar was back in the capital and apparently in favour once again, at a time when Sri Wikrama was incapacitated with small-pox. Pilima Talauva was again wielding his full ministerial powers, and some sort of peace seems to have been patched up between the two men until 1808, when Migastenna died and his office of Second Adigar passed to Ehelepola, Pilima Talauva's nephew. The dead man's *dissawa* of the Seven Korales was shared between Ehelepola and Molligoda, an unusual arrangement that alarmed the peasants, who predicted that two governors would demand double the usual services. A rebellion broke out which Pilima Talauva quelled in person, but his success revived the latent jealousy and suspicion of the King. Nettled by his monarch's manner, the Adigar had the effrontery to remind him who had placed him on the throne, and to chide him for failing to take his advice. The King's censure was bleak. 'He was not to be led by his chiefs,' he said, 'but they were to be directed by him.'[44] A further dispute arose when Pilima Talauva once again criticized his master, this time for inflicting a massive burden of public works on the people—new roads, the octangular Pattiripuwa extension to the Palace, and the Kiri Mahuda Lake, now the chief glory of Kandy.

In this manner the two men continued to quarrel for three years more, each fearing the other but neither strong enough to dispose of his opponent. The culminating point was reached when Pilima Talauva proposed a marriage between his son and the natural granddaughter of the great Kirti Sri. Seeing this union with the royal blood as a direct threat to his dynasty, the King assembled the chiefs and charged his Adigar with maladministration, accusing him of being the author of every cruel and unpopular act that had been perpetrated during the reign. For some unexplained reason the King then seemed to relent, and he forgave the Adigar his errors, but eight weeks later the King used the neglect of some trivial duty as an excuse to strip him of all his offices. He was then put in prison, but after eight days' detention the King released him and banished him to lead a private life in his native province.

The old intriguer was not a man to accept disgrace with resignation. He plotted a rebellion and bribed Asana, the Malay Mohandiram, the head of the King's guard, to assassinate his ruler. The plot miscarried. The revolt erupted prematurely, the ringleaders were taken, and Asana with sixty of his Malays fled for their lives to Colombo. Pilima Talauva and his son-in-law were arrested (the date is thought to have been June, 1812), and straight away the two men were beheaded, six minor chiefs being either hanged or impaled in a circle around them. Pilima Talauva's son and namesake was in his turn brought to the capital for execution, but the King reprieved him after some of the chiefs had interceded on his behalf. Ehelepola, despite being suspected by the King of having been implicated in the conspiracy, succeeded his uncle as First Adigar.

Although his main opponent was dead, Sri Wikrama was still not a free agent. Fearful for his safety after the plot against his life, he was said never afterwards to have slept more than two watches of the night in the same bed.[45] With justifiable misgivings as to his chiefs' loyalty, he worked to undermine their traditional power, playing off one faction against the other, constantly reallocating offices, splitting provinces, and imposing fresh financial burdens upon them. Increasingly he relied upon his Malabar relations, and he looked also to the common people for support, doing what he could to protect them from the tyranny of the provincial magnates, against whom there was more and more ill-feeling.[46] He tried to strengthen village and provincial committees so as to counteract the power of the chiefs,[47] and he made an attempt to curb corruption among officials.[48] All this, of course, further alienated the aristocracy.

The King had good reason to distrust Pilima Talauva's successors. Ehelepola had been in touch with D'Oyly ever since 1808, as had many other Kandyan nobles. By a combination of flattery and every type of bribe, from European medicines and mirrors to horses and fabrics, D'Oyly edged into their confidence and gained their goodwill. As head of intelligence, he concerned himself with the two traditional roles of the trade—subversion and the collection of information. Disguised as traders and priests, a platoon of his spies roamed the interior, keeping him informed of nearly everything of importance that happened. D'Oyly controlled a Secret Vote of £1,500 to pay for the bribes, for the wages of his men, and for fees to the messengers who maintained the links with Davie and the other captives. It was not an inconsiderable sum, but it was far less than the Dutch had spent on similar work.[49]

Soon after Maitland arrived, he ordered certain of his senior officials to keep diaries of their daily work so that the central government could check the extent of their application and energy. The practice continued right through until 1941, and it produced a profusion of the raw material of history for Ceylon's archives, much of which is still untouched. D'Oyly's own diary, discovered in 1917, is one of the prime sources for the period, but it makes the dullest of reading. It is the factual record of a hardworking and thorough civil servant, untouched by any spark that might illuminate his opinions and prejudices. Except when he describes his efforts to arrange Davie's escape, we have little idea even of the objectives towards which he was working. He provides little indication that he meddled directly in Kandyan politics or even encouraged the chiefs in their disloyalty, but he certainly provided a sympathetic ear for their complaints. 'The share of this inscrutable Englishman,' Professor Ludowyk reflected, 'who learned Sinhalese and could speak and write it, in encompassing the ruin of the Kandyan kingdom has yet to be determined.'[50] Unless new material comes to light, this question will never be answered satisfactorily. D'Oyly's diaries reveal nothing but the bare facts; the letters he received tell us much about his relatives, but little about him.[51]

On 18 July, 1811, Maitland left Ceylon prematurely, his health broken by hard work and the climate. Among the other passengers in the ship were Bombardier Alexander and the two young sons of the Mudaliyar Abraham de Sarum, whom the Governor was taking to England so that they could complete their education at Trinity Hall; as the first two Ceylonese to study in England (perhaps the first to visit the country), they mark the start of a significant process in the evolution of Ceylon as the country is today.

Maitland was an uncomprising autocrat, but he possessed just about every quality required for the post he had so ably filled. Honest, shrewd and capable, he trusted his subordinates and throve on responsibility. His aim had always been the public good.

V

On Maitland's departure, Brigadier John Wilson, the Lieutenant-Governor, took temporary charge. Not to be confused with his namesake who had entertained Macdowall's officers at the Cocoa-Nut Club, Wilson had accompanied Maitland to Ceylon as a member of his staff. Shortly after he assumed office, false rumours about French warships in Indian waters encouraged the Kandyans to hope that outside help might be forthcoming in their quarrel with the British, and D'Oyly's spies collected worrying reports about troop movement and recruits being trained up-country.[52] Wilson's reactions demonstrated that Maitland had trained him well. Resisting the temptation to anticipate this rather shadowy threat or to meddle overtly in Kandyan affairs, he did no more than strengthen his outposts and address a long and pointed letter to the King, in which he enumerated in detail his country's military successes against the French.[53]

On 11 March, 1812, Lieutenant-General Sir Robert Brownrigg succeeded Wilson. Lacking both money and influence when he was a young man, this fifty-three-year-old Anglo-Irishman had carved out a career by his own ability. He was lucky enough to catch the eye of the Duke of York during the disastrous campaign of 1794 in the Netherlands, and he became the Duke's Military Secretary the following year. In 1803 he exchanged that appointment for Quartermaster-General at the Horse Guards, a position analogous then to Chief-of-Staff. Without experience either of civil administration or of the East, this now rather elderly soldier was rewarded with the post of Governor of Ceylon.

The instructions Brownrigg received were in no way ambiguous. They read:

'If War should, after every endeavour on your part to avoid it, be rendered unavoidable by the Acts of the Candian Government, the mode of conducting it must of course be left almost entirely to your own discretion; but I trust that you will agree with me in the Opinion, that the same Principles which have induced the British Government in Ceylon to deprecate the commencement of this Contest should continue to operate in the Conduct of it; and that every Measure of offensive hostility that may be resorted to, should be undertaken solely with the view of providing for the Security of our present Possessions, and not for the Extension of them; and that, on the attaining of that Object, it will be most desirable to attempt the renewal of our former good understanding with the Candian Government with the least delay.'[54]

One of Maitland's first acts after he landed in England was to warn the Government that it should impress upon Brownrigg in the strongest terms the need to abstain from interfering in Kandyan affairs.[55] This was an unusual thing for a retiring Governor to do, and it seems more than likely that some indiscretion of Brownrigg's had alarmed Maitland, for the new Governor had ambitions to complete the work to which North had put his hand ten years earlier. The Government's instructions to Brownrigg, written a week after he had arrived in Ceylon, were probably the product of Maitland's warning.

CHAPTER 11

The Second War:
Sound Planning

I

A<small>NXIOUS</small> though Brownrigg was to crown his military career with the unification of Ceylon, he tackled the problem with patience and caution. His years of service at the Horse Guards had taught him that his country could not afford to become involved in military adventures that might distract her from her main enemy in Europe, and his instructions from Whitehall lacked nothing in clarity on the need to avoid becoming involved in an aggressive war.[1] Despite this, he found it hard to disguise his intentions from the home Government. In a manner happily ingenuous, his real aims tended to show themselves through the flim-flam of his despatches. In his reply to Lord Liverpool's initial warning when he took up his post,[2] he reported that the Kandyan court harboured no thought of hostilities, and he sent his assurances that only an attack on the coastal provinces would induce him to resort to arms; in the same despatch, however, he mentions that 'the present would be the appropriate time to emancipate the interior of Ceylon from the oppressive rule of the Kandyan King', a superfluous rider, to say the least of it. A year later he was emphasizing the military weakness of Kandy.[3] In 1814 he again returned to this theme but, by now, he was unable to restrain himself from laying bare his hopes: he first confessed that 'important as the entire Sovereignty of this Island would prove to the British Crown and naturally ambitious as

I am that such an Event might take place during the period of my being entrusted with the direction of the Government. . . .' However, he followed this admission with an assurance that it was his unceasing object to avoid giving any cause for alarm, and he asked only for instructions as to the action he should take if the headmen were to rebel against the King.[4]

In fairness to Brownrigg, the temptation to interfere in Kandy was very strong. The death of Pilima Talauva, which happened soon after the new Governor arrived, had further aggravated the country's instability. The rift between Sri Wikrama and the Kandyan aristocracy had continued to widen, all the goodwill he had gained from his victories against the British a decade earlier having, by now, been dissipated. His action in executing a natural son of the popular King Kirti Sri on a charge of treason had done him much harm, and the measures he took after Pilima Talauva's death to sever communications between the rebellious outer provinces and the more loyal central mountain core of the kingdom had increased his unpopularity:[5] bhikkhus and Moormen were expelled from the intransigent areas; women not born where they were domiciled were compelled to return to their native districts; and all court officials, whose homes were in the suspect provinces were appointed to posts in distant areas of the country. These punitive measures against Sabaragamuva and the Three, Four and Seven Korales were enforced with severity, and they reacted on the peasantry as well as the headmen and chiefs, thus nullifying much of the credit which the King had gained from certain administrative reforms he had recently introduced, such as the price-control of food and cloth, a measure to control inflation and consequent profiteering. Sri Wikrama's unwise and unconstitutional extension of *rajakariya* in order to obtain the labour to beautify his capital created further resentment among both the villagers who had to toil on the public works and their betters who had to enforce the unpopular enactments.

But resentment and disloyalty are far from synonymous, and as yet the latter seems to have been confined to the outlying provinces where the influence of the families of Ehelepola and his executed uncle, Pilima Talauva, was the strongest. Ehelepola, who had inherited not only the ambitions but much of the guile of his relation, still occupied the post of First or *mahadigar*, despite the well-merited suspicion in which he was held by the King. For a long time Sri Wikrama restrained himself from provoking too open a breach with his minister, but he chose the occasion of his marriage in February, 1813, to two fresh wives (he was childless by his previous ones) to accuse Ehelepola of extortion, misappropriation, and producing mean and unworthy gifts at his wedding.[6]

After this treatment the disgraced Ehelepola returned to his home province of Sabaragamuva in a rather disenchanted mood. In the past his correspondence with D'Oyly had been, on the whole harmless, but a change now became apparent in the tenor of his letters. The first of the series, written in August, 1813, did no more than suggest, in the most cautious manner possible, that he should send one of his officials to talk to D'Oyly, but it included a slightly odd request for the gift of a good quality shot-gun. D'Oyly's reply contained a request for news of Major Davie, a promise to make inquiries about the gun, and a suggestion that it would be better to communicate by letter rather than through an intermediary. On 3 September, D'Oyly received the answer to this letter. So cautiously was it phrased that even D'Oyly failed to produce an adequate translation of its tortuous wording. One thing, however, was clear in addition to the confirmation that Major Davie was dead: the Adigar had reason to complain about the harm that had befallen both his country and his religion. This was the signal that D'Oyly needed to tempt Ehelepola to commit himself fully. On 6 September, he wrote again in the following terms:

'Ourselves also being anxious to promote in the happy island of Lanka the Prosperity of the World and Religion, I shall rejoice to receive from you an explicit communication by what Means you propose to accomplish that beneficial Object.'[7]

It appears from the papers in the Public Record Office that D'Oyly had to wait for some months for an answer, but a letter written by Ehelepola in the February of the following year committed the Adigar unequivocally:

'Now women, Men and all other Persons residing on this side of the Limits are disaffected to the Great Gate who governs our Country. If it be said for what Cause? The Wrongs and Injustices which at this time have befallen the World are not Things which it is possible to finish relating. . . . If you have a desire for our Country, it is good that any Thing which is done be done without Delaying.'[8]

Following this letter, in March Ehelepola sent Eknelligoda, one of his principal followers, to see D'Oyly in Colombo. His instructions were to make a direct request to the British to intervene militarily to help the dissidents to seize the capital. If this help were not forthcoming, Eknelligoda was to suggest that the British might occupy Sabaragamuva, a province that readily lent itself to such an adventure, cut off as it was from the rest of Kandy by the highest range of mountains in Ceylon. With Brownrigg absent at the Pearl Fisheries, D'Oyly conducted these negotiations on his own; and, while he avoided any pledge of direct assistance, he hinted that help might be forthcoming if there was 'distinct and unequivocal proof of the general wishes of the Kandyan people': in other words, if a full-scale rebellion were to break out against the King.[9]

Ehelepola must have known that there was little hope of the King remaining ignorant of these seditious activities. When, therefore, he was summoned shortly afterwards to Kandy to answer charges that he had deprived a Malabar merchant of a large sum of money, he avoided complying with the unwelcome invitation. Instead, realizing his danger and encouraged by D'Oyly's tacit support, he started to plot with his fellow *dissawas* for a simultaneous rising of the border provinces. The news that the King was about to deprive him of his offices and supplant him by Molligoda was the signal for the plans to be put into effect, and on 1 May, 1814, he raised the banner of insurrection, at the same time sending an appeal to D'Oyly for help in the shape of men and munitions.

The rebellion was both ineffective and short-lived. Even in Sabaragamuva, his own province, Ehelepola managed to raise only some 1,000 men, ill-armed and ill-equipped. From his fellow conspirators and from the British, no help at all was forthcoming. Brownrigg was doubtful whether he possessed enough troops successfully to interfere and his misgivings about the likelihood of the rebellion gathering strength were shown to be correct.[10] Anxious though he was to see Ehelepola's revolt succeed, he was wary of being discovered to be fomenting it. The result was, as he put it himself, that he 'deemed it best to hold to a middle course of Policy, so calculated as neither on the one hand to give to the King any ground for alleging that this Government had committed any act of aggression or hostility, nor on the other so far to shut out the advance of the Adigar, as to reject those benefits to His Majesty's Colony which his undertakings promise to afford'.[11] This tightrope act had sad consequences for the people of Sabaragamuva. Molligoda, on behalf of the King, invaded the province with 1,000 men, many of whom were Tamils or Malays, and rapidly defeated Ehelepola's forces. On the night of 23 May, with some 200 men, the beaten leader fled for refuge into British territory, crossing the frontier at Sitawaka and leaving the rest of his followers to Sri Wikrama's vengeance.

This treachery by Ehelepola marked a turning point in Sri Wikrama's treatment of his subjects. Until then the King had rarely been guilty of deliberate cruelty; although Dolapilla's traditional stories suggest that a vicious strain in his character became apparent quite early in his reign, there is little or no corroborative evidence for this. The reverse, in fact, seems to have been true. His treatment of those prisoners, both European and Asian, who survived the massacres in 1803 could well be described as generous, whatever his personal responsibility may have been for the actual massacres. Despite provocation, he was forbearing towards Pilima Talauva and merciful towards his son. To Muttusamy he granted an easy death although the man had every reason to anticipate a terrible end. It was only now, in fact, that the violent side of Sri Wikrama's nature, amounting at times to near-madness, gained the upper hand. That this happened is hardly surprising. Surrounded by hostile courtiers and alienated priests, he was now isolated on his throne, able to trust only a handful of his Malabar relations. So placed, the deliberate use of terror was one of the few weapons he had left with which to control his kingdom.

A wave of arrests had started as soon as the news of Ehelepola's rebellion reached Kandy. When the victorious Molligoda returned to the capital, bringing with him a horde of prisoners, the King sentenced forty-seven of them to be impaled. So began a spate of retributive terror. Seventy important headmen, who had been involved in the previous rising in the Seven Korales, were summoned to Kandy, tried by a commission of three, one of whom was Molligoda, the man whose authority they had opposed, and flogged before being killed. The *dissawa* of Matale, found in treasonable correspondence with Ehelepola, was tortured to death, and the same fate befell Ehelepola's brother-in-law, the son of the *dissawa* of Uva. Even a priest was executed, an action nearly without precedent and one that provoked a surge of disgust among every class of Kandyan. It was, however, in his treatment of Ehelepola's family that Sri Wikrama overreached himself.[12]

Although Kandyan law stipulated that the wife and children of a traitor should be executed with him, the penalty had rarely been enforced by the Malabar kings. Many of the rebellious chiefs had taken the precaution of sending their families into British territory for safety, but Ehelepola, whose wife and children were held hostage in Kandy, made the mistake of ignoring their peril, depending for their safety on the Sinhalese aversion to maltreating women. For this error he paid horribly.

Two weeks after Ehelepola rebelled, his wife, carrying her baby and accompanied by her three young children, was led out on to the Deva Sanghinda, the square just outside the Palace, to a spot midway between the Natha and Vishnu *devalas*. There, on this sacred ground, watched it is said by the King himself from the Pattiripuwa—the octangular tower of the Palace—the mother and her children were handed over to the executioners. The various accounts of their deaths differ in detail, but it seems that the first member of the family to be ordered forward was the eldest son, a boy of eleven. Terrified he clung to his mother until the second boy, two years the younger and named Madduma Bandara, stepped out, cautioning his brother to quiet his fears. Without delay the executioners struck off the boy's head and then killed the other three children, one of whom was a girl. Last to die was the baby, from whose lips, tradition has it, milk trickled as its head was severed. Either one or all of the children's heads were then placed in a large rice mortar, and the distraught mother was ordered to pound them. Otherwise she would be violated by members of the outcast *Rodiya* sect. To avoid this unspeakable disgrace, the wretched woman is said to have lifted the pestle and let it fall on the ghastly contents of the mortar. Then with other women of her husband's family (some say it was two, some three), the executioners led her to the Bogambara Lake, where they tied stones about the women's necks and pushed them beneath the water, the traditional method by which the Kandyans executed their women on the rare occasions when they did so.[13]

The veracity of the foul business with the mortar has been challenged by P. E. Pieris, who queries the slimness of the evidence, and suggests that the story was fabricated by Brownrigg as political propaganda designed further to discredit Sri Wikrama in the eyes of his subjects.[14] This is difficult to accept. The executions were fresh in Kandyan minds, had been observed by a multitude of eyewitnesses, and were an unique occurrence in living memory. An elaboration so flagrant would have been obvious to all. The story of Madduma Bandara, now a folk-hero with his death-place marked by a rudimentary memorial, has only recently been re-told in popular form, and the mortar-incident has not been excluded from the tale.[15] Dolapihilla mentions the details more than once, and he relates that the facts came to him from his father, who in his turn had them from an eyewitness of the events, one of Sri Wikrama's page-boys, who died in 1906 at the advanced age of 106 years.[16] As confirmation of Dr Davy's and Sergeant Theon's account,[17] Dolapihilla's contribution cannot be ignored. Unpopular a figure though Brownrigg may be in Sinhalese eyes, only Pieris has gone so far as to accuse him of the deliberate invention of this story.

The death of Ehelepola's family aroused revulsion everywhere in Ceylon. In Kandy itself, the crowd which gathered to see the executions sobbed aloud as they took place and afterwards the grief in the capital was so intense that for two days no fire was kindled and no food was dressed. Except for the inhabitants of the Palace, Kandy fasted in sorrow.[18]

By now the King had alienated not only the aristocracy and the *sangha*, many of whose leaders were themselves members of the prominent families, but the peasantry as well, upon whose support he had in the past so depended. Terrified for their lives, a stream of refugees, drawn from all classes of society, was seeking refuge in British territory; at the same time, many leading members of the ruling class who had not fled, including Molligoda himself, continued to correspond with D'Oyly. Meanwhile his predecessor as *mahadigar* was supplying his hosts in Colombo with the military, economic and topographical information they needed, and was advising them on the invasion plans they were now preparing. Ehelepola's spirit at the time seems to have been all but broken by the disasters that had beset him. In an emotional scene at Brownrigg's country house, built on its rock overlooking the sea at Mount Lavinia, he burst into tears of gratitude for the kindness of his reception, asking that he might be allowed to call the Governor and Mrs Brownrigg his parents. It was an attitude which found some approval among the British officials present.[19]

Although Sri Wikrama had all but forfeited what was left to him of his people's loyalty, Brownrigg still postponed taking action. The news of Napoleon's abdication had yet to reach Ceylon and, so far as the Governor knew, the war in Europe was still in progress. The consequences to him of disregarding his instructions at such a time were likely to be serious, unless, of course, a valid excuse could be found and the subsequent success were cheap enough to justify the disobedience. The requisite pretext was not long in presenting itself. Ten Sinhalese traders, natives of Colombo, were robbed of their goods in the Three Korales and were then denounced by the robbers as being spies. Possibly the men were Ehelepola's agents, or even D'Oyly's, but there is no evidence that this was the case.[20] The King, however, believed the accusation and exacted an ugly penalty. The men were brought in October to the place of execution at Kandy. Each in turn was flung to the ground, his joints trampled upon and one arm amputated by a blow from an adze; his nose and one ear were then removed with a knife and the amputated joint cauterized. Seven men died from the torture. The survivors were despatched back to Colombo by separate routes with their severed limbs hanging around their necks.[21]

Although mutilation was a legal punishment in Kandy, it was rarely prescribed, the sole recorded instance of its use during the previous forty years having been the treatment of Muttusamy's servants. Among the Kandyans the fate of the traders aroused only sympathy. For Brownrigg it was the opportunity for which he had been waiting. Protesting to the Secretary of State that the King's action had been designed as a deliberate insult to the British Government, he declared that it was impossible to establish a proper relationship with such a government, and he advised (with some justification) that the Kandyans themselves were now looking to the British to intervene; as he saw it, there was no longer any moral objection to invading their country.[22] Nevertheless Brownrigg still moved with caution. For the time being he did no more than send Major Hook with a force of 300 men to move forward to Hanwella, while he made a start in regrouping his other troops in preparation for the invasion, the plans for which were now complete. Alarmed by these obvious threats, Sri Wikrama was also getting ready for a conflict, which seemed to be inevitable. He mobilized his irregular levies from the villages, and also managed to enlist some 700 Tamils, whom he arranged to be smuggled by devious routes from the coast into the interior.

Another revolt, led by Molligoda's brother, now erupted in the Three Korales, but this was quickly crushed by the King after the rebels had made a further fruitless appeal to the British for help. For the time being Brownrigg did no more than move Hook's force further up-country to Sitawaka, opposite Avissawella. Ehelepola now took the field with this column. One can only speculate upon the state of mind of the ex-Minister at this juncture, but he must have surely despaired that the jealousies existing between himself and his fellow chiefs, particularly Molligoda, should have resulted in such a lack of co-operation in the timings of the risings. Then, on 9 January, 1815, a handful of Kandyans, chasing a party of fleeing rebels, crossed the river into British territory. A hut was fired, possibly accidentally,[23] just the provocation for which Brownrigg had been waiting. Two days later Hook was ordered forward into Kandy.

II

Brownrigg had six infantry battalions to hold the coast and invade Kandy.[24] Four units were at their full establishment of 1,000 men. It was much the same strength that North had been able to deploy in 1803. Two of these battalions were British, one of which was the 19th Foot, now in its nineteenth year in Ceylon and once again serving on the east coast at Trincomalee and Batticaloa. The second British unit was the 1st Battalion of the 73rd Highlanders (now the Black Watch), which had arrived from New South Wales to relieve the 66th Foot in the middle of the previous year. This was the 73rd's second tour in Ceylon: in 1796, they had formed part of Stuart's original invasion force. The rest of the infantry were the four battalions of the Ceylon Regiment. The 1st Battalion, still all Malay, had been reorganized as a light infantry unit the previous July, while the 2nd Battalion was manned by Sepoys. The 3rd and 4th were both African, the last-named raised in 1811. Because slaves were in short supply and the original foundation stock unprolific, recruits for these two units were few, and both were at little more than half their strength. Four hundred Javanese recruits, collected by Captain de Bussche, had brought the 1st Battalion to its full establishment only a few months before.

In addition to this force, Brownrigg had asked for the loan of a further 2,200 fighting troops and 500 pioneers from India and his original invasion plans which, by and large, were based upon Ehelepola's advice, had taken into account these, relatively speaking, massive reinforcements. In essence, Brownrigg's design was not dissimilar to Wemyss's abortive plan of 1805. In a carefully co-ordinated movement, a series of small columns was to draw a noose around the inner Kandyan mountain stronghold, seizing all the main passes in order to thwart any attempt by the King's forces to take refuge from their attackers in an outlying area of the kingdom. The original plan was based upon nine of these columns advancing by as many routes, but this was found

o

to be impracticable. Not only did the inevitable shortage of coolies and pack-bullocks demand that the best use should be made of the navigable waterways, but the use of so many routes was in itself extravagant. Each needed supply depots and separate convoys, the guarding of which was expensive in combatant troops. As a result the number of routes to be used had to be reduced; further cuts became necessary when, at the last minute, word came from India that the departure of the Sepoy reinforcements had been cancelled because of the imminent start of operations against Scindia, the great Mahratta chieftain.

In the end Brownrigg's invasion force was organized into eight divisions marching on five principal routes. The strength of each division varied between 230 and 700 men, and all but one included a mixture of European and Asian troops. Each had its own small artillery train of two or three pieces, nothing larger being taken than a light 3-pounder. The 1st Division was Hook's, found from the Colombo garrison and directed from Avissawella upon the Balane Pass; behind him and moving on the same route came the 2nd Division, also from Colombo. The 3rd and 4th starting from Galle and Hambantota had as their objectives the Idalgashinna Pass, piercing the south-eastern corner of the massif and leading into the rugged Uva mountains, where the escarpment plunges for a sheer 4,000 feet to the hot plains below. Starting from Trincomalee, Major-General Jackson, the local commander, was ordered to prepare the 5th and 6th Divisions to march in succession through Nalanda, the way Barbut had approached and Johnston had returned from Kandy in 1803 and 1805. The smallest Division of all, the 7th, commanded by Ajax Anderson, the poet, and one of the few British survivors of the 1803 campaign, was to start from Batticaloa and follow Johnston's route up to Kandy, moving through Bintenne in the north-east corner of the mountain core of the kingdom. Lastly, the 8th Division with Captain de Bussche, Brownrigg's Swiss A.D.C., in charge, had been hastily organized at Negombo to replace the missing John Company troops, and was to follow the route Macdowall had taken in 1803. In all 2762 troops were engaged, of whom rather more than one third were European.

Brownrigg, capable and experienced soldier as he was, had ensured that the preparations for the invasion were soundly conceived. His commissariat had been well organized, the west-coast troops had been hardened by arduous route marches, the details of the transport and camp equipment thought out in meticulous detail, and all concerned possessed the self-confidence induced by the knowledge that the plans had been prepared with precision. In everything the General had been supported by his senior staff officer, Major Willerman, the Deputy-Quartermaster-General and also a Swiss. Among his other duties Willerman had supplied the Divisions with detailed topographical information about the interior, including the difficult passes which many viewed with some trepidation. The consequences of the previous war had been so disastrous that even de Bussche, whose book is a somewhat abject essay in sycophancy, was prepared to admit that some officers and officials had misgivings about the outcome of the campaign. Nevertheless, although high casualties were again expected, morale was high among both officers and men, few of whom had seen any fighting. Undoubtedly Brownrigg did a lot to sustain this. Although the old man was suffering from gout (that very painful disease) he did not spare himself in the preparatory work. Later, and despite his crippled state, he took the field with the 2nd Division, at the same time dispensing with the unwieldy luxuries common to the camps of senior officers campaigning in Asia. It is interesting that Brownrigg had read Johnston's account of his expedition to Kandy; the General can hardly have failed to benefit from the author's apt comments on the problems of fighting this type of war.[25]

III

Brownrigg wasted no time in reacting to the Kandyan foray at Sitawaka. He moved, in fact, with remarkable speed. Although the clash occurred thirty-six miles away from Colombo, the news travelled so fast and Brownrigg acted so quickly that on the very next day his Council had been persuaded to agree to war being declared, and the necessary proclamation had been put together.[26] Dr Henry Marshall's comments on this rather cynical document, typical of its genre, are worth quoting:

'This proclamation, which was translated into the Singalese language for the purpose of being circulated in the Kandyan country, or, as may be said, among our unoffending neighbours, was also intended to inform the world in general, and the countries of the East in particular, for what reasons the local government had assumed a hostile attitude towards the Kandyan government. The principal reasons assigned for invading the country were the alleged tyranny and oppression of the Kandyan monarch, his unwillingness to enter into any terms with the representatives of the British government, the mutilation of the ten cloth merchants already mentioned, and the irruption across the boundary river at Sitawaka, in pursuit of Eheylapola's fugitive adherents. The irruption of the Kandyan people into our territory had, it may be presumed, very little influence in occasioning the war—all the requisite preparations having been made long before it took place. Besides the irruption in question was obviously so unpremeditated and accidental, and really of so contemptible a character, that it deserved no consideration.'[27]

As the surgeon of Hook's 1st Division, no one was better placed to comment on the progress of events than Marshall. If one disregards a certain bias towards his English neighbours, this Scot was a man of incorruptible intellectual honesty. Not prepared to mince his words, it is understandable that he had to wait until he had long retired from the Service with the rank of Deputy-Inspector-General of Hospitals before he was able to express opinions so unpalatable from a serving officer. Others were not so slow to say what they thought. *Hermes*, writing the following year in the *Asiatic Journal*, deprecated the 'hostilities and bickering with Nipal, Candy, China, and . . . the Mahratta states'. 'The war in Ceylon,' he continued, 'has a character of its own. It is not the Company's war, and it may lead to no evil consequences. Still the principal is to be examined. We have heard a great deal of the barbarous character of the King, and all this is truly lamentable; but we are not to constitute ourselves avengers or guardians of the globe, and make the existence of wrong a universal pretext for war.'[28] Another correspondent, in replying to Hermes' protest, while not altogether disagreeing with Brownrigg's actions, expostulated against the hypocrisy with which he accused the General of clothing them. In particular, he objected to the jargon used by the Government of Ceylon in their proclamations and pronouncements. He disliked:

'. . . a certain flaunting and exuberant verbiage, a shallow sentimentality, a pert and affected style of speech; much ignorance of the forms of office, much unsoundness of political principle, and, in truth, no small portion of jacobinical thinking and acting; which are manifested in the long and endless effusions, official and literary, that have appeared in the Columbo newspaper in their regard: . . . and I do but now write, what every successive recurrance to the subject has forced upon my mind—that the whole is *Yankee*! . . .[29]

What is more, he went on to suggest, the wording of Brownrigg's proclamation was far too close to that chosen by Napoleon when announcing his intention to invade a neighbour country.

When, on 11 January, Hook's column, now strengthened to 430 men, crossed the river into Kandy and started to advance towards Ruwanwella, eight miles to the north, a number of the inhabitants of the Three Korales joined him. These men, white bands tied around their foreheads as distinguishing marks, placed themselves under the leadership of the ubiquitous Mr D'Oyly and gave a good account of themselves. Half a dozen rounds from a light field piece proved enough to dispose of the Kandyan garrison at Ruwanwella and the next evening Brownrigg was able to dine with his officers in the captured village, before he returned to Colombo the following day.

Even though the troops had not yet reached the hills, the going had proved to be abominable. The carriages of the mortars had broken, and the 1-pounder guns had to be dismantled and man-handled. Even the ammunition reserves were reduced to save transport, but the tents were retained to avoid the risk to health encountered by men sleeping in the open. The tracks were, in fact, no better than they were in 1800. Once again Ruwanwella, in those days at the navigable limits of the Kelani Ganga, forty miles upstream from Colombo, was the clear choice for a supply base. From the village the turbulent torrent could speed sick men down to the coast in only eight hours, a journey that cost three days of toil to complete in the reverse direction with supplies. Here then the 1st Division halted, building an earth-walled fort to protect the base as they waited for the other Divisions to move from their coastal stations into the interior.

The British entry into the Kandyan provinces provided the disgruntled chiefs and headmen with the impetus they needed for full-blooded rebellion. But for some, caution was still essential. Molligoda, who was commanding the royal troops in the Ruwanwella area, maintained continual touch with D'Oyly, but his family was living in the capital under the King's control and he dare not make any move. Anxious though he was to desert, he had to provide every appearance of resisting the British advance. A slight wound he had suffered during a skirmish helped him in this deception, and, a few days later, he arrived in Hook's camp, disguised unconvincingly as a messenger from himself. At this meeting he agreed to oppose the British advance to the least possible extent consistent with maintaining an appearance of loyalty to his sovereign. It was arranged that his men would discontinue loading their firelocks with ball ammunition, a compact that was to prove all but fatal to both Hook and Marshall. These two officers were leading their column through a patch of jungle when two Kandyans fired at them from a range of thirty yards. To Hook's vexation, a ball struck the ground at his feet. Later, however, it transpired that Molligoda had not been at fault; the two men belonged to someone else's command.[30]

By the end of January British columns were closing in on all the passes that led into the central core of the mountain kingdom. In the north-west de Bussche's small 8th Division was advancing through the Seven Korales and had fought only one insignificant action. This was on 29 January, the day Hook crossed the upper reaches of the Maha Oya against the feigned opposition of Molligoda's men who had been hovering noisily in front of him throughout his march. Two days later a party of his Sepoys and Malays, acting on information provided by a deserting Kandyan chief, surprised a post manned by his compatriots in the middle of the night. Some thirty Kandyans were killed and twenty weapons which had belonged to Davie's ill-fated troops were captured, a not altogether necessary slaughter that aroused their commander's disapproval and Marshall's resigned condemnation.[31] Hook was now directed northwards along the western face of the Balane mountains where a large force of the King's men was reported to be concentrating. De Bussche was threatening these Kandyans from the front, and Hook's orders were to capture the passes behind them, thus cutting off their escape route. On 3 February he did so, occupying once again the twin forts at Galagedara and Girihagama. The day before the 2nd Division had taken the famous heights of Balane without loss; Willerman, who arrived at the summit on the following afternoon could not conceive why the Kandyans had allowed them to seize so effortlessly a pass which a handful of men could have held with ease.[32] Just behind the 2nd Division was the crippled but indomitable Brownrigg, who now halted the columns on this front in order to allow the troops from Trincomalee, Batticaloa and Galle to complete the net and so prevent the King escaping.

On 8 February Molligoda entered the British camp in formal procession, bringing with him the sun banner of the Four Korales of which he was *dissawa*, the records of that province and his elephants. The *mahadigar*'s surrender had been made possible because his family had succeeded in escaping from Kandy. This was the end of the Kandyan resistance. Three days later the Three and the Four Korales, together with Sabaragamuva, were annexed to the British Crown so as to reassure the inhabitants that the British would not abandon them. According to Molligoda, the King now had with him only 200 Malabars, the same number of Kandyan militia and a few Moormen, Kaffirs and Malays.

Major Kelly's 3rd Division had by now surmounted the sheer cliffs of the Idalgashinna Pass and was moving through the mountains of Uva towards Hanguranketa. Behind Kelly, the 4th Division was marching towards Badulla but nothing had been heard about the progress of the columns from the east coast save for a single message from General Jackson to say that the difficulties of procuring the required transport were proving to be insurmountable and that no advance could be expected before the end of January. In fact Major Mackay's 5th Division managed to leave the coast only on 1 February, and it had taken the troops two weeks to reach Nalanda. The monsoon was now flooding this side of the watershed, and the soaked men often had to cut a track through the thick, low-lying jungle, wading knee-deep in viscous mud. To make matters worse, the pack-bullocks were untrained and the men unfit;[33] Brownrigg's rigorous training ideas had failed to penetrate to this side of the island. Often it was mid-day before the sodden tents were dry enough to load on to the pack-animals and the march started. It was a miserable journey, made even more so for Private John Kirner of the 19th Foot who had to endure all this with a flayed back; on the second day of the march he received six dozen lashes for drunkenness.

On 9 February, two days after Molligoda had surrendered, Brownrigg decided to set his columns in motion once again. Events now moved quickly. The next evening news came from Hook that he had reached the Mahaveli Ganga at Katugastota without encountering any opposition and that the King had fled his capital. Straight away the Governor ordered a patrol under his son, Major Brownrigg, to push forward to Kandy along the Kadugannawa route. At first light the following morning this small force crossed the river at Gannoruwa, the staging post for embassies to the capital. Extensive deserted batteries covered the ford but there was no sign of any living thing. The sole guardians of the crossing were nineteen impaled bodies, fifteen of them headmen of the Seven Korales, the agonies of their ghastly death imprinted on their contorted features.

Later that day the 2nd Division marched from Gannoruwa along a broad road, lined all the way with houses on either side, up to the gates of the deserted Palace, described by Willerman as a 'stupendous pile of buildings'.[34] As always the city was devoid of both people and valuables, occupied only by packs of half-starved dogs.

As the troops settled down to recuperate in the captured town, good news started to pour in. Brownrigg with his suite rode in on 14 February, the day that Kelly was heard to have taken Hanguranketa, together with some treasure in coin and silver ornaments and a number of women who were at first mistaken for the King's family. Flocks of Kandyans returned to the city to swear allegiance to Ehelepola and news was received that

Mackay was at Nalanda, the 4th Division in Badulla, and Ajax Anderson short of Bintenne.

Brownrigg had sound cause to congratulate himself. Derisory though the opposition had turned out to be, few campaigns had been conducted with a greater degree of economy. Not a single British soldier had been killed; the leeches had shed far more blood than the Kandyans. Deaths from sickness had been strangely few and hardly a man was in hospital. The dreaded jungle fever had failed to appear, and sore legs and rheumatism were the prevalent complaints.

A single shade of the past still haunted Kandy. Just after the 1st Division had pitched their tents outside the city, Marshall was approached by a brown-coloured man with a matted beard, dressed in Kandyan costume. It was Sergeant Theon, the German survivor of the massacre in the hospital. Treated like Major Davie, whom he had never met throughout his captivity, with kindness alternating with neglect, Theon probably managed to survive his twelve years' durance because he had a Moorish girl to care for him, whom he married and by whom he had a son.

CHAPTER 12

The Second War:
The End of an Ancient Kingdom

I

ALTHOUGH the campaign had gone so well, there had been little premature rejoicing among the British. Kandy had been invaded and captured before, and always the consequences to the intruders had been disastrous; so long as Sri Wikrama was free, it was sanguine to expect an early end to the war. Nevertheless the outlook was not too unfavourable. It was rumoured that the fugitive King had with him only a small party of Malabar troops and some relations, together with some *appuhami* guards, in all no more than 200 men. D'Oyly's spies had reported that they were somewhere in the sparsely populated eastern Dumbara, a locality which was, in itself, something of a trap. In the wild and empty country which lay to the north of it, the King would be hard put to find succour: to the west lay the Seven Korales, the province where he was the most hated. He had two choices open to him. Either he could plunge further eastwards in the direction of Bintenna, or else he could cross the Mahaveli Ganga and seek refuge among the hills of Uva, a province in which he might still find a few faithful followers ready to risk their lives for him.

From the start of the campaign Ehelepola had moved well forward with the advancing troops, leading a party of his own people and lending encouragement to the border provinces to revolt. Now Brownrigg had further use for him. On 15 February small parties of both Kandyans and troops set out in the direction which the King was said to have taken; and, among them, travelled D'Oyly and Ehelepola, the latter charged by Brownrigg with the task of urging the people of Dumbara to help in the capture of the King. Just ahead of Ehelepola a company of Malays under Lieutenant Mylius was moving parallel with the river towards the village of Teldeniya, and a further company was marching towards the Kimbutantota ferry, a key point on the main route that joined eastern Dumbara to the province of Uva. To complete the net, one of D'Oyly's ubiquitous messengers was soon to start through the wilderness towards Bintenne with a warning to Ajax Anderson to be ready to intercept the King if he moved in that direction. The scope of D'Oyly's duties during the course of the campaign had been peculiarly wide. This unusual Englishman's diary reveals that he did far more than control his network of spies and messengers and negotiate with the Kandyan leaders, as might have been expected of a civil servant in such circumstances. Much of the military planning was done by him, and he directed many of the movements of the forward columns, seemingly on his own initiative, issuing instructions not only to the various column commanders but also to Major Willerman, the senior military staff officer in the field. Anomalous though his position may have been, none of the participants seem to have criticized either the propriety or the effectiveness of D'Oyly's role, unconventional though it was. Probably this was because the arrangements worked; their failure would have produced complaints enough.

The day after Mylius's party left Kandy, it overtook fifty Malabars, led by a cousin of the King, another Muttusamy. Muttusamy had been one of the King's closest confidants but had recently felt his cousin's displeasure and had, as a result, suffered imprisonment. Despite this he turned to fight, but although the Malabars were strongly placed, their front protected by a steep rock, the Malays routed them with their bayonets, killing and wounding several and taking seventeen prisoners. Muttusamy, slightly wounded in five places, was among the captured, and although he and his men had put up a better show of resistance than most, he was ready to tell his captors as much as he knew about the whereabouts of his royal kinsman. According to Private Calladine of the 19th Foot, who had landed in Colombo with a draft just too late to take part in the campaign, but who saw Muttusamy at the coast, the latter was 'a very stout and fierce-looking man with a terrible pair of whiskers and beard. . . .'[1] The King's cousin cuts an interesting figure; one would have liked to have known more about him.

Later that day, D'Oyly and Ehelepola overtook Mylius's company, and the enlarged party pressed on into Dumbara with little confidence that the King would be overtaken before he found refuge in the mountains. Even though the men of Dumbara, at Ehelepola's instigation, were helping in the search, the troops were faced with the prospect of weeks, if not months, of exhausting toil. Already, as Willerman admitted, everyone was both mentally and physically tired.[2]

Further troops under Major Hook now arrived on the scene and, on 18 February, a variegated assembly of Kandyans and soldiers—Malay, African, British and Indian—was encamped at Teldeniya. The subsequent narrative is taken largely from the story of Don William Dias, a Sinhalese who was with the expedition as an interpreter.[3] During the afternoon, Eknelligoda, who had accompanied Ehelepola from Colombo, together with Dias and some 500 Sabaragamuva men, had wandered off in a somewhat desultory fashion in the direction of the rocky-topped mountain known as Medamahanuwara. About a mile and a half short of it a young lad was seen running away across the hills. The terrified boy was caught and immediately volunteered the startling news that the King was nearby. As he led the men to the square straw-thatched house belonging to the headman, the sight of two of the King's women confirmed the lad's truthfulness. An *appuhami* was then seen, lance in hand, pacing up and down the courtyard of the house. As the Sabaragamuva men burst in, the *appuhami*, with desperate gallantry, hurled his weapon ineffectively at Eknelligoda before he was hustled away to an unrecorded fate. One or two other of the King's men resisted, badly wounding two of the attackers, before Eknelligoda was able to hammer on the house-door and demand that the King should open it. Someone threw three silver-mounted rifles and two krises from an aperture, apparently as an act of surrender, but, as the door stayed closed, the attackers burst it open. In rushed the exultant men and bound the King like a pig with wild creepers, after stripping both him and his two wives of their clothes and golden ornaments, tearing the earlobes of the women as they ripped their rings away.[4] The two wretched women staggered outside, where Dias took charge of them and administered first-aid to their bleeding ears. Dias, according to himself, made a brave but futile protest that Sri Wikrama should be so treated by men who had but recently revered him as their king and god, but all he got for his pains was to be told by Eknelligoda that no one was asking him for his advice. Sri Wikrama, unable to walk, was then dragged along the ground into a nearby field.

Hurriedly Dias scribbled the following note to D'Oyly, hampered as he was by the two wretched women clinging closely to him for protection:

'To General D'Oyley.—The Sinhalese King has fallen into our hands, and Ekneligoda Mohottala is fetching him on and has bound him and is subjecting him to much ill-treatment and ignominy. Therefore it is of paramount importance that you should come to meet us with three palanquins. Some wearing apparel is also necessary, as the queens are almost naked.'[5]

In scarcely half an hour, Hook with a number of other officers and a body of 150 soldiers arrived on the scene. No further harm had befallen the King and the officers knelt to cut him free from his taut bonds, producing a pint of Madeira and water to revive him. Claret was provided for his women and, after some clothes had been found for them, they were lifted into palanquins and escorted with ceremony back to Teldeniya, the two senior officers riding on either side of the cortège with drawn swords. When Sri Wikrama arrived there, he found awaiting him his two other wives and his mother who had been captured previously. The next morning D'Oyly called upon him and assured him that his life was safe and that he would be treated with every degree of respect and attention.

II

Brownrigg received the news of Sri Wikrama's capture at Kandy the next day, and decided to get the King away from his erstwhile kingdom with the least possible delay. Hook was given the task of escorting him to Colombo and he took the precaution of by-passing the capital in so doing. The coast was reached on 6 March, and the King lodged in a spacious house that had been specially fitted out to accommodate him. Sri Wikrama gave the impression of being both pleased and surprised by his treatment,[6] and he soon established a reputation for both fortitude and resignation, as well as a nice sense of humour, a quality that appealed even more to his English captors. He could, however, stand on his dignity when he so wished—on entering Colombo, he insisted that the rampart should be cleared of people as it was unseemly that lesser mortals' feet should be higher than his head.[7] To the annoyance of the authorities, he did not lack sympathizers among the European community and there was some relief when, escorted by a Royal Marine guard and travelling in Brownrigg's own coach, he was driven down to Colombo harbour on 24 January, 1816, to embark with his wives, relations and dependents in the 74-gun *Cornwallis* for Madras.

Mr William Granville, one of North's original batch of civil servants, acted as escort to Sri Wikrama during the protracted four week voyage to Madras and got to know him better than any other European.[8] His account of the King's physical appearance is utterly at variance with Major Macpherson's portrayal of the vacant-looking young man he had observed in the audience chamber of the Palace sixteen years before:

'His person and manners possessed something peculiarly striking and distinguished; and no one could be five minutes in his presence without discovering a grandeur and superiority about him which it is almost impossible to define. He was about six feet in height; his limbs were of Herculean size, but beautifully formed; his head small; his features regular and handsome; his eyes large and intensely black and piercing; his hands and feet small but elegantly turned. He was unaccustomed to speak in a low tone of voice. His superiority in the presence of others was more or less manifested by the power and elevation of his voice. He thought none but the mean and humble whispered, and because he was the most despotic of kings, his voice ought therefore to be raised to the highest pitch in addressing his inferiors.'[9]

When Willerman met him he saw 'a handsome, lusty man, of a rather prepossessing aspect—not unlike Mr Fox'.[10] As has been mentioned before, he had also been likened to King Henry VIII.

At first sea-sickness tortured both Sri Wikrama and his wives, who had of necessity been hoisted on board the warship like bundles of old clothes, but the King soon found his feet and began to take a lively interest in the working of the ship. Granville who slowly gained his confidence, was impressed by the acuteness of his intellect and his sound judgement of character. Europeans who had come in contact with him at Colombo said the same thing. His violence and evil temper were apparent to all, but he had the happy knack of being able to view his defects dispassionately. 'The English Governors,' he observed to Major Hook, 'have one advantage over us kings of Kandy: they have counsellors about them, who never allow them to do anything in a passion, and that is the reason you have so few punishments, but unfortunately for us the offender is dead before our resentment has subsided.'[11] Disgusted though he was by the disloyalty of his subjects and offended by Brownrigg's refusal to meet him, his affability and sense of humour in adversity were striking.

This was the man who on his death was described by the leader writer in the *Ceylon Journal* as having 'no qualification for majesty except a portly figure' and 'scarcely a single virtue to palliate a thousand crimes'.[12] It is sad that Sri Wikrama's reputation has, in recent years, suffered further at the hands of anti-Tamil propagandists. Ruthless and cruel he could be; but, as Dr Marshall points out, he was far from being alone in this.[13] A man of culture and (when not pressed too hard) some humanity, his detractors were at pains to ensure that his crimes were not forgotten. In this Brownrigg set the lead, compelled as he was to find some justification for his disregard of his instructions in invading Kandy. The efforts Sri Wikrama made to improve the lot of his people may well have sprung from his need to win their support to counter his unpopularity with the chiefs and the priests; nevertheless he has received little credit for what he did accomplish.

III

When the news of the King's capture reached Brownrigg on 19 February, as he was dining with his officers, the old gentleman was so overcome that he burst into tears.[14] After a forty-day campaign, two thousand three hundred and fifty-seven years of Sinhalese independence was at an end. The invasion plans had worked faultlessly (so far as a military operation can), and everyone concerned had good cause to congratulate himself on the speedy and successful conclusion of the campaign. Mixed with self-satisfaction, however, was a generous measure of relief. Five days before the King had been taken, the monsoon had broken over the hills. Only a few troops were yet under shelter, and the rest, already tired, hungry and wet, were operating in the misery that would inevitably propagate disease. Rivers were in spate and the difficulties of dragging supplies from Ruwanwella up into the hills along forty-five miles of wretched tracks were becoming increasingly apparent. A long-drawn-out campaign might well have led to the disaster which some of the participants had anticipated from the beginning.

Despite the tracks and the customary shortage of coolies and pack animals, both food and the much-needed warm clothing now flowed steadily into Kandy. Brownrigg's logistic planning had been of a high order and the separate commissariat organization he now set up to supply the conquered provinces did much to ensure that there was no hold-up in supplies. Both during and after the campaign the troops stayed remarkably healthy. Only 1,600 men were retained up-country: half in the capital, 350 in Badulla and the rest scattered in small garrisons controlling the lines of communication with the coast and the main centres of population. The fact that they had enough to eat and lived in sound barracks, thrown up with remarkable speed, did much to stem disease, but the continued absence of fever, particularly

22. *Lieutenant-Colonel Lionel Hook,
19th Foot and Ceylon Regiment*

23. *Sir Thomas Maitland*

24. *Lieutenant-General David
Wemyss*

25. *Bombadier Alexander
Alexander*

26. *The Dutch Fort at Batticaloa*

27. *The late King of Kandy and his Court. A native drawing*

in Kandy itself, was conspicuous. De Bussche suggested,[15] probably correctly, that this was probably because Sri Wikrama had drained the swamp near the Palace, and replaced it by the two artificial lakes that had done so much to beautify his capital and destroy his popularity with his subjects. It is ironic that the King's aesthetic masterpiece contributed not only to the loss of his throne, but also to ensuring that the victors were, for the first time, able to occupy the capital without suffering dire consequences from so doing. In the eighteen months starting from 1 January, 1815, only ninety-four officers and soldiers died from disease in the newly conquered provinces. Although more than one-quarter of the garrison was stationed in the hills, these deaths amounted to one-sixth of the mortality in the island as a whole.[16] In July 1816, the hospital at Kandy housed only seventy-eight patients, a mere five per cent of the garrison: twenty-seven of these men were suffering from ulcers following upon leech bites, nineteen from rheumatism, three from beri-beri, seven from bowel complaints and only three from fever. A novel theory was gaining ground. The mountains were not basically unhealthy; they might even be more salubrious than the low-country. Service in the hills became popular, the wives of officers were starting to join their husbands, and the possibility of exploiting this rich and lovely country was arousing interest.[17] De Bussche, who, like his fellows, failed to understand the Sinhalese disdain for marketing their labour, was certain that the apparent indolence of the people could not be overcome, and suggested that Chinese labourers should be imported to help in the commercial development of the country; his recruiting visit to Java had put the idea into his head; there he had observed the seeming success of such a policy in a similarly fertile island.[18] Some years later, Major James Campbell had an even better idea: either British convicts or Africans could well be used to colonize the country.[19] Ceylon may have suffered much over the centuries. She was at least spared this.

On the whole the troops did not behave badly during the course of their occupation of the interior. In most of the districts through which they marched, they received a not unenthusiastic reception from the villagers, against whom they, in their turn, held no grudge, convinced as they were by the propaganda of their betters that they were delivering the land from the rule of an oppressive tyrant. Although the massacre of 1803 was still fresh in the memories of all, they were no longer looking for revenge, nor was there even a disposition to blame anyone other than the King for what had taken place. There was looting in some areas but it was certainly not widespread. D'Oyly received complaints that some African soldiers had attempted to plunder Gabadawidiya, and the 4th Division got out of hand in Uav, robbing houses and temples and commandeering elephants.[20] But, by prompt action, the elephants and much of the temple property were recovered, and a Malay captain was court-martialled for his part in the looting.[21] Other incidents must have gone unrecorded, but taking into account the standards of the time and the poor state of discipline of some of the troops, it is astonishing that there was not more trouble. Nowhere, for example, in either General Orders, diaries or memoirs, is there a mention of the 73rd Highlanders misbehaving, although this is the unit about which Brownrigg bitterly complained to the Secretary of State in the following terms:

'It is with the sincerest concern and the most mortified feelings that I am now obliged to state to your Lordship, that the conduct of this Detachment has been in the most culpable degree disorderly and mutinous and in some instances outrageous. Two privates have been convicted by General Courts Martial of assaulting their Officers and received Sentences of Death. To the first I was induced to grant a conditional Pardon from his youth and former good Character. . . . But the reoccurrence a short time afterwards of an Attack still more daring and marked with a defiance of all authority and discipline obliged me to carry the law into effect in the instance of John Stevenson, who suffered death by Military execution on the 13th of last month.'[22]

The 'conditional pardon' granted to the first condemned was, in fact, merely the commutation of the sentence to one of 1,000 lashes. In his letter, Brownrigg suggested that the trouble in this Regiment was due to the fact that during its time in New South Wales the officers had been seconded for civil duty, and so had not been able to devote enough time to looking after their men. The men besides had been allowed to work at various civilian occupations, with the result that they had been thrown into contact with convicts 'whose proliﬁgacy they cannot but be expected to imbibe'. In his last moments, the condemned Stevenson had imputed his trouble to this cause. Arrack had been a further cause of trouble among the soldiers and their criminal training had taught them how to obtain it by irregular means. In everything, they were assisted by their numerous women, who were quite as badly behaved as their husbands. After the execution the behaviour of the Regiment for a time improved, but it soon deteriorated once again and the pages of General Orders are chequered with accounts of the misdeeds of this unruly unit.

The Kandyans themselves possibly did as much damage to their compatriots as did the troops. The men of the Three Korales operating with Hook were not slow to work off old grudges against their neighbours in the Four Korales, burning and looting their villages as they progressed through their countryside.[23] Nor, when it came to taking Malabar prisoners, did they hesitate to strip them of their clothing and valuables.

Official looting was another matter. As soon as Ehelepola fled to Colombo, Sri Wikrama had foreseen the likelihood of an invasion and had started to disperse his personal and state treasures.[24] Into wooden boxes were packed his regalia, the royal jewels, his throne and footstool, the contents of the treasury in copper, gold and silver coin, state dresses of silver and gold, together with personal ornaments of every type, including such incongruities as a number of cocked hats and seventeenth-century full-bottomed periwigs. The boxes were wrapped in waxed cloths, the contents listed, and most of them were then consigned to trusted village headmen or court officials to be carried away by porter or pack-bullock for concealment in outlying villages. Some of this treasure the King retained with him on his flight, but this too he dispersed just before his pursuers overtook him, retaining only a sword of state and some boxes of gold coin and trinkets with which he could reward his helpers.

Some of this treasure was never recovered, but most of it found its way into the hands of the British authorities during the subsequent two years. After the King was captured, scarcely a day passed without news of the recovery of cash or jewels arriving in Kandy. Many of the boxes were handed over by headmen anxious to rid themselves of their responsibilities or to see the royal treasure safe from the threat of pillage. Some they handed directly to British officers but much they took to Ehelepola, who they believed was about to ascend their throne. Of the treasures he received, some, including a complete set of gold armour and a crown, Ehelepola handed over to D'Oyly in March, but many articles, including the principal crown and the sword of state, were not recovered from him until November of the following year, and then only after a protracted and rancorous argument. The King himself, in bitter disgust at the disloyalty of his subjects, played his part in helping the British to find the treasure, divulging certain hiding-places to his captors so as to frustrate Ehelepola and others from recovering it.

Sri Wikrama's ceremonial throne and footstool were discovered on the same day as he was captured. A superb piece of workmanship, the throne had been fashioned by the Dutch in 1692 as a present for the then King. Of basic European design, it was probably made either by Sinhalese or by southern Indian craftsmen.[25] Covered in gold sheeting and encrusted with jewels, its arms are a pair of lions of Sinhala, and a large sun, symbolizing the origin of the Kandyan monarchs, surmounts its back. Although it was the custom for eastern monarchs to rule from the cushioned *gaddi*, the Kandyans had used this Dutch-made throne ever since they had acquired it. Now, however, it was shipped to England, together with the lion-standard of the King, in the custody of Brownrigg's son who was charged to present it to the Prince Regent. An adornment for Windsor Castle, this throne was used throughout the nineteenth century for the ceremony of investing Knights of the Garter; but, together with the footstool, crown, the sword of state and the golden staff, commonly miscalled the sceptre, it was returned to Ceylon in 1934. These heirlooms, all that remains of the temporal glory of Lanka, are now displayed in the Colombo Museum.

The rest of the King's treasure was sold for the Prize Fund, some by auction in Colombo but the greater part at Mr Thomas King's auction rooms at King Street, Covent Garden, in a sale that realized £3,837.7.10. Included in the catalogue was a massive gold chain over 500 inches long, a cat's-eye set in gold and silver two inches wide, and the golden armour which fetched a price of over £1,000. With unfeeling vandalism, these lovely things, the summit of Kandyan craftsmanship, were sold to be broken up, despite an appeal from the auctioneer that a matchless dagger and scabbard, studded with diamonds, emeralds, rubies and pearls, should be preserved intact. It was fortunate that the main articles of the regalia were retained in the possession of the Prince Regent, and so survived.

IV

John D'Oyly's patient years of intrigue, diplomacy and espionage had shaped the bloodless British victory, and for his reward he received the post of Resident of the conquered provinces. Kandy was fortunate in the choice. This dedicated man was fluent in Sinhala, sympathetic towards the people, and appreciative of their culture. Every hour of the fourteen years he had spent in Ceylon had been devoted towards preparing himself for this role.

With at first only two British subordinates to assist him in revenue and judicial matters, D'Oyly was superimposed upon the existing Kandyan administrative organization which was retained unchanged except that in the place of the King, D'Oyly ruled through the chiefs in the name of the Governor and the Prince Regent. The retention of the existing machinery of Government was not popular with everyone. D'Oyly records two cases of headmen petitioning that they should be ruled by white men in the fashion of the low country; even a soldier, they said, would be acceptable to them.[26]

The Convention to establish the new order was signed on 2 March, 1815, in the ancient audience hall of the Kings.[27] Here, in the place where Sri Wikrama had received General Macdowall, de Bussche was a spectator of the brilliant scene:

'When we took possession of Kandy, not a human being was to be seen in that great city. Not a week had elapsed when many houses were again occupied by their owners, and before the second of March all the numerous streets of Kandy were filled with people, who came from distant provinces, to witness the ceremonies of that day. Early in the morning, the spacious courts of the palace began to fill with headmen, called Mohottales, Corales, Vidahns; generally speaking, men advanced in years, of good and intelligent appearance, with long black or grey beards. Many of them had never seen a European face; none, or very few, any of our military; their astonishment was great when at the usual hour the daily guards were relieved. It was a fine clear day, and, by the brightness of the arms, the musick, the correct and uniform movements of the troops, their curiosity was alternately gratified. At four o'clock our friend Eheylepoola, with the first and second Adikars, and all the Dessawes, arrived with numerous retinues at the palace. The two Adikars were preceded, like the Roman consuls, by lictors, who instead of fasces were armed with immense whips made of hemp, which they constantly cracked with great noise, and which served as a warning for all the people to clear the way for them.'[28]

Despite his gout, Brownrigg rose to receive the chiefs and continued so to stand throughout the subsequent lengthy ceremonies. Ehelepola, whom Marshall described as 'a remarkably fine intelligent-looking man',[29] took the place of honour on Brownrigg's right-hand side. First came the prerequisite formal compliments from both parties, during which the Kandyan notables assured His Excellency that his arrival and that of his army had rescued them from tyranny and oppression. Next the Convention was read, first in English and afterwards twice in Sinhala by both D'Oyly and by Abraham de Saram, the Modeliar of His Excellency's Gate. The Union Jack was then hoisted to the accompaniment of a royal salute reverberating around the encircling hills, fired by cannon that had been dragged so laboriously into the mountains. A tradition exists that British soldiers had previously tried to raise the flag, but that a *bhikkhu* had dragged it down, protesting that it should not be allowed to fly until the Convention was signed, an attractive but rather improbable account of the British soldiery yielding to moral coercion.[30]

A few days later D'Oyly and James Sutherland, Brownrigg's private secretary and afterwards Secretary to the Kandyan Provinces, signed the Convention on behalf of the British, while Ehelepola and nine major chiefs attested as representatives of the Kandyan people, writing their names in a mixture of Sinhalese,

Nagri and Tamil scripts. This Convention[31] postulated a novel and much-criticized doctrine. The King, by his arbitrary and unjust acts, was held to have forfeited all claims to his title. Consequently both he and his line, together with the Malabar race as a whole, were for ever to be excluded from the throne. Kandyan sovereignty was to be vested in the British Crown, to be exercised through the Governor, and all chiefs and subordinate headmen, lawfully appointed by the British Government, were confirmed in their rights, privileges and powers. Property, civil rights and immunities were guaranteed to all classes of people according to the established laws, institutions and customs. Buddhism was declared inviolable, an unfortunate choice of words that was to get Brownrigg into trouble with William Wilberforce and his companions in the evangelical pressure-group,[32] and the rights, ministers and places of worship of the faith were to be maintained and protected. Torture and mutilation were both prohibited, and the powers of capital punishment were reserved to the Governor. Subject to these conditions, the administration of justice over the Kandyans was to be exercised according to established forms and by the usual authorities, but special arrangements were introduced for non-Kandyans, whether military or civilian. Revenues and royal dues were appropriated to the British Crown, to be collected under the superintendence of agents of the British Government. Finally the right was reserved to the Governor to regulate trade for the benefit of the inhabitants.

As usual, it is difficult to improve on Dr Marshall's comments on the Convention:

'The Kandyan chiefs appear to have tacitly acquiesced to the usual unlimited assumption of power which conquest is presumed to confer in India. Few persons present at the solemn conference gave the chiefs credit for acting with sincerity and honesty of purpose in lending their sanction to the transfer of the dominion of the Kandyan provinces to the Sovereign of the United Kingdom of Great Britain and Ireland, it being generally believed that in seeming to do so, they submitted with reluctance, but with admirable grace, to the force of circumstances, and did as they were desired, leaving to time the development of the result. The Kandyans, it may be observed, considered all innovation as subversive of their ancient government, which, as in like cases, was in their estimation the best of all possible constitutions. As to the reason assigned to seizing the country, namely, to relieve the inhabitants from oppression, it may be observed, that civilized nations assume a sort of inherent right to regulate the policy of the more barbarous communities, humanity being frequently assigned as the pretext for subjugating a country, while conquest is the real and ultimate object of commencing hostilities. There seems to be room to suspect some lurking fallacy in an argument which gives a specious colour of humanity and benevolence to the gratification of a passion so strong and so general as the love of conquest.'[33]

A few days later it was the turn of the *sangha* to meet the Governor. At nine o'clock in the evening the *adigars* and *dissawas* again assembled in the pillared audience chamber and asked leave from the Governor to go to meet the *bhikkhus* and conduct them to the meeting. About an hour later the sound of drums, trumpets and whip-cracking heralded the approach of the procession. Into the courts on either side of the audience hall de Bussche saw flooding a vast concourse of people, lit by nearly a thousand torches, in the centre of which he could see the minute and decrepit figure of Kobbakaduva Nayaka, the seventy-year-old High Priest, so infirm that two young priests had to support him on either side. Behind him followed his train of some ninety other *bhikkhus*, shaven-headed and fan in hand, their rich yellow silk robes contrasting with the velvet one worn by the High Priest. After an exchange of felicitations, the Nayaka assured the Governor of the attachment of the *sangha* to the new government and its appreciation of the measures which had been taken to safeguard the faith of the country. Towards midnight the old man and his retinue withdrew, accompanied at his own request by the Kaffir band of the 3rd Ceylon, which he retained for several hours while it played outside his living quarters.[34] But despite this outward show of goodwill, the *sangha* were only too wary of their new rulers. Brownrigg's assurances that their rights and privileges would be respected were all very well, but, as Colvin R. de Silva put it, a Christian government was no satisfactory substitute for a Buddhist king and any relationship between the *sangha* and such a government was intrinsically anomalous.[35]

At the same time as Sri Wikrama dispersed his treasures to

hide them from the British, the *bhikkhus* removed their sacred Relic of the Tooth from the Dalada Maligava. This symbol of Buddhism, more holy to the Sinhalese even than the Sri Mahabodhi, the Bo tree that has flourished at Anuradhapura for more than two millennia, had been brought to Lanka early in the 4th century A.D. Throughout the centuries it had become, not just an object of the deepest religious veneration, but the symbol of the divine right of the Kings of Lanka to their throne. Wars were fought to possess it, fine temples built to house it, and bodyguards formed for its protection. When a monarch moved his capital, the Tooth went with him. In the seventeenth century the Portuguese were said to have seized and destroyed this sacred relic for the greater glory of their Christian god, but every true Buddhist knew that it was not the Tooth upon which the invaders had laid their sacrilegious hands.

After Brownrigg had left Kandy for Colombo on 20 March, escorted in regal state by the *dissawas* of the provinces through which his route lay, D'Oyly was faced with the task of persuading the priests to return the Relic to its home in Kandy. After protracted arguments, which included a demand that a Sinhalese king was necessary for the maintenance of their faith, a contention probably encouraged by Ehelepola's adherents, D'Oyly at length prevailed; and, on 24 April, the Tooth Relic was escorted back to the Dalada Maligava in the precincts of the Palace with a *perahera* little different to that still enacted in Kandy each July or August at the time of the full moon. Tusker elephants, clad in gold and silver, magnificently garbed dignitaries, acrobats, drummers and disciplined troops of the famous Kandyan dancers, the gold of their head-dresses and ornaments matching the sheen of their sweating torsos, coalesced into the vivid throbbing pageant, unsurpassed as a spectacle by any other faith. At the drawbridge entrance to the Palace, opposite the spot where Ehelepola's children had died, the Relic was lowered from its elephant and conducted between the moated walls, escorted by *bhikkhus* and chiefs. D'Oyly, invited within the sanctuary, removed his shoes and offered at the shrine a fine musical clock in the Governor's name, an act of respect that aroused some of his evangelical compatriots to further wrath.[36] Here, despite a further excursion, the story of which will be told later, the *Dalada* is still treasured.

In the forefront of every ceremony which was held in Kandy could be found Ehelepola, the man who shared with D'Oyly the credit for the British victory. The influence the late Adigar had exercised on behalf of the British, the advice he had given them and the active part he had played in the operations had all been invaluable. Like many of his fellow Kandyans he had made the mistake of assuming that he would be rewarded with Sri Wikrama's throne, even though he would be ruling as the client-king of the victors. In this manner he would succeed, where the old Pilima Talauva had failed, in establishing once again a Sinhalese dynasty. His confidence in his future was such that, a few days after Sri Wikrama's capture, when a palace official brought him some of the treasures which the late King had entrusted to his care, Ehelepola donned the golden hat and coat of royalty. Rebuked by the official for the impropriety of the action, Ehelepola replied that he would in a few days be King.[37] But now his ambitions were in ruins. There was not to be another king. The Kandyans had once too often called in outside help to solve their problems. In his disappointment, Ehelepola behaved with exemplary dignity, refusing all honours except the title of *Friend of the British Government*. He was granted precedence over all other chiefs and, as a tangible token of respect, was promised a jewelled likeness of 'Prinny'. The most talented man in Kandy, still in his prime of life, Ehelepola took up residence in the capital, where he lived in near-regal state, marrying once again, this time the widow of Migastenna, the sister of Kapuvatta, also named Pilima Talauva.

To Molligoda went once again the high office of *Mahadigar*, together with the *dissawa* of the Seven Korales, while Pilima Talauva, Ehelepola's brother-in-law became Second Adigar and *dissawa* of Sabaragamuva. Anyone advanced by the King during the later years of his reign was removed from his post and the vacancy filled by a member of one of the great families. The Kandyan oligarchy still ruled but now its power was tempered, not by the Malabar, Sri Wikrama, but by the Englishman, D'Oyly.

CHAPTER 13

The Third War: Rebellion

I

EARLY in the month of August, 1817, Brownrigg (who had been rewarded for his economical victory with a baronetcy) set out from Colombo to tour his newly acquired provinces, the second such peregrination he had made since the signing of the Convention. With him went Lady Brownrigg, carried like her crippled husband in a tomjohn (an open, single-poled sedan-chair, cooler than a palanquin), which the coolies lugged up precipices of the nature of the Balane Pass, places in Dr Davy's opinion where 'it is possible, though not humane or considerate, to ascend on horseback'.[1] Attending His Excellency was the usual horde of servants, camp-followers, staff officers and local worthies, with gaily decorated elephants leading the vast retinue. But the Governor's military escort was, in contrast, diminutive: no more than a small party of the Ceylon Light Dragoons, on at least one occasion reduced to less than half a dozen troopers,[2] was thought sufficient to guard him from the perils of the journey. In every way Kandy seemed to be tranquil.

Since the signing of the Convention two years before conditions in the conquered provinces had in no way given any cause for alarm. British rule was mild, if not indulgent, and relations between the European officials and the Kandyan ruling classes, superficially at least, were sound. The last-named, retaining all their age-old splendour and exercising possibly even greater power

235

than they had done under the King, continued to occupy themselves with their internecine quarrels. Only rarely did one of them commit the error of giving his new rulers cause to question his loyalty. Between the rest of the population of Kandy and the handful of British officials and military officers language formed a near impenetrable barrier. Contact between the two races was minimal, and even D'Oyly, with his still-busy network of spies, had little idea what was happening beneath the outwardly placid surface of the country.

But as Dr Marshall emphasized in retrospect, it was not sufficient for a government to be just, it had to be palatable as well.[3] For over 2,000 years the Sinhalese had resisted foreign invaders, and for the past three centuries they had been given good cause to loathe the succession of Europeans who had held the littoral of their country and tried to subjugate the interior. United though all classes had been in wishing to remove Sri Wikrama, the possibility of a faceless foreign bureaucracy replacing their monarchy had not been contemplated, even though they might have anticipated that mutual jealousies would continue to prevent their ruling families from choosing one of themselves, even Ehelepola, to replace the King.

Marshall described this relationship between the ruled and their rulers:

'The Kandyans used to enquire when the English intended to return to the maritime provinces. "You have now," said one, "deposed the king, and nothing more is required—you may leave us." The people showed no dislike to us individually, but as a nation they abhorred us. They seemed to entertain a superstitious notion that the English could not live in Kandyan territory. They made no complaint of oppression or misrule, contenting themselves with expressing a wish that we should leave the country. Conversing on this subject, a subordinate chief observed to an officer, that the British rule in the Kandyan country was as incompatible as yoking a buffalo and a cow in the same plough.'[4]

If the British had perhaps ruled Kandy with greater firmness, the coming troubles might have been avoided. As it was they held the country in a light grasp, but managed, at the same time, to treat the inhabitants in a manner unfortunately insensitive. To blame them for this lack of tact is easy; but different in race, language, religion, custom and mode of thought as they were, they had as many difficulties in understanding the Kandyans as the latter in understanding them. Offence was often given unwittingly: temples would be entered without showing proper respect; priests would be treated without the deference which was their due; because the British knew nothing about caste distinctions, they tended to handle all classes of Kandyans in a similar fashion. Understandably the chiefs were offended the most. As Davy put it:

'Before, no one but the king was above them; now they were inferior to every civilian in our service—to every officer in the army. Though officially treated with respect, it was only officially; a common soldier passed a proud Kandyan chief with as little attention as he would a fellow of the lowest caste. Thus they considered themselves degraded and shorn of their splendour.'[5]

The novel impartiality of British justice the chiefs found particularly galling. Not only did it fail to take note of their position and caste but it also ignored their cherished privileges, in effect a breach of the Convention which they had signed with Brownrigg's representatives.

The British task was hard. There was no way of placating men who, having flung out their own ruler, were prepared neither to select one of themselves to replace him nor to accept the dominion of foreigners. But, if the chiefs were difficult to placate, the *bhikkhus* were impossible. Unable to reconcile a Christian government with a Buddhist state, they predicted the menace the new religion was to become to their own faith. They had seen Christianity at work in the Maritime Provinces, and they realized that they could not withstand the spread of a proselytizing religion, supported by a ruling minority which controlled the civil patronage. Under the terms of the Convention, Brownrigg had been conscientious in protecting their faith, but this did nothing to mollify them, nor to make them less implacable in their opposition to British rule.

The British were no more successful in establishing a *rapport* with the general mass of the Kandyan people than they were with the chiefs and the priests. All classes were accustomed to the presence of a king in their capital, to the splendour of his court and the fascinating complexities of its ceremonial. They were traditionalists, and the court of their ruler and the lesser courts of his *dissawas* provided the mainspring for their traditions. Despotism was the only rule they knew and under this despotism, tempered by its many checks and balances, they had far less cause than most races to complain about their government. A shadowy King of Great Britain ruling thousands of miles away was little more than a name, and certainly no substitute for a monarch before whom any peasant might prostrate himself and plead the justice of his cause.[6] Even less of a substitute was King George's representative in Kandy, the scholarly John D'Oyly. Popular and respected though he was, he lived as a recluse in the style of a simple Kandyan gentleman, avoiding all the normal pro-consular trappings. He was, as Brownrigg complained to the Secretary of State, 'a private Gentleman of very retired and unostentatious habits. . . .'[7]

The Governor was, in fact, becoming more and more exasperated with D'Oyly. His despatches were peppered with derogatory comments on his subordinates, including the damning condemnation that he 'had to arouse him into that energy of which he is so capable when the Occasion appears sufficiently interesting to require it',[8] and that D'Oyly's mild and complacent habits were such that he seldom left his chambers.[9] Brownrigg's complaints were not unjustified. Probably D'Oyly's fire was in the process of being dampened by the continual overwork and sickness which were to take his life in 1824. Perhaps he was a better subordinate than a principal, and his wider responsibilities as Resident were too much for him. Whatever it was, the task of ruling his wide territories seems to have been too onerous for him.

Not long after the signing of the Convention, the size of the civil administration had to be increased and Government Agents were posted to Uva, Sabaragamuva and the Three Korales, while reluctant low-country Sinhalese and Burgher clerks and interpreters were tempted by offers of double pay to serve in the interior.[10] Barracks and forts were needed to house more than 1,000 soldiers, and work had to be put in hand to provide the much-needed road between Colombo and Trincomalee and improve the mountain tracks to make them fit for pack animals. All this cost money and Whitehall was quick to complain at the cost. The King, Bathurst argued, was able to maintain his unpopular rule without spending all this money. Why, then, was this expenditure necessary to support the British, who, he had been told, were received so enthusiastically by the people of the country?[11] Brownrigg answered this query in a lucid and well-reasoned manner, demonstrating his grasp of the problems of ruling Kandy, and emphasizing the need for a military presence in the interior to overawe a latently hostile population.[12] But reductions could not be avoided, and the 3rd Ceylon Regiment was disbanded in March, 1817, following the 4th Battalion which had gone the same way at the end of the 1815 campaign. The African soldiers were passed on to the 2nd Battalion, which now became a mixed unit with five companies of Sepoys and five of Kaffirs. This latest reduction left only four infantry units in the island: the two local Battalions, the 73rd Highlanders and the 19th Foot, the last-named waiting to be relieved by the 83rd Foot in the middle of October. Scattered around the coastal forts and dispersed into eleven small up-country garrisons, it was not a large force to control such a country.

II

Brownrigg's journey brought him to Kandy in time for the great *Esala Perahera*.[13] After attending the ceremonies and coping with a massive accumulation of business, the Governor left the capital on 26 September *en route* for Trincomalee. So far it had been a light-hearted and pleasant tour, the entourage meandering through the picturesque countryside, passing comfortable looking villages and encampments of bronzed and healthy soldiers, the staff officers reminiscing about their experiences of 1815 as they passed well-known landmarks. Wherever they stopped a gay and enthusiastic welcome awaited the Governor and his lady, and the people showed every sign of carefree and happy contentment. Dr Davy, who was with the party, found only the one thing to criticize. Kandy, which the British had intended to improve as a city, looked much the worse for wear after its two years of occupation. Many buildings had been pulled down and little put in their place; the temples, Davy noted, seemed to be very neglected indeed. A mere three buildings had been erected since 1815: a house for the Governor, another for the military commandant and a jail. The last was the finest building in the country, a fact that surprised the Kandyans.[14]

Near Lake Minneriya, on the return journey,[15] the peaceful atmosphere prevailing in the Governor's party was shattered.[16] From the capital arrived a messenger with the news that eastern Uva and the province of Vellassa were in revolt against the Government. A large number of Veddas lived around Bintenna in Vellassa. Some of these people were still hunters; others had settled down to an agricultural life, and the Sinhalese villagers of the area were little more advanced than their aboriginal neighbours. Although the King's government in Kandy had never exercised more than a tenuous control over this remote part of the country, the villagers had always been in the habit of displaying a staunch loyalty to the person of the monarch. Uva had never been ruled by a foreign power, and the Portuguese had been bloodily repulsed on the sole occasion they had penetrated into the interior of the province. When, therefore, the British columns arrived in 1815 from Batticaloa and Hambantota, the people fled into the jungle, to reappear only slowly and reluctantly. They made no effort to co-operate with the intruders; and, to make matters worse, the most serious looting by the troops happened around Badulla, so antagonizing the inhabitants even further. The situation was so serious that Brownrigg visited the area himself in 1816 and decided, as a result, to place a civil servant in charge of the province in the post of Government Agent.

During September, 1817, Mr Silvester Wilson was Agent at Badulla. Worried by the rumours that a mysterious stranger, dressed sometimes as a Malabar and on other occasions in the yellow robes of a priest, had been seen in the jungles of Vellassa with a retinue of eight priests, Wilson despatched a Moorish official, the Haji Mohandiram, to apprehend the man. There were several Moorish

28. An Execution by an Elephant

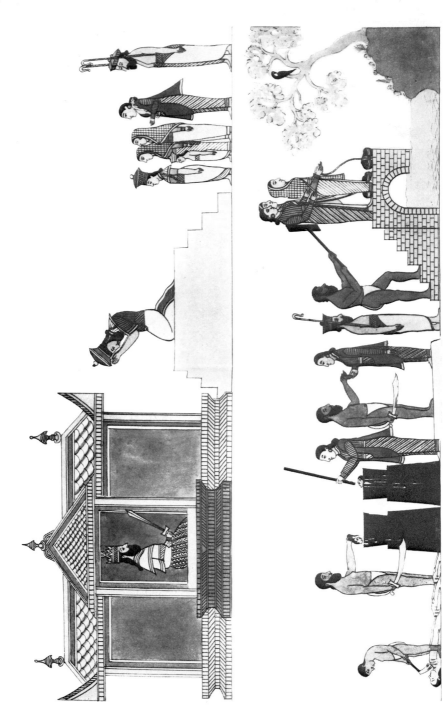

29. The Execution of Ehelepola's children. An engraving published by T. W. Boone in 1843.

communities scattered around this part of the country, inter-spersed among the Sinhalese and the Veddas, and much wealthier than their neighbours because the trade and transport of the district was in their hands. The British had made good use of their carriage-bullocks during the 1815 campaign, and the Moors had welcomed the arrival of the invaders, in contrast to the atti-tude of the Sinhalese and Veddas. As might have been expected, the Sinhalese chiefs mulcted these prosperous Muslims in every way possible, with the result that the latter saw in the British occupation a means of rescuing themselves from the oppressions of their masters. They petitioned Brownrigg to replace the Sinhalese official, to whom their headmen were answerable, by a member of their own community, and to this Brownrigg had agreed, appointing this Haji Mohandiram to the post. It was hardly surprising that Brownrigg's action angered the leading Sinhalese families in the area, who lost, at a single stroke, both valuable perquisites and a part of their traditional authority.

Soon after the Haji set out, he received news that the Malabar's retinue had been increased by 200 Veddas, armed with bows and arrows. Having only a handful of armed men with him, he decided that this was now too much for him to tackle and started to beat a retreat towards Badulla. On the way back he clashed with some armed followers of the stranger and a little later he was taken prisoner.

While the Haji was out looking for the Malabar, news was received in Kandy that the stranger had proclaimed himself King. Wilson heard of his subordinate's capture on 12 October and set out to rescue him two days later, taking as an escort Lieutenant Newman and twenty-four Malays and Caffres of the 1st Ceylon. The day after he left Badulla, as he was travelling through a deserted countryside, Wilson met two Moormen who told him that their Haji had been flogged and sent captive to the Malabar, who had now moved to Bintenna and was commonly known in the countryside as *diyo*, or God, the terms used to describe a king or a member of his family. Later that afternoon Wilson sighted a party of 200 men, armed with bows and arrows. Anxious to avoid bloodshed, Wilson advanced alone to talk to them but the Kandyans fled after discharging a few of their missiles. The next morning Wilson encountered a larger company of some 500 men, with whom he managed to confer for about fifteen minutes, but without any success. Deciding that he was accomplishing nothing, Wilson turned back towards Badulla. On the return journey, a few miles south of Bibile, he allowed his escort to draw ahead of him while he stopped for a drink. A few minutes after he had halted, as he was washing his face and hands, several hundred Kandyans appeared. Making a further attempt to establish contact with them, Wilson beckoned them forward to talk. Their reply was to shoot two arrows through his head.

Wilson's interpreter, who had halted with him, managed to escape, and the man met Newman who was returning to find out what had happened to his superior. In a short skirmish Newman drove the Kandyans off, but his men could find no trace of Wilson's body. Later it was established that the corpse had been hidden in the bushes, less the head which had been sent to Bintenna, a grisly offering to the newly-acclaimed King. Wilson's cool courage was not untypical of his kind, but there was perhaps an element of carelessness in his behaviour. Six months before, Sophia, his twenty-four-year-old wife, had died of malaria in Badulla. Possibly he was indifferent to his own safety.

Brownrigg had heard something of the activities of this odd stranger before he started from Colombo towards Trincomalee, but at the time the news seemed to be of little significance. During the two years the British had held the country, signs of unrest had been uncommonly rare. Soon after the Convention was signed, the chiefs were said to have been conspiring to expel the invaders, but this was never proved. Then in 1816, Eknelligoda, Sri Wikrama's captor, had informed D'Oyly that some *bhikkhus* had approached him with a proposal that he should join with certain other chiefs in a plot to revolt against the Government. At the inquiry that followed Eknelligoda's allegation, only two men were incriminated, a chief called Madugalle and the Malay Mohandiram who had fled from Sri Wikrama's wrath at the time of Pilima Talauva's death in 1811. The Malay was deported to Batavia and a court of his fellow chiefs found Madugalle guilty. He was sentenced to two years' imprisonment and the confiscation of his goods, but Brownrigg released him at the time of the 1817 Perahera. There were further rumours of unrest in 1816 also, but the reports on this occasion originated from William Tolfrey, the probable author of *Gentleman on the Spot*, who had replaced D'Oyly in the post of Chief Translator. Tolfrey, however, died insane in February, with the result that Brownrigg discounted the truth of his warnings.

The situation of the Governor's party when the news of the revolt was received seemed to be critical. Lake Minneriya was a long way from Kandy, and somewhere in the vicinity was Ehelepola with two or three thousand followers. The Governor's escort, on the other hand, consisted of only four light dragoons. D'Oyly trusted Ehelepola, but Brownrigg, suspicious of the extent of his ambitions and knowing the vast influence he exercised, entertained strong reservations about his loyalty. Molligoda, now *mahadigar* and still hating Ehelepola, did all he could to encourage the Governor's doubts. When it was heard that Ehelepola had, during his progression through Matale, quarrelled with the local *dissawa*, an adherent of Molligoda, and forcibly removed his insignia of office, fears for the safety of the Governor and Lady Brownrigg were intensified. The late Adigar's action was both unwarranted and illegal, but probably resulted from a blind flash of rage directed towards Molligoda. Understandably, however, it was taken to be an indication that he was on the verge of joining the insurrection, but when he met Brownrigg at Nalanda he apologized for his inexcusable behaviour, making amends which Brownrigg wisely accepted with good grace.

The Governor was back in Kandy on 26 October, having taken only six days on the road from Trincomalee, his speed perhaps being a measure of his disquiet. Heavy rain was falling and much of the country was inundated and impassable, but D'Oyly had already taken a number of counter-measures against the insurgents, as they must now be called, a prouder and so more expressive term than the 'freedom-fighters' of today. Parties of troops from Batticaloa and Kandy were already on their way to reinforce the small garrison stationed in Uva, and Mr Simon Sawers, the Revenue Commissioner, had been sent to replace the unlucky Wilson at Badulla. Molligoda, with a party of his

243

people from the Seven Korales, was also travelling towards the disaffected areas to lend his weight in the restoration of law and order.

The local *dissawas*, who tended to spend much of their time at the centre of things in Kandy, leaving their satrapies to the care of their assistants, had also left for their provinces. Among them was Keppitipola, the *dissawa* of Uva, one of the half-dozen leading Kandyan chiefs, brother of Ehelepola's murdered wife and related to nearly every prominent family. Soon after Keppitipola arrived in his province, the British heard that this vigorous and active leader had been captured by the rebels, together with several of his leading headmen, and had then thrown in his lot with Doresamy, the name by which the Pretender was now known, who had designated him as *mahadigar*. The capture was contrived by Keppitipola, although both D'Oyly and Sawers believed at the time that it had not been premeditated. Brownrigg, however, had strong doubts about the *dissawa*'s innocence, justifiably as it turned out. From now on, Keppitipola became the mainspring of the revolt, and all but led it to a victorious conclusion.

Ehelepola professed himself horrified at his brother-in-law's desertion. To Brownrigg he sent word that he felt too ashamed to come into the Governor's presence, and he swore in front of D'Oyly an oath of unshaken fidelity to the British Government. Then, as if to produce a hostage for his own good behaviour, he called his wife to Kandy and brought Keppitipola's family to live with her.

No evidence has come to light to suggest that either Ehelepola or any other Kandyan chief was instrumental in starting this rebellion, which was more in the nature of an expression of local dissatisfaction than a direct challenge to British rule. It came about, in fact, more by accident than design. Nevertheless Brownrigg, like North before him and the Portuguese and the Dutch before that, complained with a deep bitterness that the perfidious Kandyan race were 'almost without exception systematically treacherous' and that he could never rely upon the good faith of a single chief.[17]

III

Commanding the garrison at Badulla was Major Macdonald, a capable officer of the 19th Foot. Seeking to avenge Wilson's death and put a quick end to the revolt, on 25 November he marched his small force towards Vellassa, and the following day made contact with Captain Fraser, Brownrigg's A.D.C., who had left Kandy with a column of sixty-four men only four days earlier. These heavily equipped men were able to move with singular rapidity although they rarely engaged in any form of energetic training. In a couple of days Macdonald's soldiers covered twenty-four miles *as the crow flies* across the grain of the most rugged mountains in Ceylon, fighting on the way a sharp action which cost the Major some casualties and resulted in his twice being slightly wounded by arrows himself. Fraser had moved just as quickly. His force had marched over twice the distance across equally harsh country. 'In all their marches,' Brownrigg reported, 'through narrow roads, close jungles, over steep mountains, among rocks and precipices our gallant soldiers pressed on, regardless of the dastardly enemy, who lurked in secure hiding places to discharge their arrows and muskets, for some had firearms, and little injury sustained, not a single man was killed after the one at Kiwulgedera, and only a very few slightly wounded.'[18] Since the Peninsular War, the word 'guerrilla' had become part of the English military vocabulary, but still there was the imputation that this type of fighting was unethical, despite the help the British Army had received from its Spanish allies.

Near the place where Wilson died, Macdonald's troops found a man's head impaled on a stake and beside it an *ola* proclamation, wrapped in a white cloth, announcing the pretender's kingship and enjoining his subjects to put every white man to death. This was the signal for the British to revive the weapon they had used in 1804.

'Major Macdonald now thought an example of severity should be shown, the houses all round were therefore burnt, and all the property found, cattle, grain, etc, etc, was either carried off or destroyed. This terrible sight appeared to dismay the natives, they ceased to shout or skirmish at a distance and only ventured upon the skirts of the plain to gaze in silence upon the flames which consumed their habitations. They seemed panic-stricken at the rapidity and undaunted courage with which our troops had advanced upon them, . . . they saw the hopelessness of their course and were driven to despair.'[19]

The ruthlessness had the desired effect. Several headmen surrendered to Molligoda, together with their followers, declaring that they would hand Doresamy and Wilson's murderers over to the British. All were pardoned so as to encourage further defections.

Many officers thought that Macdonald's rapid swoop had crushed the rebellion but Brownrigg was far less sanguine. Well appreciating the probable consequences of Keppitipola's defection, he established his headquarters at Kandy and threw himself into the task of capturing the pretender and his minister. Every combatant soldier who could be spared was ordered up country, 700 to Uva and more than 1,000 to the neighbourhood of Kandy, not counting pioneers and gun lascars. Martial law was declared in the insurgent provinces, and the huge reward of 2,000 rix dollars was placed on Doresamy's head.

Private Calladine of the 19th Foot was among the reinforcements who marched from Batticaloa into Vellassa. In the middle of October he and his comrades were daily expecting the arrival of the 83rd Foot from the Cape to relieve them. After twenty-one years' service in the island, their Regiment was due at last to return to England, and the women of the Company were already on their way to join the Headquarters at Trincomalee when news of Wilson's death arrived. Calladine remembered the morning the women sailed:

'What high spirits we were all in, thinking soon to follow them to Trincomalee, and from there to embark for old England; but alas! very few, if any, of these women ever saw their husbands again, and poor Mrs Jones was the first of them to become a widow, as the Captain was the first man of the Company that died.'[20]

Calladine's company set out from Batticaloa, following much the same route as that covered by Johnston in 1805. Forcing their way through hot, dreary scrubland and thick forest, interspersed at times by lovely stretches of park-like country, the men were tormented in turn by mosquitoes and leeches. Soon they marched barefoot to avoid the delay of removing their boots and gaiters at every stream. Always there was the threat of sniping Kandyan arrows, and the putrid corpse of a Moorish bullockdriver hanging from a tree warned them of the perils of straggling.

These sweating, swearing, red-coated Europeans must have been a terrifying sight, and their arrival in Vellassa caused all but a few Moormen to flee for safety into the jungle. Jones, admired by Calladine as a firm but just officer, took care, however, that his men did not molest anyone they caught. The result was that when the Company established its permanent post in the hills, the villagers soon trickled back to their houses to sell their fruit and vegetables to the soldiers. Discipline in these conditions could not have been easy to enforce, despite the barbarous punishments which could be inflicted. When Jones's men made contact with another column which had come up from Galle, the new arrivals plundered the arrack store before it could be placed under proper guard, and so drunk did some soldiers of the 2nd Ceylon become that they had to be tied to bullocks' backs when the march was resumed.[21]

Soon there were few villages left standing. Nearly all were to meet the fate of the one destroyed by Macdonald. The British had no other weapon which they could use to subdue the country. The Kandyans moved too quickly to be caught, and the way they dealt with their traitors discouraged their countrymen from helping their enemies. The small British columns, chasing to and fro across the wild, rough country between Bintenna and Badulla, making vain efforts to lay their hands on the leaders, rarely lost more than the odd man from rebel bullets or arrows. On the other hand the perpetual hardships sapped the strength of the soldiers, and lowered their resistance to disease. The Kandyans, Brownrigg complained, would not stop to be defeated. 'There is,' he wrote, 'no resource left but to burn and lay waste the property of the headmen, their leaders—revolting as such vigorous measures are to my heart, they are the only means left to reduce the refractory to submission.'[22]

IV

At the turn of the year, the rebellion started to spread outside the eastern provinces. It was the usual sequence of events. Stern measures were deemed necessary to suppress the revolt, but repression had the opposite effect. Embittered homeless men took to the jungle and their neighbours rose in sympathy or were terrorized into helping them. Savagery was met by savagery. The Kandyans tortured captives. The Government treated as brigands all men they took in arms and sometimes those without.

Soon more of the chiefs, seeing that the revolt could succeed, followed Keppitipola's example and added their influence and leadership to the struggle. First Dumbara, then Sabaragamuva and soon the Seven Korales rose against the Government. By February all Kandy, except for lower Sabaragamuva, the Three and the Four Korales, and the country lying between the capital and the Balane Pass, was in revolt. On the 21st of that month martial law had to be extended to the whole of the country and soon every chief of consequence, except for Molligoda and Eknelligoda, had joined the insurgents.

The Four Korales started to waver and could well have changed its allegiance if Molligoda had not been recalled to his home province from Uva. The *mahadigar*'s continued loyalty to the British was providential; if the Four Korales had been lost, the main supply route between Kandy and the coast would have been cut and the British would probably have been forced to evacuate the interior.

Molligoda never ceased to poison the Government's mind about Ehelepola's loyalty, but Brownrigg was reluctant to believe the accusations, aware as he was of the enmity between the two men. What is more, the Governor was not disposed to forget the debt he owed Ehelepola for the help he had provided in 1815. Although Doresamy and Keppitipola continually asserted that Ehelepola was supporting them, there was no evidence of the truth of their claim and the ex-Adigar himself gave no indication that he was sympathetic towards the insurgents. Nevertheless most Kandyans believed the claims of the rebel leaders, and the danger that Ehelepola might join them was more than Brownrigg could entertain. On 2 March, therefore, Brownrigg arrested him and removed him out of harm's way to Colombo. It was a difficult decision for Brownrigg to make, and it is to his credit that he dealt with the matter honestly and made no attempt to concoct spurious charges against the Kandyan. His action was justified. When the rebellion was over evidence came to light to confirm the truth of Molligoda's accusations and the claims of the insurgent leaders.[23]

The same night that Ehelepola was arrested, an attempt was made also to take Pilima Talauva, *dissawa* of the Seven Korales and son of the old Adigar, evidence having come to light that he was in correspondence with the insurgents. The chief escaped, however, through the back of the house while his uncle Kapuvatta (who was also named Pilima Talauva), the Second Adigar, held the arresting officers in conversation at the front door. For his pains Kapuvatta was taken in place of his nephew, who now joined the insurgents. Given command of both Matale and the Seven Korales, Pilima Talauva became second only to Keppitipola among the Kandyan leaders.

By the end of February, the British were beginning to feel the strain. Although the 83rd Foot had arrived and the 19th Foot had been retained in the island, a force of five infantry battalions was scant to fight such a war. As the British tired, the Kandyans became bolder, concentrating their forces and attacking British posts. At Paranagama, Macdonald with eighty men was besieged by 7,000 or 8,000 Kandyans, about half of whom were armed with muskets. Keppitipola himself led them. It was 1803 all over again. From a weak position on a low, gently-sloping hill, the 19th held the enemy at bay by counter-attacking them time after time with minute parties of men. Ten days later the Kandyans withdrew when the defenders had not suffered a single casualty, exhausted though they were. Shortly afterwards a permanent fort was constructed half a mile away from the hill and named Fort Macdonald after the Major. Later he was stationed here and it must have given him some satisfaction to write his own name as his address at the top of his correspondence.

Similar attacks were mounted elsewhere, including one as close to Kandy as Hanguranketa. All failed. Massing their forces to attack their enemies' defended posts was an error the Kandyans had made before. Because they never pressed an assault and discharged their muskets from a distance, their losses were not serious. But the damage to their morale when they withdrew with nothing accomplished was critical. If their forces in Uva had continued to fight in the manner for which they were equipped, as the men of Matale did, the outcome might have been different. The British communications between Kandy and Nalanda had been cut in early March in this northern province. Major Delatre, with a force of 100 men, marching up from Trincomalee, was faced by Kandyans fighting the type of warfare for which they were best suited. In torrential rain, with his bullock-drivers deserting, Delatre had to carve his way through successive ambushes, clearing the blocked track of obstacles as he moved. Severely wounded himself and burdened by his casualties, the loss of his transport forced him to destroy his reserves of ammunition. So tenacious was the opposition and so tired his men when he reached Nalanda that Delatre decided to evacuate the garrison and make for Kurunegala in the Seven Korales instead of continuing to try to force his way through to Kandy.

Three days after Nalanda had been abandoned, Captain Raper of the 19th Foot marched from his post on the Atgalle Pass, just above Kandy, to discover what had happened to Delatre. Fighting his way through opposition similar to that met by the Trincomalee column, Raper reached Nalanda to find the place abandoned. After only a five-hour halt for a rest and a hot meal, Raper started back to Atgalle, carrying his wounded with him. He arrived there after covering forty terrible miles in fifty-six hours, fighting nearly all the way. A week later every man of Raper's detachment was in hospital.

For the first months of the campaign, the Army, although tired, had kept remarkably healthy, a point reiterated by Brownrigg in his despatches with something of a suggestion of surprise. In mid-February, the hospitals held only 267 men, one-third of whom were sick with leg ulcers, but by March disease was spreading and in April the Kandyans' old ally had become once again the crucial factor in the fighting. One-fifth of the British troops were now in hospital.

The average annual mortality rate for the troops stationed in the United Kingdom was, at the time, 15 per 1,000. Even in Ceylon, the average death rate of the 19th Foot between 1811 and 1813 was no more than 20 per 1,000. In 1818, however, this Regiment lost 114 men, a rate of 152 per 1,000, and this did not start to compare with the casualties among the 73rd Highlanders. In the same year the losses of that Regiment had reached the terrible proportion of 412 per 1,000, and the figure had dropped only to 283 per 1,000 in 1819, most of the men dying from diseases they had contracted during the fighting of the previous year. The 83rd Regiment, which did not have one man on the sick-list when it landed from the Cape, fared just as badly as the Highlanders.[24] Only a negligible proportion of these losses were caused by Kandyan bullets and arrows. During April, May and June, the British suffered only 100 battle casualties.

Calladine fell ill with yellow fever in April, went down to the coast to recover, then returned to duty to catch a fresh fever, and so down to Batticaloa once again, this time in a doolie slung on a pole between two coolies. There he watched the 73rd Highlanders die:

'During the time I was in hospital I had the cots on my right and left cleared three times by men dying, and I suppose there were between thirty and forty who died in the ward in the time. . . . All the barrack rooms in the Fort were turned into hospital wards, and even the canteen verandah. What few men there were in health were in tents outside the Fort, so that the whole garrison had become a hospital, and the burial ground, where a grave was seldom opened, had now become like a ploughed field.'[25]

No sooner had Calladine flung off this fever than he contracted dropsy and the fever returned once again. But he lived, convinced that he had cured his beri-beri by drowning it in arrack.

On 21 February, Brownrigg wrote to Mr Hugh Elliott, the Governor of Madras, asking for 2,000 troops and 4,000 coolies to be sent from India as reinforcements, one-quarter of that number to be despatched without delay. Elliott complied, acting with the speed Maitland had displayed in the past when India asked for help. On 22 March, the 1st Battalion of the 15th Madras Native Infantry landed in Ceylon and half the 2nd Battalion of the 7th Regiment followed less than three weeks later. At about the same time the 2nd Battalion of the 18th embarked, but the unit was delayed at sea and did not put into Trincomalee until the end of May. After six weeks of being cooped up in their ships, the Sepoys were then marched straight across the hills to Badulla. Four companies stayed there, and the rest of the unit pushed on through the mountains of Uva towards Kandy, encumbered by massive baggage and harassed nearly all the way by the Kandyans. It speaks well for this newly arrived Indian battalion that it did not disintegrate on the way.

These reinforcements arrived just in time. By the end of March the Kandyans controlled the whole of Matale, and Brownrigg had been forced to withdraw his small detachments scattered around the outskirts of the capital into the safety of the city and evacuate a further series of posts running along the line of communication between Sabaragamuva and Badulla. The likelihood that the newly conquered provinces might have to be relinquished was dear, and Brownrigg felt it necessary to remind the Secretary of State that Kandy was a country worth fighting to retain and that the disgrace of allowing a great military nation to be expelled by a horde of semi-barbarians (as he called them) could not be countenanced.[26]

CHAPTER 14

The Third War:
The Old Order Ends

I

DURING April and May, the British were compelled to evacuate more of their posts. Their scattered little garrisons had melted into the sick-bays, and there were no men left to escort the supply-laden coolies along the winding mountain tracks. Because the troops had either eaten or destroyed all the food in the villages, they were now dependent upon whatever rations the commissariat could manage to carry forward to them; often this was less than a quarter of a pound of salt meat and a pound of unhusked paddy daily, and the consequent lack of proper food further weakened the overworked men and reduced their resistance to disease. The British had despoiled the land, and now their weapon had recoiled upon them.

By the middle of May, the Kandyans were in complete control of large stretches of their country. The British had abandoned eastern Dumbara and Matale in the north. They had quit Bintenna (it would be more accurate to say the place where Bintenna once stood), withdrawing the garrison to Alupota in the foothills, and taking with them the local chieftain who had remained loyal and could not now be abandoned to starvation or summary execution. The entire line of posts between Badulla and Kandy had been given up, and the troops remaining in Uva were now dependent for all their food and stores upon the tenuous supply line from Sabaragamuva. For a time in April even the

253

communications between Kandy and Colombo had been severed, but this crisis was short-lived. Within three weeks the British were again in control of the route, so firmly so that it was declared safe for unarmed travellers. Nevertheless there was an ever-present threat that this part of the country might fall into the hands of the insurgents. The thought haunted the British. They knew only too well what would be the outcome of any withdrawal they might have to conduct down this road, short of coolies and encumbered by their hundreds of sick men.

In Kandy alone there were at times as many as five hundred hospital patients, and each evening at sunset they were issued with the arms and ammunition with which to defend themselves in the event of the hospital being attacked during the night. So close did the Kandyans press to the town that, in April, it was thought wise to evacuate Lady Brownrigg and the other wives from the capital, an operation which involved the greater part of the fit men left in the garrison. Morale was low. Davy afterwards wrote that it 'was a melancholy time to those who were on the scene of action; and many began to despond and augur from bad to worse, and to prophesy (what indeed was far from improbable) that the few districts not yet against us, would join the enemy. . . .'[1] A steady stream of defeatist letters reached England, the never-ending pessimism of which annoyed the editor of the *Asiatic Journal*. 'Their musing of deep gloom,' he scoffed, 'prepared us to expect that the arduous trial for British arms was about to close in triumph; for those who resign their doubts and feelings to the influence of an amiable melancholy never grow in earnest till their willing despondency is without hope.'[2]

If the British had realized the full effect their devastation of the countryside was having upon its people, they might have been somewhat less despondent. Already the heart was going out of the Kandyan resistance. Davy, discussing in retrospect the miseries suffered by both sides, described what happened:

'We suffered most from the harassing nature of the service; from fatigue and privation; and from the effect of these, and of night-marches, and of an unwholesome climate, producing disease. The sufferings of the natives were of a more severe kind and complicated nature. In addition to the horrors of war in its most appalling shape, they had to encounter those of disease, want and famine, without chance of relief.'[3]

Davy estimated the British deaths during 1818 at 1,000 men, or one-fifth of the force employed. 'The loss of the natives,' he went on to say, 'killed in the field or executed, or that died of disease or famine, can hardly be calculated; it was, probably, ten times greater than ours, and may have amounted, perhaps, to ten thousand.'[4] Regretting that his countrymen had ever entered Kandy, he declared that the evils resulting from the occupation had greatly exceeded the benefit conferred on the people by the removal of Sri Wikrama.

The critical Marshall was even more outspoken than his fellow physician. Comparing the British deeds in Ceylon with the Duke of Cumberland's reprisals against his own countrymen after Culloden, he reported that:

'Neither of the belligerents seemed much disposed to take prisoners, and that the atrocities of a force trained in the usages of civilized warfare, were not less flagrant than those of an uncivilized population. White and black races, the invaded and the invaders, Christian and Pagan, vied with each other in promoting the horrors and barbarities of mutual destruction. Probably this was considered the only effective mode of carrying on the war, and that the end justified the means. Did not the means condemn the end?'[5]

Marshall can be excused for his use of 'civilized'. Dialectics on the meaning of the word were not yet fashionable.

Davy's criticism, although the less outspoken, carries more weight because he was not only an admirer of Brownrigg but owed his position to him. He may well have been correct in exculpating the Governor and his senior officers from personal knowledge of the worst excesses committed by the troops. It was hard to keep track on the actions of a score of Africans or Malays, operating in the wilds of Dumbara under the command of an exhausted subaltern or sergeant. For Brownrigg, running the war from his bed, it was all but impossible. Crippled in turn by a violent skin disease and by the gout, which now affected a hand as well as his feet, he had to be lifted each morning from his bed to a chair. The lucidity of his despatches and orders reveal his grasp of the problems confronting him, but he was never able to see for himself what was happening in the jungles. Perhaps Davy was a little fulsome when he described his patron as 'not less remarkable for his mildness and forbearance, than for consistency and determination, and unremitting exertion',[6] but he was not too far from the mark.

It was not only the doctors who castigated the conduct of their fellow-countrymen. Major Campbell, who arrived in Ceylon when the fighting was over, wrote that he had heard that many of the Kandyans had been barbarously treated, and that the soldiers, exasperated by their sufferings, had even put their prisoners to death when they were out of sight of their officers.[7] Private Calladine merely reported that 'seldom a day passed but we had parties out scouring the country for a distance around, burning all they came across and shooting those they could not take prisoner'.[8] Captain Ajax Anderson had no moral qualms about the methods of warfare needed to beat the Kandyans. In his *Ode to an Old Camp Cloak*, the 'companion of his way' through the tangled thickets of the island, he promises that,

> 'We'll track the savage to his den,
> With famine, sword and flame;'[9]

The final word can be left to another soldier in the 19th Foot, whom an officer overheard to say, 'When I am discharged, I intend to become a highwayman; for one thing, after what I have seen in Kandy, taking the life of a man will give me no concern.'[10]

II

Gradually the British began to gain the upper hand. They still lacked the troops to hunt the insurgents down, but the grasp of the Kandyan leaders upon their people was starting to slacken, despite the penalties exacted from waverers and the disloyal. Death by torture, mutilation (Keppitipola was accused of favouring this particular form of punishment), and the ravaging of women by the Rodiyas were among the horrors which the unlucky peasant caught up in the struggle had to suffer from his compatriots. And by no means all the devastation was inflicted by the British. The insurgents likewise burned and looted any district slow to rally to them, but this was a weapon which rebounded upon them. Often when the British managed to scrape together enough troops to garrison a new post, the villagers would gather around it, seeking protection from their fellow-countrymen.

By mid-July the tide had turned in favour of the British. The country between the south-east tip of Sabaragamuva and the north-eastern border of the Seven Korales—half of the Kandyan dominions and the richer half as well—was quiet. Even Vellassa and the surroundings of Badulla, but a short time before the main centres of resistance, were peaceful, so much so that even the Moor bullock-drivers could go about their business in safety again. Matale and Dumbara, however, were still in insurgent hands.

Two incidents did much to hearten the British. Towards the end of June a mixed patrol of six Highlanders from the 73rd, with six Malays and the same number of Africans of the Ceylon Regiment, was ambushed in thick jungle two miles outside Badulla. Two of the Highlanders were killed and Lance-Corporal McLoughlin, the patrol commander, leaving ten of his men to guard the bodies, fought his way to Badulla with the rest to bring help. A relief force arrived at the scene to find the survivors still keeping the Kandyans at bay. It might well be said that McLoughlin should have been criticized for splitting his force in this way, but because of the Kandyan habit of mutilating the dead and impaling their heads on spikes within view of their comrades' camps, everything possible was done to avoid a dead man's body falling into insurgent hands. Often when a man was killed, the column would be halted and the body burnt, a measure that caused delay and risked the lives of other men.

To mark this action, for which McLoughlin received high praise, a medal was struck for the survivors (see Plate 20). At the time this was a rare honour, but the Corporal and his three surviving Highlanders had no benefit from it. All died of fever before they could receive their medals.

No mention is made of the weapons used by the Kandyans

in this action. At the start of the revolt the people of Vellassa were armed with little more than bows and arrows, but as the war spread to the richer provinces, more and more of the insurgents were found to be armed with muskets or gingals. Soon every other Kandyan fighting man was seen to be carrying a firearm, and the number captured during the war, or surrendered afterwards, seems to confirm that this was so; the British recovered over 8,000 muskets, pistols or gingals, and with a total Kandyan population estimated at some quarter of a million persons, it is doubtful whether more than 16,000 men could have been in the field at any one time. As in so many societies, the Kandyans seem to have used the musket in preference to the bow, a perplexing choice. Silent, cheap, light and accurate, the latter was a far more suitable weapon for use in the jungle than the clumsy, slow-to-reload musket, the gunpowder for which was hard to obtain. The Veddas, particularly, were skilled archers, able to hit a mark at sixty yards and kill an elephant with the special fourteen-inch bladed arrow.[11] Even the light bow carried in war was a powerful weapon. Calladine, who for much of the campaign worked as a medical orderly, saw many arrow wounds; he described the case of a Malay who walked into camp with a blade sticking in his head just behind his ear:

'The doctor told Captain Jones that he would soon have a dead man in the camp. I held the man's head between my knees, and the doctor, by main strength with the artillery knipper (with which they cut the port fores in two), pulled out the arrow, which was buried not less than between three and four inches in his head; but, contrary to the doctor's expectations, there were very few drops of blood following the blade, and the man, instead of dying, walked back the same day to Hansenwelle.'[12]

The second incident that heartened the British concerned their Malay troops. A Moorman approached the commander of one of the posts in Vellassa with the information that an insurgent chief had several times suggested to him that he should persuade a party of Malays to desert with their weapons. A plan to simulate such a desertion was concocted; and, on the appointed day, the Moorman led thirty soldiers to the rendezvous. Among them were a Malay officer and several N.C.O.s, all dressed in private soldiers' uniforms. There are different versions of what followed, but the more accurate story is likely to be that told by Calladine, who was a member of the garrison of the post and had no special axe to grind.[13] That evening as the Kandyans shared their meal with their new allies, the Malays drew their krises at a given signal and plunged them into their hosts. Some thirty men were left dead on the spot, but the life of the chief who had been instrumental in suggesting the deal was preserved, and he was brought back as a prisoner. Medals and a cash bounty were awarded to each of the Malays, and their lieutenant was promoted to the rank of captain. According to Calladine the British had been wary. His detachment had been moved to the camp as a precaution against the Malays double-crossing their own side.

Despite this slackening tempo of Kandyan resistance, Brownrigg realized that the insurgents were still sustained by three sources of strength.[14] First there was the expectation that history would repeat itself: soon enough disease and starvation must destroy their foes. Then there was the upsurge in morale produced by the coronation of the so-called king in May. Keppitipola had organized this before a gathering of 3,000 people at a ceremony in which the pretender had assumed the famous name of Kirti Sri, in itself an inspiration to the Kandyans to continue their resistance. Finally there was the Relic of the Tooth, the mystical affirmation of a king's regality, abstracted from the Dalada Mandapa by a *bhikkhu*, and exhibited in July by Keppitipola at Hanguranketa. Brownrigg, however, had doubts about Keppitipola's claim that he held the true Tooth. He found it hard to understand how it could have been stolen from the Temple, closely guarded as it was by British troops, but the only way to test the truth of the insurgents' claim was to investigate the Dalada Mandapa to see what it held. But there was a difficulty. No one could recognize the Tooth, and Molligoda had doubts as to whether the British had, in fact, ever been in possession of it. Had a fictitious article been deposited in Kandy in 1815? The real Relic, the Adigar suggested, might well have been hidden by Ehelepola for use when he might need it to support his ambitions. It was D'Oyly who produced the solution to the dilemma.

259

A state of uncertainty, he suggested, might well be preferable to confirming that Keppitipola did indeed possess the true Relic. The advice was shrewd, and Brownrigg accepted it, albeit a little grudgingly.

Brownrigg badly needed still more troops to fill his depleted ranks and so enable him to invade Matale and Dumbara. He had raised some independent companies of Malays and Moormen and again embodied the Burgher militia, so freeing the few troops left around the coast for service up-country. But trained regular soldiers were wanted for work in the jungle. As long ago as April he had asked the Governor General at Calcutta, the Marquis of Hastings (he is better known as the able and experienced soldier, Lord Moira) for a battalion of British infantry, three Indian units and a proportion of gunners to be held ready to reinforce him at short notice should the need arise. The following month, Brownrigg petitioned Governor Elliott at Madras to let him have these troops without further delay, but the latter refused, pleading that he had already sent everything he could spare to Ceylon. Although Hastings was finding it difficult to raise the necessary men to put the finishing touches to the subjugation of the Mahrattas, as soon as he heard of Elliott's refusal, he ordered the 89th Regiment, a battalion of the Bengal Native Infantry, and a company of Indian Artillery (the quaintly named Golundauze) to be made ready to sail from Calcutta. It was a wise and generous gesture, and when the news reached him, Elliott relented and put the 86th Foot under orders for the island. Some delay occurred in arranging the embarkation, and it turned out that the first of these units did not arrive in Ceylon until September, by which time things had so improved that Brownrigg was already considering returning a part of his Indian loan.

III

The enthusiasm aroused by the coronation and the display of the Relic encouraged Keppitipola to a rash venture into the Four Korales. The foray ended in disaster and destroyed any remaining hopes of a Kandyan victory. Crossing the Mahaveli Ganga on 16 July, the force of 2,000 Kandyans was straightway put to flight by a small detachment of the 83rd and fled back over the river. The next day the insurgents crossed once again, but in pursuit of them was a column of British troops, one hundred and fifty strong. Following Keppitipola's men for ten days and moving through the jungle as quickly, if not more so, than their quarry, the column at last succeeded in ambushing the Kandyan advanced guard and killing ten insurgents. This was enough. Once again the Kandyans fled, and by the twenty-third of the month they were back across the river once more. Their leader, with a few men, moved in the opposite direction, travelling through the Seven Korales and seeking refuge in Matale. Again Keppitipola had neglected to make use of the advantages provided by his environment and had indulged in an ill-considered and hopeless enterprise. It had been particularly significant that the people of the Four Korales, far from helping their countrymen, had provided the British with intelligence on the whereabouts of Keppitipola's men.

This defeat virtually ended the resistance in Uva. For two months past a steady flow of chiefs and headmen had been bringing bands of their armed followers in to surrender. Keppitipola's defeat quickened the rate, and on 21 August Brownrigg, to speed it still further, offered a pardon to all who submitted within the month. The proclamation recapitulated the state of the country:

'The people of Ouva and Wellassy in which the Rebellion commenced, having felt the evils consequent on their folly and wickedness, have repented, and with very few exceptions implored forgiveness from Government. The People of Weyeloowa are doing the same, the few of the Province of Saffragam, who dared to stir up Rebellion in that loyal Country, are dismayed and wish to submit; excepting a few evil-minded Persons, the People of the 7 Corles are all attached to the Government of the King of England, from which they derive benefit; the loyal and distinguished Chiefs and People of Oodanoora, Yatte-noora, the 4, and 3 Corles, have remained faithful—such being the case, the Governor is also informed that the greater number of the Kandyan People in other Districts, having learnt by experience, that resistance is useless, and only produces ruin to themselves, are desirous to return to obedience, but are prevented by the influence and threats

261

of those Rebel Chiefs, who are conscious they themselves cannot expect Pardon, and therefore tell the People that they also will not be forgiven.'[16]

The Proclamation went on to warn the insurgents that reinforcements were on their way from India, and that, once they had arrived, no forgiveness could be expected; anyone who surrendered straight away with their 'Fire Arms, Gun Powder, Balls and Sulpher'[17] could expect a pardon.

There was no mention of either Matale or Dumbara in the Proclamation. The insurgents had held these two northern provinces since March. Now Brownrigg waited for the expiration of his period of grace before tackling them. The more important target of the two was Matale, to the north of which lay Anuradhapura, the still venerated capital of the ancient kings of Sinhala.

The operations against Matale were planned as a three-pronged advance, directed from Kandy, the Seven Korales and from Trincomalee, every soldier who could be spared from the garrisons being swept together for this final effort. On 22 September, the day following the expiration of Brownrigg's period of grace, two divisions of troops, each some two hundred strong, left Kandy and started to advance towards Nalanda, one by way of the Balakaduwa and one by the Atgalle Pass. On the same day, two other divisions, commanded by Lt-Col Hook, entered Matale from the south-east. In the unaccountable manner of the campaign, each division was made up of small detachments of men from as many as half a dozen different regiments. The lightest of equipment was carried, packs being left behind; each man brought in his haversack only a clean shirt and a pair of woollen trousers, together with a spare pair of shoes in the case of the Europeans, and a 'cumblie' (the locally-made blanket) strapped on top.

Matale, as yet, was hardly touched by the war. To the invading troops the border districts seemed lusher and even more lovely than the Seven Korales. This was soon remedied. Even though the Kandyans were doing everything possible to surrender and hand over their weapons to the advancing columns as quickly as they could, any village found deserted was looted and burned. So little resistance was encountered that the invasion devolved into a punitive march. The sole battle casualty was a Kandyan who was wounded when surprised carrying a gingal. Pilima Talauva, who had headed the resistance in Matale, fled from his base in the ancient rock-temple at Dambulla, as Hook's columns approached the shrine on 25 September. He took refuge in Anuradhapura, but five days later a British patrol entered the old city, after making a final spurt in which thirty-four miles were covered in twenty-four hours in an attempt to surprise the enemy leader. Pilima Talauva just escaped, begging his people not to accompany him as his only hope of safety was to travel alone. Nevertheless he still retained a retinue large enough to shoulder his palanquin.[18] Major Jonathan Forbes, who probably knew him, described him as a weak and indolent man with none of the ability and energy of his redoubtable father.[19] The Kandyans were not fortunate in their leaders; they had little of the physical fortitude needed in guerrilla fighters. Keppitipola was noteworthy among them for travelling on foot and wearing only a single cotton cloth around his loins.

At the end of a nearly bloodless campaign, resistance in Matale had been brought to an end. In a similar advance into Dumbara, which was supported by a rapacious horde of Sabaragamuva Kandyans, led by the loyalist Eknelligoda, the British overran the final refuge of Kandyan resistance. The war was all but over.

As always, dissensions between their leaders had contributed towards the Kandyan defeat. The discord in Kandy between Molligoda and Ehelepola was mirrored by the clash between Pilima Talauva and Keppitipola in the field. In September this came to a head. Madugalle had joined the revolt in its early days, soon after his release from prison, and had become the focal point for resistance in his native province of Dumbara. In August, he persuaded Keppitipola, who had found his way back from Matale into Uva, to cross the Mahaveli Ganga into Dumbara, bringing with him the man whom he had appointed king. The tale goes that Madugalle, or it may have been Pilima Talauva, then discovered that the king was not Doresamy, the royal Malabar, but a Sinhalese *bhikkhu* named Vilbava, a native of the Seven Korales. Whereupon Pilima Talauva sent instructions from

Matale to Madugalle to arrest both Vilbava and his sponsor Keppitipola. Madugalle complied and then exposed both men to public ridicule in the stocks.[20] But it is hard to believe that the two Kandyan leaders were ignorant of the true identity of the so-called king. As far back as February, Brownrigg had discovered that the real Doresamy was living quietly under police supervision in Madras, and the Governor already suspected that the stranger was a Sinhalese. His suspicions were soon confirmed, and he spread the news by means of a public proclamation that a priest, not a Malabar, was playing the part of the king. It is more likely that Vilbava's arrest was provoked by Pilima Talauva's ambition rather than his indignation, because no sooner had the deed been done than he produced a Tamil of his own as a candidate for the throne.

Some sort of uneasy peace was patched up between the three main Kandyan leaders, because Keppitipola was soon released and Vilbava was either set free or escaped, to seek refuge among the Veddas of Vellassa and disappear from public view for twelve years. Madugalle and Keppitipola fled westwards when the British overran Dumbara and somehow made contact with Pilima Talauva. But none of them were to remain at liberty for much longer. During the night of 29 October, news of their whereabouts was brought to Captain Fraser, who was searching the country to the south of Anuradhapura for them. At 4 am the next morning, a party of thirty men led by an ensign of the 83rd Foot was despatched in pursuit. After a march of fourteen miles through pouring rain, an armed Kandyan was captured who immediately agreed to show the soldiers the hiding place of his leaders. In a nearby hut they found Pilima Talauva, lying lame and sick on a cot, together with Keppitipola, who seized the hand of the British ensign, repeating his name as he did so. For some time past both men had been making their separate overtures to the British and they were now only too ready to surrender.

Madugalle, who had been with the other two, managed to escape in the confusion with a number of his men, but three days later he was taken, after being betrayed by the local villagers, who not only revealed his whereabouts to the British but helped to capture him as well. That same evening the soldiers caught a *bhikkhu* lurking among some trees. Inside a bundle of clothing he was carrying they found the Relic of the Tooth in its jewelled container. This was the final blow to Kandyan resistance. The people, already crushed into submission, saw in the loss of the Tooth a divine demonstration that the British were destined to rule them. In two thousand years, it was the first time their Relic had passed from their possession.[21] Afterwards Molligoda observed that 'whatever the English might think of the consequence of having taken Keppitipola, Pilimé Talawé, and Madugallé, in his opinion, and in the opinion of the people in general, the taking of the relic was of infinitely more moment'.[22]

IV

During the course of the insurrection, forty-seven captured insurgents had been sentenced by courts martial to capital punishment. Of these, twenty-eight had been executed and the balance either reprieved or pardoned. Now it was the turn of the three great rebel leaders to be tried, and all, in November, were sentenced to death. Brownrigg reprieved Pilima Talauva but deported him to Mauritius, together with twenty-four of his fellow chiefs. Some faced sentences of five years' banishment; others were exiled for life; all were permitted a considerable degree of freedom and lived in some comfort, dining each month with the Governor, where they earned a reputation for good humour and conviviality.[23] Exile from his native hills was a harsh fate for a Kandyan but their treatment might well have been worse.

Neither Keppitipola nor Madugalle was reprieved. Before the outbreak of the revolt, Dr Marshall had attended the former professionally, and he saw him again in gaol several times after his conviction.[24] The Kandyan admitted to Marshall that his mistake had been not to surrender before Brownrigg's pardon expired on 20 September, and he asked the Doctor to use his influence to try to get his sentence commuted. 'Although life was full of trouble,' he confided to Marshall, 'existence was still desirable.' Keppitipola attributed his misfortunes to delinquencies dating from a former existence. Buddhism, the cynical Scot mused, was a belief which is able to repudiate responsibility for offences committed in this life.

On the morning of 26 November, the two condemned men were taken to the Dalada Mandapa to perform their last devotions. Madugalle, a man who had shown great bravery during the insurrection, lost his nerve towards the end and dived into the shrine room, claiming sanctuary, but was dragged out again. The undignified scene shocked his fellow Kandyan, who was himself behaving with the firmness and self-possession expected from a member of his class. To Sawers, who was present, he criticized Madugalle's behaviour as being the action of a fool.

The two chiefs were then taken to the Bogambara Lake, where Keppitipola's sister, the wife of Ehelepola, had died four years before. After performing the final rites of his faith and making his formal ablutions, Keppitipola tied his long hair in a knot on the top of his head and sat down upon the ground, grasping a small bush between his toes. As he began to repeat some Pali verses, the executioner swung his sword into the back of his neck. Two blows were needed to kill him. Madugalle died less bravely; an executioner was needed to hold his head steady to receive the sword cut.

Marshall roundly condemned the barbarity of the occasion, but intent on the pursuit of scientific knowledge, he made off with the two severed heads. In due course, he presented Keppitipola's skull to the museum of the Phrenological Society of Edinburgh, by which accident it was preserved for posterity. After Ceylon gained her independence, it was returned to its native land, and now rests on the Esplanade at Kandy underneath a rather paltry memorial. A further monument to the man who is now honoured as one of Lanka's national heroes stands on the road running from Nuwara Eliya to Badulla. Keppitipola, in his costume of ceremony, stands with his back to the ravaged hills among which he fought, caught in the action of drawing his sword to repel the invaders approaching from the plains below.

By the turn of the year the more wealthy of the Kandyan provinces were already starting to recover from the effects of the war,[25] as they had done equally quickly from the even greater damage they had suffered ten years before. It was different in the mountains of Uva where the soil was thinner and the warfare had been more savage. For two seasons no crops had been planted; the cattle were either slaughtered or stolen; and the fruit trees had been destroyed. Soon an epidemic of smallpox, arriving from India and spreading up from the coast, attacked what Brownrigg described as 'the miserable remains of the population',[26] now dragging themselves from their hiding places in the hills and jungles to try somehow to sow a few wretched patches of kurakkan. Dr Davy, in March and April of 1819, on a solitary tour of Uva and its neighbourhood, journeyed through an empty countryside in which he saw only a few starving souls. 'Its cottages in ruins,' he wrote, 'its cattle destroyed, and its population fled,—all effects of the rebellion, of which this province was the principal theatre. Had the country never been inhabited, its desert appearance would be little thought of. . . .' Instead there were associations of every kind of human misery that war and famine can inflict.[27] Returning to Colombo by the less ravaged north-west, he found the country around the Girihagama Pass merely a wreck of what it had once been.[28] Matale, on the other hand, looked untouched.[29]

Seventy-five years later, the effects of the war were still felt in Uva. A civil servant of many years residence in the province wrote:

'This kind of warfare finds no place in military history, properly speaking, but it left indelible marks on the face of the country, for it was partly owing to the stern methods of repression, that Uva has been, considering the character of its soil, its climate and its people, the most backward, the most stagnant of any portion of Ceylon.'[30]

The troops had suffered also. Only forty-four officers and men had been killed by Kandyan bullets and arrows, but one in five of the Europeans in the island died from disease during 1818. And among the survivors, the germs of disease had taken root which were to kill most of them during the next two or three years. Nineteen officers of the 73rd Highlanders died during or shortly after the campaign; only twelve soldiers of their Light

Company survived to return to Scotland in 1821. Losses among the Indian and Ceylonese regiments can only be guessed as their casualty returns cannot be traced.

Many of the officers and men who died from fever, dysentery and the dropsy contracted in the jungles of Ceylon were veterans of the European War. The 2nd Battalion of the 73rd Foot, which had shared in the victory at Waterloo, was disbanded at the end of the War and the men who did not choose to take their discharge were posted to their sister battalion in Ceylon. They arrived at the start of the insurrection and most must have perished. Captain James McGlashan of the 19th Foot, who died at the end of 1818, after marching from Trincomalee to Kandy, had survived not only Waterloo, but the bloody battles of Busaco and Albuera as well. His brother officer, Ajax Anderson, may have been thinking of him when he wrote:

> 'The meed of the distinguished few
> Who nobly bled at Waterloo!
> But heav'n the hapless youth denied
> This guerdon of a warrior's pride,
> And on this unfrequented spot,
> He died unhonour'd and forgot,'[31]

It is usually forgotten that the soldiers' wives died as well as their husbands. No one counted their deaths. Medical statistics, the new science of the army surgeons, was not yet used to analyse the chances of survival of the camp-followers. Sometimes children survived both parents. The result was that:

'. . . the number of European fatherless children was so great to excite general sympathy, and induce the benevolent Lady Brownrigg to prevail on an elderly medical officer to transfer to the local Government his right of property in a house and grounds at Colpetty to be converted into an Asylum for these poor orphans, on condition that a small Government annuity should be paid him for his life, which has long since ceased.'[32]

Later the civil Government tried to sell the house and remove these orphans' successors elsewhere, but it is pleasant to relate that their plans failed on a legal technicality.

V

On 25 November, Brownrigg, at long last, could return to Colombo. His short tour of inspection of the hills had been prolonged into an absence of eighteen months. He was a fortunate man. Defeat had been close; like Waterloo, it had been 'a close-run thing'. But the bed-ridden old soldier had again given proof of his determination and acumen. When he invaded Kandy, he acted against the judgement of his colleagues on the Council; rumour had it that they all opposed the venture. Then, in adversity, the pressure had been strong to withdraw from the newly acquired territory and leave the insurgents in possession. Too many of his subordinates remembered their history too well and anticipated disaster. Support from home was not to be expected. Even as he drove into Colombo, a despatch was on its way, castigating him for not having yet restored tranquillity, and emphasizing that he should withdraw if he could not beat the insurgents quickly or if there appeared to be a widespread desire among the Kandyans to revert to their old system of government.[33] Faced with the problems of the post-war recession and the need to cut spending, Lord Liverpool's Cabinet was not prepared to risk becoming involved in a long-drawn-out military adventure, the moral issues of which were so shaky.

It says much for Brownrigg's self-confidence that throughout the year he had been engaged in planning a new system for governing Kandy which would break the power of the chiefs and bring the interior under the direct control of the Government. In this he had been helped by George Lusignan, now Secretary for the Kandyan Provinces, who had justified Maitland's faith in his capacity by once again climbing to senior rank in the service. Because of the disloyalty shown by the chiefs, Brownrigg considered himself justified in putting aside the provisions of the 1815 Convention, and he issued, on the day he left Kandy, a Proclamation setting out in fifty-nine sections his newly-formed plans for ruling the Kandyan provinces.

In each province a Government Agent was to assume powers of direct rule, similar to those exercised by the Collectors in the coastal districts. To these Government Agents and to the Board of Commissioners in Kandy, the chiefs were, in future, to be in every way subordinate, and they were to exercise no powers except those which they derived from the Government. Their traditional fees were abolished, and they became, in effect, salaried officials, subject to dismissal either by the Board of Commissioners or by the Governor, according to their rank. In the administration of justice they were relegated to a minor role. Except for bridge- and road-making, *rajakariya* was abolished, and taxation was at the same time simplified, the new basic levy being a tithe on agricultural produce.

Kandy and the Maritime Provinces, in short, were to be ruled alike. The powers of the chiefs were reduced, in theory at least, to those of petty civil servants. Nevertheless, their influence remained considerable, their social importance was little changed, the outward trappings of their ceremonial remained as it was before, and in the absence of a European official their word could still be law. For all that, the ancient social structure of the country, so well suited to its people, had been undermined. D'Oyly understood the implications and probable results of the measures. For months he and his fellow commissioners argued with Brownrigg on the details of the scheme. But it is likely that he realized, from his profound knowledge of Kandy and its people, that it would be many years before the changes—radical though they were—would make much difference to the daily life of the cultivator in his village.

In the meantime, Ceylon was once more a single country—one of Britain's smaller and less-considered colonies. As such she was to remain for rather more than a hundred years. In terms of the nation's long history it was but a short interval to the Sri Lanka of today.

EPILOGUE

Sri Wikrama lived out a comfortable exile at Vellore in Madras until 1832, when he succumbed to a dropsy at the age of fifty-two. He left an only son, who had been born in captivity to his youngest wife, but the young man outlived his father by only eleven years.

On Sri Wikrama's death the surviving Kandyan leaders still exiled in Mauritius were allowed to return to Ceylon on condition that they lived in the coastal provinces and never returned to their home provinces.[1] The ineffective Pilima Talauva was not among them; he had died, it was said, from the effects of alcohol.[2] Ehelepola too perished in the Isle of France. The British were not prepared to risk trusting him, and they never dared to allow him to return home. Until 1825, he had been held under comfortable restraint in Colombo, but he was then banished, in the company of his servants and relations, to join his compatriots in exile. He died four years later, little more than fifty years of age, but seemingly a mild and listless, white-haired old gentleman. He had outlived his bitter enemy, Molligoda, by six years.

The capture in 1830 of the harmless pretender Vilbava, who had been living for twelve years as a fugitive among the Veddas, proved to be something of an embarrassment to the Government. He was brought to trial and convicted on a charge of high treason, but the irregularities of the proceedings were such that he was granted a free pardon, a conclusion which was by no means unwelcome to the authorities, for reasons both of equity and expedience. The poor man had been no more than a tool of the

271

chiefs, and there were no advantages to be gained from punishing him after such a lapse of time.

Brownrigg was allowed to retire two years after the insurrection ended, and he provided proof of the toughness of his constitution by surviving in retirement in Monmouthshire until 1833, despite the illnesses from which he had suffered in Ceylon.

North also enjoyed his last years. Surviving his two elder and more robust brothers, he succeeded to the family title as the fifth Earl of Guilford, and spent much of his time re-visiting familiar places on the continent of Europe until he became Chancellor of the newly founded Ionian University in Corfu. In this role he was able to fulfil himself, devoting his life and his fortune to his beloved Hellenes. With his usual enthusiasm he dressed not only his students but himself as well in classical robes, his bizarre appearance in flowing purple drapery and a gold fillet encircling his bald pate serving to make him an object of condescending ridicule to his austere fellow-countrymen.[3] He left Greece when his University failed in 1827, and died in England the same year.

In his Mediterranean retreat, Guilford once again encountered Thomas Maitland. Like his two fellow Governors, the latter's health had improved when he escaped from the tropics, and by 1813 he was fit enough to take up the appointment of Governor of Malta. Two years later he gained promotion as Lord High Commissioner of the Ionian Islands, where he did little to support, and something to hinder, the Chancellor's ambitions for his University. In both these last two appointments, Maitland added to his reputation: he was undoubtedly one of the most capable pro-consuls of his time. In 1824, he died in Malta of an apoplexy. Famed for the quality of his table, Maitland was to the last a notorious glutton.

Of the major protagonists, only John D'Oyly died in Ceylon. In 1821 he had been created a baronet in tardy recognition of his services, and three years later he had worked himself to death. He had served in Ceylon for twenty-two years. During this time he never visited England, and he never married. His mother's letters, in which she urges him to come home and enjoy the comfortable pension he had earned, are poignant, both in their sadness and their lack of any understanding of the motives that drove him to kill himself in exile for what he judged to be the good of his adopted people.[4] On his death he was found to be paying monthly bounties to 115 indigent Ceylonese, among them the natural son of Major Adam Davie.[5] D'Oyly was buried at Kandy in the Old Garrison Cemetery, just behind the Palace in a spot across which Sri Wikrama's soldiers had surged forward to attack Davie's soldiers. The broken fluted masonry column that marks D'Oyly's grave has now all but disappeared under the secondary jungle which, in tropical fashion, has engulfed the small burial ground.

When Dr Henry Marshall retired in 1832 with the rank of Deputy-Inspector-General of Hospitals, he became famous as an advocate of the cause of army reforms to improve the wretched lot of the soldier, producing a stream of articles and books on medical, sociological and military matters, all marked with the imprint of his inquiring and liberal mind.[6] Of the two soldiers who, between them, contributed so much to our information about the life of the serving man in Ceylon, Alexander Alexander, after taking his discharge from the Royal Artillery, enlisted as a mercenary to fight with the British forces aiding the South American liberation movement, where he found himself as unpopular with his officers and his comrades as he had been in Ceylon. Calladine retired from the army with the rank of Colour-Sergeant in the year of Queen Victoria's accession to the throne, having survived a further overseas tour with his Regiment in the West Indies. After a respectable career as master of a workhouse and a poor-rate collector, he died at Derby in 1876 in his eighty-fourth year.

Calladine's regiment, the 19th Foot, sailed for England in January 1820 after a term of twenty-four years in the island, unusually long even by the standards of the time. They left behind them fifty of their officers and 1,500 soldiers in their graves;[7] there were only two men still with the unit who had landed in Ceylon in 1796. Most of the casualties were caused by disease, not battle. But they must have learned something from their militarily unorthodox experiences for no less than five of their officers later reached the rank of lieutenant-general or higher.

T

Calladine's description of their leave-taking reflects a certain attitude of mind:

'. . . we had such a number of black women coming alongside, who were left behind, some with three and four children, and although they were only blacks, still I conceive that they felt as keen a sorrow as if they had been white. I suppose the 19th Regiment left more children than any regiment leaving the country before, as it was so long in the island, between twenty-four and twenty-five years. Some of them were grown up and the girls were married, while boys who had been brought up at the Government School at Colombo were filling respectable places as clerks, or otherwise had entered the army.'[8]

It is not surprising that 220 men decided to transfer to other regiments in the island, thus forfeiting their chances of seeing England or Ireland again.

In due course other regiments took the place of the 19th and the 73rd, but they never had anything really serious to do. Ceylon was spared any further insurrections of any consequence against British rule. During the early 1820s there were one or two minor outbreaks of violence in the highlands; there was a bloodless travesty of a revolt in 1834; and fourteen years later a rather more serious, but nevertheless feeble disturbance erupted in Matale and the Seven Korales. Otherwise Ceylon was free of bloodshed until the communal rioting between Tamils and Sinhalese swept through the country in 1958, which was followed by the tragic insurrection of young people in 1971. Few countries, other than the smaller nations of Europe and those protected by a powerful empire, have been fortunate enough to enjoy a span of nearly a century and a half free from communal strife or the consequences of external wars.

This freedom from strife is an item that can well be entered on the credit side of the colonial balance sheet. The tally of such items is trite, but bears repeating: a measure of impartial justice; the material progress that brings a fifty-fold surge in population in 150 years; access for a few lucky ones to the science, art and philosophy of the western world. But, above all, the removal of the ever-present threat of violence gave men peace of mind; colonial subjection allowed them to live a normal span, to have their children, and to see them grow to adulthood in a world perhaps a fraction less hostile than that into which their parents had been born. Certainly colonialism could rob a people of its dignity, and the harm perpetrated to the culture, religion and way of life of the subject race was often irreparable, as was the damage done to the character of many of those who administered the system and benefited from it. But we are far too close to the end of the British occupation of Ceylon to try to strike a balance between the evil and the good which stemmed from it. Another century must pass before the problem can be viewed in impartial perspective. Perhaps by then the scale of world events will have reduced it to a forgotten irrelevance?

Senkadagala Nuvara (Kandy) in 1803

Tuesday (March) 22nd, 1803.

This morning I rode into Candy and the following is my idea of the town.

It is situated in a bason and surrounded by steep hills on every side. The entrance to it from the road is through a rude attempt at a barrier gate, to which you ascend by a number of steps; and advancing a few hundred yards, you come to another of the same kind; you may then be said to be at the entrance of the town, which consists of one broad street, about two miles in length, from the second barrier to the palace, which is at the upper end, but in an open space, a little to the left of the street. From the main street a number of smaller ones branch off in various directions. The houses, or rather huts, are all raised ten or twelve feet from the level of the streets, and have flights of steps leading up to them, they are built of mud and thatched; a few only, belonging to the headmen, are tiled and white-washed. Near the upper end of the street is a square choultry, supported by square wooden pillars most curiously carved and painted. There are also two large pagodas or temples, which are named the east and west temples, but I had not an opportunity of examining them.

The palace is a building of immense extent, though a good deal damaged by fire. It forms three sides of a square, and has a square enclosure in the centre, containing the tombs of the Rajahs, as I imagine; they are immense circular piles of brick and chunam, rising gradually to a point, something like the dome of a church; there were a number of very small buildings close to them, just big enough to contain a man, the walls of which were filled with figures of men and animals, the size of life, but most grotesquely painted. The first thing that attracts your attention on your entrance to the palace through the principal gate (for there are three or four) is an open hall supported by square stone pillars curiously carved; between the intervals of which are placed wooden spikes, about three feet high on which elephant's teeth were stuck on state occasions; through this hall you pass to the temple that contains a number of images of Buddha, all in a sitting posture, as large as life; some of white marble, neatly gilt, and others of brass. Upstairs, directly over this, is the throne, which is covered with thin brass plates, and set round with stones; the walls are covered with fine pier glasses; it is situated in a room without windows, and to come at it you are obliged to pass through two others, the doors of which are covered with brass and ivory; in short it appears merely calculated to make a very dazzling appearance at night, which is the only time the King ever gives audience to anyone.

The walls of the temple and the anti-chambers to the throne, are profusely covered with inscriptions and paintings. This appears to be the most ancient part of the palace, for it has evidently been built at very different periods of time.

In some rooms were immense quantities of bows, darts, spears, arrows, etc. beautifully painted; in others immense brass lamps of all kinds of fanciful shapes, such as men, elephants, birds, etc., one room was full of glassware in cases, and appeared never to have been opened since they were received from the Dutch: another room was hung round with Dutch paintings and mirrors, and the ceiling hung with lustres, globe lamps, etc.

Many brass guns were found, two or three pounders, the carriages of which were most curiously ornamented, and a number of ginjalls commonly called grass-hoppers; these were small iron guns carrying a ball of six to ten ounces, and mounted on three wooden legs, exactly like a common stool; these they carry from one bush to another with great celerity as occasion requires.

I saw a few of those whips that make such an uncommon noise and which they crack always before the King or Adikar, whenever they stir out. They are made of fibres of the aloe stained of various colours, the thong is near two yards and an half long, tapering gradually to a point from the handle, where it is the thickness of your wrist. The handle is about a cubit in length and made of the same material. The walls of many of the buildings attached to the palace were covered with grotesque paintings of giants, elephants, etc.

It would be an endless task to describe all the various apartments of the palace, which is, taken altogether, a mean-looking irregular building; suffice it to say that the King had removed everything valuable some time before our arrival.

The only living animals that I saw in the palace were five white deer.

Source: Thomas Ajax Anderson: *Poems Written Chiefly in India.*

Corporal Barnsley's Deposition

Made 27 June, 1803, before Captain Madge and Captain Pierce, of the 19th Regiment, and Assistant-Surgeon Gillespie, of the Malay Regiment.

'That on the 23rd June, a little before daylight, the Candians commenced an attack on the hill guard, in rear of the palace, on which was a 3-pounder, and took it. That soon after a strong body of the enemy, headed by a Malay chief, made a charge on the eastern barrier, to endeavour to take a gun which was there; they were opposed by Lieutenant Blakeney, at the head of a few men of the 19th, who himself fell in the conflict. That an incessant fire was kept up until two o'clock in the day, when, as the enemy was endeavouring to break in at the rear of the palace, Major Davie hung out a flag of truce, offering to surrender the town, on being permitted to march out with his arms. This they consented to; and Major Davie, after spiking the guns, marched out about five o'clock, and proceeded to Wattapologo, where he was obliged to halt all night, being unable to pass the river. Next morning the Candians sent out four Modiliars to propose, that if Major Davie would give up Boodoo Sawmy (the King whom Governor North placed on the throne of Candy, and who retreated with our troops), they would assist him with boats and rafts to cross the river; on which Major Davie gave him up by his own consent. After which another message was sent, that there were plenty of bamboos and other materials at hand, and they might make rafts for themselves. All that day was employed in endeavouring to make rafts, but they could not succeed in getting a rope across the river, owing to the depth and rapidity of the current; but next day, about ten o'clock, Captain Humphreys, of the Bengal artillery, came and reported that he had succeeded in getting a rope across. About this time some of the Malays and gun Lascars began to desert in small parties; upon which Major Davie ordered the remainder to ground their arms and follow him, with all the officers, back to the garrison. As soon as they had proceeded two hundred yards on their way thither, the Candians stopped them, took the officers on one side, and kept them prisoners for half an hour; when this declarent says, he heard shot in the direction of the place where the officers were prisoners, and which was followed by their massacre. That immediately after, they took the European soldiers two by two, and leading them a few yards along the road, knocked them down with the butt end of their pieces, and beat out their brains. That this declarent was also led out with his comrade, and received a blow under the right ear, and a wound on the back of his neck, which the enemy conceiving to be sufficient, then proceeded to the murder of the remainder. That he lay as dead for some time, and in that situation distinctly heard the firing, which he supposes to be the putting them all to death. That he took the opportunity, while this was doing, of crawling into the jungle,* where he lay till night, and then proceeded to Fort Macdowal to give the information to Captain Madge.

(Signed)

'GEORGE X BARNSLEY,
'Corporal, 19th Regiment.'

Source: Arthur Johnston: *Narrative of an Expedition to Candy in the year 1804.*

* Forest

Proclamation by General Brownrigg, 1815

Proclamation by His Excellency Lieutenant-General ROBERT BROWNRIGG, Governor and Commander-in-Chief in and over the British Settlements and Territories in the Island of Ceylon, with the Dependencies thereof.

In Council

His Excellency the Governor and Commander-in-Chief of the British Settlements in the Island of Ceylon could not hear with indifference the prayers of the inhabitants of five extensive provinces, constituting more than one-half of the Kandyan Kingdom, who, with one unanimous voice raised against the tyranny and oppression of their ruler, taking up arms in defence of their lives, or flying from his power, implored the protection of the British government, while the most convincing circumstances indicated corresponding sentiments, from the same causes, in other provinces less within the reach of direct communication. Neither could his Excellency contemplate, without the liveliest emotions of indignation and resentment, the atrocious barbarity recently perpetrated in Kandy upon ten innocent subjects of the British government—seven of whom instantly died of their sufferings, and three miserable victims were sent, in defiance, with their mutilated limbs, across the limits, to relate the distressing tale, and exhibit the horrid spectacle to the eyes of an insulted government, and an indignant people in the capital of the British settlements.

In the perpetrator of these acts, His Excellency convincingly recognizes the true author of that implacable animosity which has constantly been opposed to every approach of friendly intercourse, so often attempted on the part of His Majesty's government.

No shadow of doubt now remains that the rejection of all relations of amity originated and continues with the king alone, and that the people are not otherwise parties to such a policy, than as they are compelled to become so by a coercion alike hostile to the British interests, and intolerable to themselves.

To him and his advisers is imputable the impossibility, proved by

281

repeated trials, of terminating, by any just or defined conditions, a state of relations unsettled and precarious beyond all precedent—which bears no essential character of a peace, nor has any title to that appellation—which yields no solid tranquillity or safe intercourse, but perpetuates the alarms of war without its remedies—and which, to continue any longer, after a public unequivocal act of hostility, would be to sanction injury and encourage insult.

By the irresistible influence of these feelings and considerations, His Excellency had become convinced of the unavoidable necessity of resolving to carry his Majesty's arms into the Kandyan country. In this, however, he has been anticipated by the irruption of an armed Kandyan force into the British territory; who, having pursued the fugitive inhabitants across the boundary river of Sitawaka, fired upon them from the opposite bank, and finally, crossing that river in arms into the Hewagam Korle, proceeded to commit depredations on His Majesty's subjects.

This measure, therefore, supersedes every deliberative consideration, and leaves no choice but that of repelling the hostile forces from the British frontier.

But it is not against the Kandyan nation that the arms of His Majesty are directed; His Excellency proclaims hostility against that tyrannical power alone, which has provoked, by aggravated outrages and indignities, the just resentment of the British nation, which has cut off the most ancient and noble families in his kingdom, deluged the land with the blood of subjects, and by the violation of every religious and moral law, become an object of abhorrence to mankind.

For securing the permanent tranquillity of these settlements, and in vindication of the honour of the British name; for the deliverance of the Kandyan people from their oppressions; in fine, for the subversion of that Malabar dominion, which, during three generations, has tryannized over the country, His Excellency has resolved to employ the powerful resources placed at his disposal.

His Excellency hereby proffers to every individual of the Kandyan nation the benign protection of the British government; exhorts them to remain without fear in their dwellings, to regard the armed forces who pass through their villages as protectors and friends, and to co-operate with them for the accomplishment of these beneficial objects.

In their march through the country, the most rigorous discipline will be observed by the British troops; the peaceable inhabitants will be protected from all injury in their person and property, and payment will scupulously be made for every article of provisions which they furnish. Their religion shall be sacred, and their temples respected. The power of His Majesty's arms will be exerted only against those who, deserting the cause of their country, oppose the progress of His Majesty's troops, and of their own countrymen united in arms—for their deliverance.

Source: Henry Marshall: *Ceylon.*

The 1815 Convention

At a Convention, held on 2nd day of March, in the year of Christ 1815, and the Singalese year 1736, at the Palace in the City of Kandy, between His Excellency Lieutenant-General Robert Brownrigg, Governor and Commander-in-Chief in and over the British Settlements and Territories in the Island of Ceylon, acting in the name and on behalf of His Majesty George the Third, King, and His Royal Highness George Prince of Wales, Regent of the United Kingdom of Great Britain and Ireland, on the one part, and the Adikars, Dissaves, and other principal chiefs of the Kandyan provinces, on behalf of the inhabitants, and in presence of the Mohottales, Coraals, Vidaans, and other subordinate head men from the several provinces, and of the people then and there assembled, on the other part, it is agreed and established as follows:

1st. That the cruelties and oppressions of the Malabar ruler, in the arbitrary and unjust infliction of bodily tortures, and the pains of death, without trial and sometimes without an accusation or the possibility of a crime, and in the general contempt and contravention of all civil rights, have become flagrant, enormous, and intolerable; the acts and maxims of His Government being equally and entirely devoid of that justice which should secure the safety of his subjects, and of that good faith which might obtain a beneficial intercourse with the neighbouring settlements.

2nd. That the Rajah Sri Wickreme Rajah Sinha, by the habitual violation of the chief and most sacred duties of a sovereign, has forfeited all claims to the title, or the powers annexed to the same, and is declared fallen and deposed from the office of king; his family and relatives, whether in the ascending, descending, or collateral line, and whether by affinity or blood, are also for ever excluded from the throne; and all claim and title of the Malabar race to the dominion of the Kandyan provinces is abolished and extinguished.

3rd. That all male persons being, or pretending to be, relations of the late Rajah Sri Wickreme Rajah Sinha, either by affinity or blood, and whether in the ascending, descending or collateral line, are hereby declared enemies to the government of the Kandyan provinces, and excluded and prohibited from entering those provinces, on any pretence whatever, without a written permission for the purpose, by the authority of the British government, under the pains and penalties of martial law, which is hereby declared to be in force for that purpose; and all male persons of the Malabar caste, now expelled from the said provinces, are, under the same penalties, prohibited from returning, except with the permission before mentioned.

4th. The dominion of the Kandyan provinces is vested in the sovereign of the British empire, and to be exercised through the Governors or Lieutenant-Governors of Ceylon for the time being, and their accredited agents, saving to the Adikars, Dissaves, Mohottales, Coralls, Vidaans, and all other chief and subordinate native head men, lawfully appointed by authority of the British government; the rights, privileges, and powers of their respective offices, and to all classes of the people the safety of their persons and property, with their civil rights and immunities, according to the laws, institutions, and customs established and in force amongst them.

5th. The religion of Boodhoo, professed by the chiefs and inhabitants of these provinces, is declared inviolable; and its rights, ministers, and places of worship, are to be maintained and protected.

6th. Every species of bodily torture, and all mutilation of limb, member, or organ, are prohibited and abolished.

7th. No sentence of death can be carried into execution against any inhabitant, except by the written warrant of the British Governor or Lieutenant-Governor for the time being, founded on a report of the case made to him through the accredited agent or agents of the government resident in the interior, in whose presence all trials for capital offences are to take place.

8th. Subject to these conditions, the administration of civil and criminal justice and police, over the Kandyan inhabitants of the said provinces, is to be exercised according to established forms, and by the ordinary authorities, saving always the inherent right of government to redress grievances and reform abuses, in all instances whatever, particular or general, where such interposition shall become necessary.

9th. Over all other persons, civil or military, residing in or resorting to these provinces, not being Kandyans, civil and criminal justice, together with police, shall, until the pleasure or His Majesty's government in England may be otherwise declared, be administered in the manner following:

First, All persons, not being commissioned or non-commissioned military officers, soldiers, or followers of the army, usually held liable to military discipline, shall be subject to the magistracy of the accredited agent or the agents of the British government, in all cases except of murder, which shall be tried by special commissions, to be issued from time to time by the governor for that purpose. Provided always, as to such charges of murder wherein any British subject may be defendant, who might be tried for the same by the laws of United Kingdom of Great Britain and Ireland, in force for the trial of offences committed by British subjects in foreign parts no such British subject shall be tried on any charge of murder, alleged to have been perpetrated in the Kandyan provinces, otherwise than by virtue of such laws of the United Kingdom.

Second, Commissioned or non-commissioned military officers, soldiers, or followers of the army, usually held amenable to military discipline, shall, in all civil and criminal cases, wherein they may be defendants, be liable to the laws, regulations, and customs of war, reserving to the governor and commander-in-chief, in all cases falling under this ninth article, an unlimited right of review over every proceeding, civil or military, had by virtue thereof, and reserving also full power to make such particular provisions, conformable to the general spirit of the said article, as may be found necessary to carry its principle into full effect.

10th. Provided always, that the operation of the several preceding clauses shall not be contravened by the provisions of temporary or partial proclamation published during the advance of the army; which provisions, in so far as incompatible with the said preceding articles, are hereby repealed.

11th. The royal dues and revenues of the Kandyan provinces are to be managed and collected for His Majesty's use, and the support of the provincial establishment, according to lawful custom, and under the direction and superintendence of the accredited agent or agents of the British government.

12th. His Excellency the Governor will adopt provisionally and recommend to the confirmation of his Royal Highness the Prince Regent, in the name and on behalf of His Majesty, such dispositions in favour of the trade of these provinces, as may facilitate the export of their products, and improve the returns, whether in money, or in salt, cloths, or other commodities, useful and desirable to the inhabitants of the Kandyan country.

God save the King!
By His Excellency's command,
JAMES SUTHERLAND,
Dep. Secretary.

Source: Henry Marshall: *Ceylon.*

NOTES

Chapter 1

1. Ribeiro, 2.
2. *Services of Herbert Beaver*, 437.
3. *The Travels of Fa-Hsien*, 71, ed. by H. A. Giles, Routledge and Kegan Paul, 1956.
4. In Sinhala, *kanda* means mountains, and Kanda Uda Pas Rata means 'The Five Lands above the Mountain', used to describe the five districts in the vicinity of the capital which the King governed through district chiefs, rather than the *dissawas* or provincial viceroys who ruled the outlying areas. The Portuguese corrupted the Sinhala name to Candia, which the British then shortened to Kandy. The Sinhalese refer to the capital as Maha Nuvara (the Great City) or Senkadagala Maha Nuvara. The use of Kandy to describe the whole of the King's dominions, as well as the capital, became usual among the British, but was never acceptable to the Sinhalese.
5. Pliny, *The Natural History*, 2, vi, 24. John Bostock and H. T. Riley, George Bell & Sons, 1890.
6. Pieris, *Ceylon and the Portuguese*, 25. *Parangi* (from ferengi) is Sinhala for Portuguese. It is frequently said that the Portuguese were responsible for bringing venereal disease into the island. *Parangi* is also *yaws*, a disease similar in its symptoms to syphilis.
7. Ibid, 23.
8. Ibid, V.
9. De Couto, quoted in Ribeiro, 65–6.
10. Ibid, 76–7.
11. In Sinhala *balane* means look-out. The place Balane is so named because the Kandyans for centuries used it as a look-out point from which they watched for invaders approaching from the low country.
12. Pieris, *Ceylon and the Portuguese*, 217.
13. Ribeiro, 265–7.

Chapter 2

1. *Johan Jacob Sarr's Account of Ceylon, 1647–57*, J.R.A.S.C.B., 11 (39), 1889, 299.
2. Ribeiro, 379.
3. For the account of the Dutch war I have depended upon Pieris, *Ceylon and the Hollanders*; Raven Hart, *The Dutch Wars with Kandy* and *The War with the Singalese*.
4. Raven Hart, *The War with the Singalese*, 10 (privately printed ed.).
5. H. A. Colgate, *The Royal Navy and Trincomalee, c. 1750–1958*, The Ceylon Journal of Historical and Social Studies, 8 (1), 4.
6. Raven Hart, *The Pybus Embassy to Kandy*.
7. Welsh, i, 26.
8. The primary sources for the British occupation of the Maritime Provinces are C.O. 59, 56; W.O. 1, 362; Cleghorn, Chap. 28; Percival, 113–9; and Welsh, i.

Chapter 3

1. Knox, xxxiii.
2. Ibid, 168–9.
3. Ibid, 102.
4. Chapter 1, p. 9.
5. Marshall, *Ceylon*, 21.
6. Knox, 36. The writer suggests that Raja Sinha introduced some of the more brutal punishments, but this is a matter of great doubt. Knox never, in fact, set eyes on the King, despite the portrait in his book.
7. Lawrie, *Kandyan Law and Punishments*, 334–7, deals with Kandyan legal punishments and penalties.
8. *The Travels of Marco Polo*, trs. and ed. William Marsden, Longman, Hurst, Rees, Orme and Brown, 1818, 669–70. This place of pilgrimage is shared by Muslim, Christian and Hindu (as well as Buddhist). The first two see the footprint as that of Adam, while the Hindu believes that Shiva left it there.
9. Knox, 60.
10. Pybus, 79.
11. The details of the audience are from Pybus, 53–61. The royal audience chamber is hardly changed today. It is now used for Supreme Court sittings.
12. Pybus, 26.
13. Knox, 20.
14. Ibid, 45.
15. Percival, 319.
16. Marshall, *Ceylon*, 11.
17. Knox, 102.

18. Marshall, *Ceylon*, 19.
19. Knox, 103.

Chapter 4

1. W.O., 1, 362, Stuart to Dundas, 21 February, 1796.
2. Colvin R. de Silva, i, provides essential background to these negotiations. This erudite and unbiased account of the British occupation of Ceylon is, in every respect, unequalled.
3. Douglas, 158.
4. Details of this rebellion are sparse. The evidence available in 1918 was summarized in L. J. B. Turner, *The Madras Administration of Ceylon*, C.A.L.R., 4 (1), July 1918, 6–53. To this Colvin R. de Silva, i, 59 and 197–202, has added further evidence obtained from the Madras Military and Political Proceedings in the India Office Library.
5. *The Wellesley Papers*, C.L.R., 2, 1888, 223.
6. Mills, Chapter 4, and Colvin R. de Silva, i, Chapter 7, deal in detail with Dual Control.
7. In 1802 North introduced Jenner's cow serum into Ceylon for vaccination against smallpox. It had been developed only six years before.
8. Edward Atkinson, for example, the Paymaster-General of the Troops, was also Commissary of Grain and Provisions. He kept no accounts and before a military board he stated that he considered that the deriving of pecuniary advantages to himself by sending in a false return was an allowable though not an avowed emolument of the office. He was also suspected of defrauding the soldiers of their pay. Quoted by Mills, 33.
9. Davy, 312.
10. In the absence of Kandyan sources covering the latter years of their history, one is left with little more than a few poems and the oral traditions handed down in families. Only during the past two decades has Sinhalese history been taught seriously in schools, and with their language so neglected that many of the better brains in the country were incapable of writing it, many, if not all, of these traditional stories would inevitably have been lost if Mr. Punchinbandara Dolapihilla had not collected them into his book. Many of these stories Mr Dolapihilla heard at only one remove from eyewitnesses of the events. Much is fictional or semi-fictional, but through them runs a sturdy thread of obvious truth which can be disentangled from the embroidery of the proud old men who inspired their juniors with the deeds of their ancestors. It may not be the most reliable raw material for history but it cannot be disregarded. From these stories came the suggestion that Kannasamy was Pilima Talauva's son. It is widely believed.

11. Cordiner, ii, 160.
12. Quoted by Pieris, *Tri Sinhala*, 2–3.
13. C.O. 54, North to Secret Committee, 26 November, 1798.
14. Ibid., 21 February, 1799.
15. Ibid and Cordiner, i, 168.
16. Valentia, i, 235.
17. Douglas, 30.
18. Cordiner, ii, 160.
19. Valentia, i, 235–49, gives a detailed account of the twelve interviews between Pilima Talauva and the British representatives, North's despatches are in C.O. 54, 2. Pieris, *Tri Sinhala*, Chapter 2 is important for an understanding of the events.
20. Macdowall's despatches and the diary of Captain Macpherson are in *Macdowall's Embassy to Kandy*, C.L.R., 3rd Series, 2, 1932, and 3, 1933 and 1934. Macpherson's diary is also reproduced in Cordiner, ii, 287 ff.
21. Percival, 377 ff. Much of this book, including the account of the embassy, is inaccurate, but the author's description of the early days of the British occupation of Ceylon is vivid. Percival was a shameless plagiarist.
22. Jonville, *Macdowall's Embassy.*
23. Pieris, *Tri Sinhala*, 165–66.
24. To see the west coast rivers in their monsoon spate or reduced to their narrow channels during dry weather is to wonder how they could have been used as supply routes. The answer is that hillsides, denuded of their forests for tea and rubber plantations, no longer hold the rain which instead pours in uncertain torrents along what were once navigable waterways.
25. Percival, 388.
26. Ibid, 394.
27. Ibid, 388.
28. Jonville, *Macdowall's Embassy*, 9.
29. Cordiner, ii, 305.
30. Ibid.
31. Percival, 404.
32. *Macdowall's Embassy to Kandy*, C.L.R., 3rd Series, 3, 1933–4, 263.
33. C.O. 54, 10, North to Hobart, 30 January, 1803.
34. Ibid, North to Macdowall, 2 February, 1803.

Chapter 5

1. Marshall, *Ceylon*, 85. Dr Henry Marshall did not arrive in Ceylon until 1808, so he was describing these events at second-hand. A cynical and outspoken Scot, he was the first British medical officer to compile statistics on the health of British troops. Because at the time such information was available only in the armed forces,

naval and military medical men both in the United Kingdom and on the continent of Europe initiated some of the most important movements in preventive medicine. (See Blanco, *Henry Marshall*). Historian and naturalist, as well as physician and surgeon, Marshall was the first writer to criticize North. Both Cordiner and Valentia were adulatory and obtained a lot of their material from North himself; Percival took the same line, but his book was published in 1805 and it was difficult for a junior officer to do otherwise.

2. Cordiner, ii, 169–9.
3. Coehorns, also spelt cohorns, were light brass mortars, easily manhandled. They were named after their inventor, Baron Coehorn, a Dutch military engineer.
4. Slightly different estimates of the strengths and compositions of the two columns are contained in De Bussche, 65; Cordiner, ii, 168–70; Percival, 427; and Ajax Anderson, *Poems*, 159. Anderson, an officer of the 19th Foot, published two volumes of lively, doggerel verse based on his experiences in India and Ceylon. A few copies of *Poems* contained an appendix which included the journal of Barbut's column and a series of letters written to Anderson by his friends in Kandy, after he had been evacuated sick to Trincomalee. The only existing copy of this book with the appendix is in the Colombo Museum. Excerpts from the appendix have been published in The Green Howards Gazette, 80 (937), April, 1972, 1087–1095.
5. Cordiner, ii, 262.
6. Percival, 82.
7. Cordiner, ii, 262.
8. *Memoirs of John Shipp*, T. Fisher Unwin, 1890. The book has recently been republished by Chatto & Windus, 1969.
9. Douglas, 142.
10. Cordiner, i, 143.
11. Percival, 175.
12. Marshall, *Notes on the Medical Topography of Ceylon*, 77.
13. Percival, 171–2.
14. Quoted by Elizabeth Longford, *Wellington: The Years of the Sword*, Weidenfeld and Nicholson, 1969, 101, from *The Wellington Papers*.
15. Douglas, 158.
16. Cordiner, i, 92–3.
17. The primary sources for the First Kandyan War up to the middle of June, 1803, are Cordiner, ii, 168–205; C.O. 54, 10 and 11; A.A.R. for 1803; and the appendix referred to in Note 4 above.
18. Dolapihilla, 114.
19. C.O. 54, 10, Macdowall to North, 5 February, 1803.
20. Quoted by Elizabeth Longford, op. cit. 74.
21. C.O. 54, 10, North to Clive, 30 January, 1803.

22. The only account of the Kandyan military organization is that of Ralph Pieris, Part 3. My description owes much to this book but is based also on Johnston, 31–3, part of whose information was culled from Knox; most of his material, however, was obtained by personal observation. Dolapihilla, Jonville and D'Oyly all include many references to the subject.
23. *The Travels of Marco Polo*, trs. and ed. William Marsden, Longman, Hurst, Rees, Orme and Brown, 1818, 622.
24. These were probably old Portuguese weapons which littered the Kandyan plateau. Their names had a fine ring: Nags, Camels, Falcons, Lions, Serpents, Basilisks, Savages, Culverins, Bombards, Pedreiros, Spheres, Roqueiros, Passamuros, Mortars and Bercos are all mentioned by Pieris, *Ceylon and the Portuguese*, 101.
25. Cordiner, ii, 177.
26. Ajax Anderson, *Poems*, 163.
27. Ibid, 165.
28. The pass is now not named on the Ordnance Survey maps. Balakaduwa village was located near the summit in the middle of the last century but has now disappeared. The name survives only in a neighbouring tea estate.
29. Dolapihilla, 117.
30. Ibid, 119.
31. A description of Kandy, as seen by a British officer who arrived there in March, 1803, is at Appendix A. This is taken from the appendix to Ajax Anderson, *Poems*.

Chapter 6

1. The Sinhalese version of this letter, delivered to the King and rescued from the burnt Palace, is one of the few contemporary Sinhalese documents to survive, other than the palm-leaf *olas*. It aroused contempt among the Kandyans because the translation was so unimpressive, lacking lucidity, style and refinement. See Karunartna Wijetunga, *A Letter from Governor North to the King of Kandy*, Vidjodoya Journal of Arts, Science and Letters, i, (1), January 1968, 79–83.
2. At the time Sabaragamuva was more often than not written as Safragam.
3. These gingals were light, artillery pieces, man portable, and mounted on a tripod (hence 'grass-hopper'). They fired a ball of about one inch diameter.
4. 'They aim principally at the Coolies, who carry the ammunition and provisions, well knowing that, without these, a regular force can make but little progress.' Johnston, 5.
5. Cordiner, ii, 189 and 191.
6. L. J. B. Turner, *Pilima Talawuwé*, 222.

7. Patches of this high jungle are now rare. The depredations of rubber and tea have proved fatal. John Still, *Jungle Tide*, should be read for a description of this high jungle, and I acknowledge my debt to his account.

8. Johnston, 104–116, and C. G. O., 2 February, 1814 and 17 December, 1815.

9. Johnston, 111.

10. *Memoirs of John Shipp*, T. Fisher Unwin, 1890, 37.

11. Cecil C. P. Lawson, *A History of the Uniforms of the British Army*, v, Kaye and Ward, 1967, 135–6.

12. *Services of Herbert Beaver*, 706.

13. Kaffir (Arabic for infidel) was nearly always used to designate the African. I have found it impossible to avoid the word, unpleasant though it sounds to the modern ear.

14. Wheeler, 51; *Journal of a Soldier of the H.L.I.*, Edinburgh, 1819, 110; and Oman, 145.

15. Sometimes the cartouche was worn on the back. De Meuron's Regiment wore it so.

16. Cordiner, ii, 188.

17. The only Dutch-built canal in Ceylon connects Colombo to Negombo.

18. This is on the railway at Mirigama. The Kandyans were making use of an old Dutch or Portuguese fort.

19. *Services of Herbert Beaver*, 706.

20. V. M. Methley, *Letters of Herbert Beaver*, 70.

21. Valentia, i, 273.

22. Cordiner, ii, Part Second, V, *Extracts from the General Medical Report of the Troops Serving in Ceylon, for the Month of April 1803*, provided a vivid description of the medical state of each individual unit in the island. See also Marshall, *Notes on the Medical Topography of Ceylon*.

23. Valentia, i, 252.

24. As opposed to the eight 'line' companies of an infantry battalion, the light and grenadier companies were known as the 'flank' companies. These flank companies of the 19th Foot had come up from Colombo at the start of the war but now rejoined the rest of the Regiment in Trincomalee.

25. Lewis, *Ceylon in Early British Times*, 30–1; and Valentia, i, 231.

26. Cordiner, ii, 199.

27. Ajax Anderson, *Poems*, 181–2.

28. Ibid, 182.

29. A rix dollar was at the time worth 8p. There were twelve fanams in one rix dollar.

30. Cordiner, ii, 201.

31. Ajax Anderson, *Poems*, 183.

32. Ibid, 185.

33. Ibid, 189.
34. Pieris, *Tri Sinhala*, 61.
35. Macdowall to North, 3 June, 1803. Quoted by Pieris, *Tri Sinhala*, 60.
36. Pieris, *Tri Sinhala*, 61.
37. Marshall, *Ceylon*, 108.
38. Davie to Macdowall, 31 May and 1 June, 1803. Quoted by Pieris, *Tri Sinhala*, 60.
39. Ajax Anderson, *Poems*, 189.
40. Arbuthnot to Davie, 25 June, 1803, Quoted by Pieris, *Tri Sinhala*, 64.

Chapter 7

1. Various prints and drawings *circa* 1820 show the hill either nearly bare of trees or lightly wooded.
2. This chapter is based on the stories of the survivors of the massacre. The first man to arrive in Colombo was Milhanage Joannes, a Sinhalese lascarin, who was followed by Mohamed Gani, a Malay. Their accounts are in C.O. 54/11, North to Hobart, 8 July, 1803. Corporal Barnsley's formal deposition was published as an appendix to Johnston, *Military Expedition to Kandy*, and is reproduced as Appendix B to this book. These three narratives were the basis for Cordiner, ii, 207–20. Barnsley dictated a more detailed narrative to Alexander Alexander (i, 112–26). Sergeant Theon's narrative was printed as an appendix to Ajax Anderson, *The Wanderer in Ceylon*, 182–203. Assistant Surgeon Greeving's story (not very reliable) is in J.R.A.S.C.B., 26 (71), 1918, 160–181; it had first been published in the *Colombo Observer* in 1848 and extracts had appeared in the *Illustrated London News*, 17 August, 1850, but it was then lost sight of until rediscovered by Miss V. M. Methley in C.O. 54, 12, and published by her in J.R.A.S.C.B. Greeving was the only educated man to tell the story, and Miss Methley has possibly depended rather too much upon his account for her monograph on Major Davie. On balance Barnsley's account seems to be the more reliable. Three of Muttusamy's servants who reached the coast were examined by a magistrate. Their evidence is reproduced in Pieris, *Sinhale and the Patriots*, Appendix W, *The Fate of Muddu Svami*, 674–83.
3. A.A.R., 1803, Chronicle, 10–12.
4. C.O. 54, 12, Memorandum to the Horse Guards, 20 April, 1803.
5. D. P. E. Hettiaratchi, *The Chief Executioner of Major Davie's Detachment*, J.R.A.S.C.B. 29 (76), 1923, 183–5.
6. Cordiner, ii, 211–2.
7. Pieris, *Sinhale and the Patriots*, 682.
8. Eight of Muttusamy's servants managed to make their way to

the coast. Five of these were the survivors of those who were
surrendered with their master. The other three were captured
by the Kandyans at a later stage and then released after being
mutilated.

9. Ajax Anderson, *The Wanderer in Ceylon*, 188–9.
10. Ibid, 184.
11. Joannes reported that Blakeney was killed in the struggle with
Sangunglo, and his account has gained acceptance. Greeving, however, describes Blakeney's wounds in detail and his eventual death.
When Greeving's diary was published in J.R.A.S.C.B., this para-
graph was omitted. D. P. E. Hettiaratchi, *Note on 'Greeving's
Diary'*, J.R.A.S.C.B., 29 (77), 1924, 325–6, notices this point.
12. Alexander Alexander, i, 117.
13. See Appendix B.
14. Marshall, *Ceylon*, 106.
15. D'Oyley, 11.
16. C.O. 54, 18, Maitland to Camden, 22 November, 1805, Encl.
17. Ibid.
18. 'Davie's Road' which runs from Kandy down to the river, is not
the route taken by Davie's men. Nor is the tree, known as 'Davie's
Tree', which stood at the end of this road (the site of which is now
marked with a small monument), the place of the massacre. The
road is thought to have been so named because it is the way he
walked each evening during his incarceration.
19. C.O. 54, 23, Brownrigg to Liverpool, 29 March, 1812, Encl.
20. C.O. 54, 11, North to Hobart, 8 July, 1803.
21. Marshall, *Ceylon*, 117.
22. A.A.R., 1804, *The War in Ceylon*, 16–18.
23. D'Oyly, 42.
24. Valentia, i, 253.
25. Davy, 314.
26. Cordiner, ii, 211.
27. Greeving, 166–7.
28. *Granville's Journal*, 545.
29. D'Oyly, 42.
30. Davy, 314, and Pieris, *Tri Sinhala*, 69.
31. Greeving, 172–3.

Chapter 8

1. The main primary authorities for this chapter are the Colonial
Office records, Cordiner ii, Beaver and A.A.R., 1804.
2. C.O. 54, 11, Blackall to Arbuthnott, 8 July, 1803.
3. Ajax Anderson, *Poems*, 86–7.
4. Cordiner, ii, 218.
5. These figures are based upon De Bussche, 65. Clearly, however, he

has underestimated the casualties of the 19th Foot during June in Kandy.

6. Cordiner, ii, 221.
7. A.A.R., 1803, *Chronicle*, 84.
8. Marshall, *Ceylon*, 42.
9. C.O. 54, 11, North to Hobart, 8 July, 1803.
10. *The Wellington Despatches*, Vol. 1, ed. Colonel Gurwood, Parker, Furnival & Parker, 1844, 596.
11. *Services of Herbert Beaver*, 710.
12. Ibid, 711.
13. C.O. 54, 11, North to Hobart, 20 April, 1803.
14. Cordiner, ii, 225.
15. Ibid, 229–30 and Valentia, i, 279.
16. Ajax Anderson, *The Wanderer in Ceylon*, 192.
17. Pieris, *Tri Sinhala*, 72.
18. Cordiner, ii, 240.
19. C.O. 54, 18, Maitland to Camden, 18 August, 1805.
20. C.O. 54, 15, Gordon to Cooke, 15 November, 1804.
21. 80,000 parahs (or pala) of paddy is about 100,000 bushels.
22. Marshall, *Ceylon*, 121.
23. Pieris, *Tri Sinhala*, 80.
24. Ibid, 73.
25. C.O. 54, 13, North to Hobart, 1 January, 1804.
26. In the end, the West Indians were never sent.
27. C.O. 55, 62, Hobart to North, 29 March, 1804.
28. Pieris, *Tri Sinhala*, 72.
29. North hoped to obtain 40 Africans from the disbanded force of the Nawab of the Carnatic. C.O. 54, 11, North to Hobart, 17 June, 1804.
30. C.O. 59, 56, *Military History of Ceylon*.
31. C.O. 54, 58, Wilson to Bathurst, 4 March, 1815.
32. C.O. 54, 18, Maitland to Camden, 19 October, 1805.
33. A.A.R., 1804, *Ceylon Military Establishment*, 147.
34. Campbell, ii, 9.
35. C.O. 54, 13, North to Hobart, 1 January, 1804.
36. Ibid.
37. C.O. 54, 12, Instructions to General Wemyss dated May 1803.
38. C.L.R., 2 (28), 1888, 222.
39. C.O. 54, 15, North to Camden, 26 December, 1804.
40. Ibid.
41. C.O. 54, 17, North to Camden, 13 April, 1805.

Chapter 9

1. C.O. 55, 62, Hobart to North, 29 March, 1804.
2. C.O. 54, 14, North to Hobart, 3 March, 1804.

3. Pieris, *Tri Sinhala*, 70.
4. Ibid, 74–5.
5. The account of Johnston's march is based primarily upon his own book; Alexander, i, 148–66; Marshall, *Ceylon*, 123–30; and C.O. 54, 16, North to Camden, 8 February, 1805.
6. Johnston, 38–9.
7. Ibid, 42–4.
8. The handsome, compact, little Kandyan pack-bullocks carried a load of one hundredweight. They can still be found in use in the hills around Hanguranketa.
9. I have been guided by the interpretation of Johnston's route compiled by Mr Frederick Lewis, *Johnston's Expedition to Kandy, in 1804*, J.R.A.S.C.B., 29 (78), 1925, 43–69.
10. Ajax Anderson, *The Wanderer in Ceylon*, 198.
11. Johnston, 61
12. Ibid, 65.
13. Marshall, *Ceylon*, 123.
14. Forbes, i, 40–41.
15. Alexander, i, 164.
16. J. P. Lewis, *A Ceylon Centenary: Lt.-Col. A. Johnston*, C.A.L.R., 6 (3), January 1921, 155.
17. Cyrus D. F. Abayakoon, *Where did Colonel Johnston Die? Ceylon Fortnightly Review*, 2 (2), 20 May, 1949. The writer's theory that there were two Colonel Johnstons who served at this time in Ceylon can be discounted.
18. Johnston, 94–130.
19. Percival, 203.
20. C.O. 54, 16, North To Camden, 8 February, 1805.
21. Cordiner, ii, 258.
22. A.A.R., 1805, 99–100.

Chapter 10

1. C.O. 54, 11, North to Hobart, 6 October, 1803.
2. C.O. 54, 16, North to Camden, 8 February, 1805.
3. Quoted by Hulugalle, 16. I have failed to trace the original reference.
4. Quoted by John Cannon, *Lord North, The Noble Lord in the Blue Ribbon*, Historical Association, 1970, 26. This recent assessment of Lord North first drew my attention to the similarities in the characters of the two brothers.
5. C.O. 54, 18, North to Camden, 10 July, 1805.
6. C.O. 54, 17, Camden to Wemyss, 21 February, 1805.
7. Frewen Lord and Willis Dixon have provided much of my material on Maitland's background and character. The former is a little too eulogistic and is, in some respects, not too accurate.

8. C.O. 55, 62, Camden to Maitland, 21 February, 1805.
9. C.O. 54, 18, Maitland to Camden, 19 July, 1805.
10. Ibid.
11. C.O. 54, 18, Maitland to Cooke, 19 July, 1805.
12. C.O. 54, 18, Maitland to Camden, 19 October, 1805.
13. Pieris, *Letters to Ceylon*, 49.
14. C.O. 59, 56, *Military History of Ceylon*.
15. Ibid.
16. C.O. 54, 18, Maitland to Camden, 19 October, 1805.
17. Major Honner and Captain Madge, both of the 19th Foot, were court-martialled at Colombo in January, 1806, for publicly criticizing Maitland. The former was cashiered and the latter reprimanded and instructed to send in his papers. Madge was the officer who had evacuated Fort Macdowall, while Honner was reputed to be a sadistic bully, whom Alexander describes (i, 167–170) as gloating over and mocking his soldiers as they were flogged. When he got back to England, Honner tried to sell a fabulous piece of jewellery, which he claimed had been given to him in Kandy by Muttusamy. It consisted of a very rare white spinel, weighing 74¼ carats, set in gold and rubies; later Louis XVIII of France bought it for £23,000. (Louis Kornitzer, *The Bridge of Sighs*, Geoffrey Bles, 1939). Fortescue (v, 162) describes the poor state of discipline of the 19th Foot and Alexander (i, 169) suggests that they were moved from Trincomalee to Colombo because of their ill-conduct. J. P. Lewis, in an unpublished letter in possession of the Regiment, wrote that he considered that Fortescue's strictures were not fully substantiated.
18. C.O. 54, 22, Maitland to Minto, 21 September, 1806.
19. Alexander, i, 191.
20. C.O. 59, 56, *Military History of Ceylon*; L. J. B. Turner, *Some Aspects of the Economics of Ceylon, 1797–1805*, C.A.L.R. 4 (4), April 1919, 187–8, and 5 (2), October, 1919, 68.
21. C.O. 64, 18, Maitland to Camden, 19 October, 1805.
22. Fortescue, iv, 496.
23. See Chapter 9, p. 165.
24. Calladine, 139.
25. Cordiner, i, 275.
26. Ibid, 274.
27. Alexander, i, 109–11.
28. Calladine, 43.
29. Percival, 131.
30. Ibid, 330.
31. Calladine, 46–7.
32. Marshall, *Notes on the Medical Topography*, 76.
33. Campbell, i, 227.
34. Wheeler, 195.

35. Cordiner, i, 75.
36. Campbell, i, 50–2.
37. Percival, 162–5.
38. C.O. 55, 62, Hobart to North, 21 April, 1807.
39. Cordiner, i, 87.
40. Percival, 236.
41. Campbell, ii, 33.
42. Mockley Ferriman, 93.
43. The account of Pilima Talauva's downfall is from Davy, 317–9.
44. Ibid, 319.
45. D'Oyly, 156.
46. Ibid, 86 and 136.
47. De Silva, 126.
48. D'Oyly, 104, describes the impalement of two officials for accepting bribes to release people from their *rajakariya*.
49. C.O. 54, 25, Maitland to Wyndham, 28 February, 1807.
50. Ludowyk, *The Story of Ceylon*, 149.
51. Pieris, *Letters to Ceylon*.
52. C.O. 54, 40, Wilson to Liverpool, 16 July, 1811.
53. Ibid.
54. C.O. 55, 62, Liverpool to Brownrigg, 31 March, 1812.
55. C.O. 54, 45, Maitland to Peel, 29 January, 1812.

Chapter 11

1. C.O. 55, 62, Liverpool to Brownrigg, 31 March, 1812.
2. C.O. 54, 44, Brownrigg to Liverpool, 3 November, 1812.
3. C.O. 54, 48, Brownrigg to Liverpool, 30 November, 1813.
4. C.O. 54, 51, Brownrigg to Bathurst, 20 March, 1814.
5. Davy, 319.
6. Ibid.
7. C.O. 54, 48, Brownrigg to Bathurst, 30 November, 1813, enclosures.
8. C.O. 54, 51, Brownrigg to Bathurst, 10 February, 1814, enclosure. 'The Great Gate' was one of the King's numerous titles.
9. C.O. 54, 51, Brownrigg to Bathurst, 20 March, 1814, enclosure.
10. C.O. 54, 52, Brownrigg to Bathurst, 16 August, 1814, and enclosures.
11. Ibid, enclosure of 1 June.
12. Davy, 321–3.
13. The Bogambara Lake was below the bund of the present lake in Kandy. The market now stands near the further (or western) shore.
14. Pieris, *Tri Sinhala*, Appendix H.
15. T. Vimalanda and F. R. Jayasuriya, *The Child Hero of Ceylon*, M. D. Gunasena & Co, Colombo, 1966.
16. Dolapihilla, xii and 289.
17. Davy 322 ff and Ajax Anderson, *The Wanderer in Ceylon*, 201.

18. Davy, 323.
19. *Gentleman on the Spot*, 6.
20. Marshall, *Ceylon*, 142.
21. C.O. 54, 53, Brownrigg to Bathurst, 30 October, 1814, enclosures.
22. Ibid and 31 December, 1814.
23. Marshall, *Ceylon*, 146.
24. The account of the Second Kandyan War is based on the following primary authorities: C.O. 54, 55, Brownrigg to Bathurst, 16 January and 25 February, 1815; De Bussche; Marshall, *Ceylon*; D'Oyly, 179–269; Jonville, *Narrative of 1815*; *A Gentleman on the Spot*; *The Journal of the March of the Fifth* (written by another surgeon); and the diary of Captain Lockyer, who commanded the detachment of the 19th Regiment in the 5th Division, published as Appendix V of Pieris, *Sinhale and the Patriots*, 662–73.
25. The Library of the University of Ceylon possesses a copy of Johnston, *Narrative of an Expedition to Kandy*, 1st ed., in the front of which is pasted a letter from the then Commandant of the Senior Division of the Royal Military College at High Wycombe to Brownrigg, forwarding to him a presentation copy of the book and commending it to him. The letter is dated 22 June, 1810, when Brownrigg was employed at the Horse Guards. As he was not appointed to Ceylon until 11 October of the same year, when news was received of Maitland's illness, it is doubtful if either the writer of the letter or Brownrigg then knew who Maitland's successor was to be.
26. See Appendix C.
27. Marshall, *Ceylon*, 147.
28. *Asiatic Journal*, 1, January to June, 1816, 105–8.
29. Ibid, 210–14.
30. Marshall, *Ceylon*, 151.
31. Ibid, 153.
32. Manuscript letters from Major Willerman to the Hon Sir Alexander Johnston, then Chief Justice of Ceylon, in the India Office Library. MSS Eur. D. 667.
33. *Journal of the March of the Fifth Division*, 67.
34. Willerman letters.

Chapter 12

1. Calladine, 39.
2. Willerman letters.
3. Dias's narrative was published for the first time in English in 1896 in two separate translations: Don V. Dias, *Capture of Sri Wikkrama Rajasinha by the English*, in M.L.R.S.: T. B. Pohath-Kehelpannala, *How the Last King of Kandy was Captured by the British*, in J.R.A.S.C.B. The authenticity of the account was challenged on the

NOTES

grounds that Dias would have been about 80 years of age in 1860, the year when the account was said to have been written; that there was no record of Dias in the archives; and that his account did not correspond in detail with that of de Bussche. P. E. Pieris (*Tri Sinhala*, 158) accepts the narrative and identifies the writer with Don William Adrian Dias Bandaranayaka, one of the three Mohundirams of the Gate in the year 1819, when Brownrigg presented him with a gold medal and chain. I see no reason to disagree with Pieris. The account certainly bears every mark of authenticity.

4. A blood-stained garment, supposedly worn by one of the two Queens, is exhibited in the Colombo Museum. The description infers that the women were robbed by British troops, an accusation which cannot be substantiated.
5. Don V. Dias, 21.
6. *Gentleman on the Spot*, 31.
7. Calladine, 39.
8. *Granville's Journal*.
9. Ibid, 544.
10. Willerman letters.
11. *Gentleman on the Spot*, 32.
12. The *Ceylon Journal*, 13, 18 February, 1832.
13. Marshall, *Ceylon*, 137–9 and 142, contrasts Sri Wikrama's actions with the behaviour of Cumberland after Culloden and the English criminal code in the reign of George III.
14. Ibid, 158.
15. De Bussche, 71.
16. Ibid, 67.
17. Ibid, 77–8.
18. Ibid, 94–106.
19. Campbell, i, iii-vi and 92.
20. D'Oyly, 234.
21. Pieris, *Sinhala and the Patriots*, Appendix G, 614–17, *Looting by the Military*.
22. C.O. 54, 52, Brownrigg to Bathurst, 17 August, 1804.
23. D'Oyly, 183.
24. Pieris, *Tri Sinhala*, Appendix M, 220–36, assembles most of the material on the capture and disposal of the Kandyan royal treasures. There is some further information in *Gentleman on the Spot*, 34–7.
25. Father S. G. Perera, *The Throne of the Kings of Kandy*.
26. D'Oyly, 224 and 233.
27. The Hall of Audience, with its magnificently carved pillars, still stands in the centre of the area that used to be occupied by the complex of Palace buildings, one of the few survivors. It is now used as a Court of Justice.

301

28. De Bussche, 40–1. The account in Marshall, *Ceylon*, 163, varies slightly. The latter states that the Kandyans took no interest in the ceremonial.
29. Marshall, *Ceylon*, 160.
30. Dolapihilla, 274.
31. See Appendix D.
32. Pieris, *Sinhala and the Patriots*, Appendix C, 596–9, *The Fifth Article of the Treaty*.
33. Marshall, *Ceylon*, 164–5.
34. De Bussche, 43–50.
35. Colvin R. de Silva, i, 171.
36. Pieris, *Sinhale and the Patriots*, 452, Note 47, mentions the adverse comment on this act in *The Christian Observer*, January, 1816.
37. Deposition of Welleygedera Apoohamy Sattambi quoted by Pieris, *Tri Sinhala*, 233.

Chapter 13

1. Davy, 360.
2. *Asiatic Journal*, v, June, 1818, 614.
3. Marshall, *Ceylon*, 178.
4. Ibid, 175.
5. Davy, 326–7.
6. Ibid.
7. C.O. 54, 61, Brownrigg to Bathurst, 5 September, 1816.
8. Ibid.
9. C.O. 54, 66, Brownrigg to Bathurst, 25 September, 1817.
10. C.O. 54, 51, Brownrigg to Bathurst, 5 September, 1816.
11. C.O. 55, 63, Bathurst to Brownrigg, 7 August, 1816.
12. C.O. 54, 65, Brownrigg to Bathurst, 28 February, 1817.
13. *Asiatic Journal*, v, July, 1818, 19–23, provided a contemporary account of the Perehera, written by Millawa, the *dissawa* of Vellassa. Millawa had been a close adherent of the deposed King, and he was noted for his distinguished appearance, his courtly manners, and his learning. He was poet, astrologer and historian, and was accepted generally as the most able of the Kandyan leaders.
14. Davy, 371. The dilapidated appearance of the Palace is reflected in Plate 9.
15. The main primary sources used for the Third War are Brownrigg's despatches in C.O. 54, Volumes 66, 70, 71 and 73; the *Asiatic Journal*, v and vi; Colombo General Orders for 1817 and 1818; Marshall, *Ceylon*, Davy, Calladine; and Major Macdonald's Order Book.
16. Brownrigg recorded that he received the first accounts of the disturbances when he arrived back in Kandy on 26 October (C.O. 54, 66, Brownrigg to Bathurst, 7 November 1817). This,

however, is contradicted in Davy, 394; Marshall, *Ceylon*, 184, and *Asiatic Journal*, v, June 1818, 613.
17. C.O. 54, 66, Brownrigg to Bathurst, 27 November, 1817.
18. Ibid, 7 November, 1917.
19. Ibid.
20. Calladine, 49.
21. Ibid, 49–55.
22. C.O. 54, 66, Brownrigg to Bathurst, 27 November, 1817.
23. C.O. 54, 74, Brownrigg to Bathurst, 8 July, 1819. Annexure dealing with the interrogation of the Maha Betme of Kataragame.
24. Marshall, *Ceylon*, 42 and 210–12.
25. Calladine, 69.
26. C.O. 54, 70, Brownrigg to Bathurst, 12 April, 1818.

Chapter 14

1. Davy, 329.
2. *Asiatic Journal*, vii, April 1919, 444–5.
3. Davy, 330–1.
4. Ibid.
5. Marshall, *Ceylon*, 204–5.
6. Davy, 332.
7. Campbell, i, 53.
8. Calladine, 55.
9. Ajax Anderson, *The Wanderer in Ceylon*, 121.
10. Marshall, *Ceylon*, 206.
11. For a description of Kandyan skill with the bow see Pieris, *Sinhale and the Patriots*, 208.
12. Calladine, 58.
13. Ibid, 60–2. The official version (C.G.O. 1 May, 1818) describes the Malays seizing the chief during the march, when he was surrounded by several hundred armed followers, and bayoneting thirty-three of their opponents.
14. C.O. 54, 71, Brownrigg to Bathurst, 24 July, 1818.
15. Ibid.
16. Ibid, 9 October, 1818, Encl.
17. Ibid.
18. Forbes, i, 233.
19. Forbes, i, 52.
20. Accounts of the incident are in Marshall, *Ceylon*, 195–7, and C.O. 54, 71, Brownrigg to Bathurst, 9 October, 1818, Encls.
21. The Portuguese claimed to have captured and destroyed it but the Sinhalese denied that it was the true Tooth.
22. Davy, 369.
23. For an account of the life of the banished chiefs, see Brohier, *The Uva Rebellion*, 51–3.

24. Marshall, *Ceylon*, Appendix X, *The Execution of Kappitapola*, 277–81.
25. C.O. 54, 73, Brownrigg to Bathurst, 8 January, 1819.
26. Ibid, 2 November, 1819.
27. Davy, 406.
28. Ibid, 442.
29. Ibid, 467.
30. Herbert White, 109–10.
31. Ajax Anderson, *The Wanderer in Ceylon*, 91.
32. James Stewart, *Notes on Ceylon*, Privately printed, 1862.
33. C.O. 55, 63, Bathurst to Brownrigg, 25 July, 1818.

Epilogue

1. Forbes, i, 234.
2. Marshall, *Ceylon*, 200.
3. Ferriman, 75–109, provides an excellent description of North's life before and after the Ceylon period.
4. Pieris, *Letters to Ceylon*.
5. Lewis, *Tombstones and Monuments*, 298–9.
6. Blanco, *Henry Marshall*.
7. Marshall, *Ceylon*, 42.
8. Calladine, 77.

SELECT BIBLIOGRAPHY

MANUSCRIPT SOURCES

Colonial Office and War Office Records in the Public Record Office in the series C.O. 54 and 55, and W.O.1.

History of the Services of His Majesty's 1st Ceylon Regiment (Riflemen). Material for an unpublished volume of *Cannon's Histories* in the Ministry of Defence (Central) Library, London.

Lawrie, Archibald Campbell. *Kandyan Law and History.* Unpublished manuscript in the India Office Library. There is a typewritten copy in the Library of the University of Ceylon

Letter books of Major Macdonald, 19th Foot, 1815–1820, covering his tour in Uva. In the Green Howards' Museum.

Letters of Major William Willerman in the India Office Library (MSS Eur. xxx D 667 (part)). They have now been published in C.J.H.S.S., 1 (2), July–December, 1971 (Ed. by Geoffrey Powell).

PRINCIPAL JOURNALS, ETC.

Asiatic Annual Register, 1800–1812.

Asiatic Journal and Monthly Register, 1816–1820.

Ceylon General Orders, 1814–1820.

Ceylon Government Gazette, 1802–1820.

Ceylon Literary Register, 1st Series, Vols. 1–7, 1887–1893.

Monthly Literary Register and Notes and Queries for Ceylon, Vols. 1–4, 1893–1896.

Ceylon Antiquary and Literary Register (Ceylon Literary Register, 2nd series), Vols. 1–10, 1915–1924.

Ceylon Literary Register, 3rd Series, Vols. 1–4, 1931–1936.

Journal of the Royal Asiatic Society (Ceylon Branch), Vols. 1–36 (Nos. 1–100), 1845–1945; (new series). Vol. 1–13; 1946–1969.

CONTEMPORARY PRINTED SOURCES

The Life of Alexander Alexander. Ed. by John Howell. Vol. 1. William Blackwood, Edinburgh, and T. Cadell, London, 1830.

Anderson, Captain Thomas Ajax. *Poems Written Chiefly in India*. Philanthropic Society, 1809.

Anderson, Captain Thomas Ajax. *A Wanderer in Ceylon*. T. Egerton Military Library, 1817.

Andrews, Robert. *Journal of a tour to Candia in the year 1796*. Ed. by J. P. Lewis. J.R.A.S.C.B., 26 (70), 1917, 172–229, and 26 (71), 1918, 6–31.

Letters of Captain Herbert Beaver (*H.M. 19th Regt.*), *March–April, 1803*. Ed. by Violet M. Methley. C.A.L.R. 4 (2), Oct. 1918, 65–75.

Sketch of the Services of the late Major Herbert Beaver. United Service Journal, 1829, Part II, 431–8 and 705–15.

Brownrigg, Sir Robert. *Taking of Kandy by the British*. M.L.R.C. 1 (9), Sep. 1893, 202–7.

The Diary of Colour Sergeant George Calladine, 19th Foot, 1793–1837. Ed. by Major M. L. Ferrar. Eden Fisher & Co., 1922.

Campbell, Lieut.-Col. James. *Excursions, Adventures and Field Sports in Ceylon*. Two vol. T. & W. Boone, 1843.

The Cleghorn Papers. Ed. by the Rev. William Neil. A. & L. Black, 1927.

Cordiner, The Rev. James. *A Description of Ceylon*. Two vol. Longman, Hurst, Rees and Orme, 1807.

Davy, John. *An Account of the Interior of Ceylon*. Longman, Hurst, Rees, Orme, and Brown, 1821.

de Bussche, Captain L. *Letters on Ceylon*. J. J. Stockdale, 1817.

Dias, Don V. *Capture of Sri Wikkrama Rajasinha by the British: an account alleged to be from an eyewitness*. Trs. by D. K. William. M.L.R.C. 4 (1), Jan. 1896, 20–2.

The Douglas Papers. Ed. by Father S. G. Perera. Ceylon Observer Press, Colombo, 1933.

Diary of Mr. John D'Oyly. Ed. by H. W. Codrington. J.R.A.S.C.B., 25 (69), 1917.

Forbes, Major Jonathan. *Eleven Years in Ceylon.* Vol. 1. Richard Bentley, 1840.

Graham, Maria. *Journal of a Residence in India.* 2nd ed. Archibald Constable, Edinburgh, and Longman, Hurst, Rees, Orme and Brown, London, 1813.

Granville, William. *Deportation of Sri Vikrama Rajasinha.* C.L.R., 3 (11), Nov. 1934, 487–504, and 3 (12), Dec. 1934, 543–50. (First published Wesleyan Mission Press, Colombo, 1830.)

Greeving's Diary. Ed. by Violet M. Methley. J.R.A.S.C.B., 26 (71), 1918, 166–80.

Johnston, Major Arthur. *Narrative of an Expedition to Candy in the year 1804.* James McGlashan, Dublin, and Wm. S. Orr and Co., London, 1810.

Jonville, J. E., *Journal and Narrative of the Military Expedition of 1815.* Ceylon Miscellany, 1, 1842, 33–45 and 140–55.

Jonville, J. E. *Narrative of the Embassy of Major General Macdowall in 1800.* J.R.A.S.C.B., 38 (105), 1948, 1–21.

Knox, Robert. *An Historical Relation of Ceylon.* Introduction by S. P. Saparamadu. Ceylon Historical Journal, Vol. 6, 1958. (First published Richard Chiswell, London, 1681.)

Macdowall's Embassy to Kandy. C.L.R. 2, 1932, and 3, 1933 and 1934.

Marshall, Dr. Henry. *Notes on the Medical Topography of the Interior of Ceylon.* Burgess and Hill, 1821.

Marshall, Dr. Henry. *Ceylon.* William H. Allen & Co., 1846.

Methley, Violet M. *The Ceylon Expedition of 1803.* Transactions of the Royal Historical Society. 4th Series. Vol. 1, 1919, 93–128.

Mockler-Ferryman, Lieut.-Col. A. F. *The Life of a Regimental Officer During the Great War 1793–1815. Compiled from the Correspondence of Colonel Samuel Rice, 51st Light Infantry.* William Blackwood & Sons, 1913.

Percival, Captain Robert. *An Account of the Island of Ceylon.* Printed by and for G. & R. Baldwin, 1805.

Philalethes. *The History of Ceylon.* Joseph Mawman, 1817.

Pieris, Sir Paulus Edward (editor). *Letters to Ceylon 1814–1824, being correspondence addressed to Sir John D'Oyly.* W. Heffer & Sons, Cambridge, 1938.

Pohath-Kehelpannala, T. B. *How the Last King of Kandy was Captured by the British.* J.R.A.S.C.B., 14 (47), 1896, 107–114.

The Pybus Embassy to Kandy. Transcribed by R. Raven Hart. Government Press, Colombo, 1958. (First published William Skeen, Colombo, 1862.)

Raven Hart, R. *The Dutch Wars with Kandy, 1764–1766.* Ceylon Historical Manuscripts Commission Bulletin No. 6, Government Press, Colombo, 1966.

Raven Hart, R. *The War with the Sinhalese.* Spolia Zeylanica, 29 (2), 1961, 315–340, and privately printed, 1961.

Ribeiro's History of Ceilao. Ed. and trs. by P. E. Pieris, The Colombo Apothecaries Co., Colombo, 1909.

Valentia, George (First Earl of Mountmorris). *Voyages and Travels to India, Ceylon, the Red Sea, Abyssinia and Egypt,* Vol. 1. Printed for F. C. and J. Rivington, 1811.

Vimalananda Tennakoon. *The Great Rebellion of 1818.* Gunasena & Co., 1970. (Extracts from the Colonial Office Records, 1816–19.)

Welsh, Colonel James. *Military Reminiscences,* Vol. 1. Smith, Elder & Co., 1830.

The Letters of Private Wheeler, 1809–1828. Ed. by Capt. B. H. Liddell Hart, Michael Joseph, 1951.

Anon. *A Narrative of Events which have Recently Occurred in the Island of Ceylon.* T. Egerton, Military Library, 1815. (Variously attributed to Edward Tolfrey, Edward Jeffrey and William Willerman.

Anon. *Kandy, 1815. Journal of the Fifth Division.* United Services Journal, Vol. 43, 1911.

Anon. *The Uva Rebellion 1817–1818 with full Details of Military Operations throughout the Kandyan Country.* A. M. & J. Ferguson, Colombo, 1889. (Reprinted from the Ceylon Government Gazette.)

Anon. *The Ex King of Kandy, Sree Wickrama Rajah Singha.* Colombo Journal, No. 13, Feb. 18, 1832.

LATER WORKS

Archer, Mildred. *British Drawings in the India Office Library.* Two vol. H.M.S.O., 1969.

Balkis. *Pseud. A Forgotten Tragedy.* Cornhill Magazine (3rd series), 27, Oct. 1909, 544–556.

Blanco, Richard L. *Henry Marshall (1775–1851) and the Health of the British Army.* Medical History, 14 (3), July 1970, 260–276.

Brohier, R. L. *The Golden Age of Military Adventure in Ceylon. An Account of the Uva Rebellion, 1817–1818.* Platé, Colombo, 1933.

Brohier, R. L. *Ancient Irrigation Works in Ceylon.* Pts. I–III. Ceylon. Govt. Press, Colombo, 1934–5 (Reprinted twice).

Burne, Alfred H. *The Noble Duke of York.* Staples Press, 1949.

Cave, Henry W. *The Book of Ceylon.* Cassels, 1908.

Colgate, H. A. *The Royal Navy and Trincomalee.* The Ceylon Journal of Historical and Social Studies, VII (1), 1964.

Cowan, H. L. *History of the Ceylon Regiment.* United Services Magazine, Nov. 1860, 323–7.

De Quincey, Thomas. *Ceylon.* Collected writings ed. by David Masson, Vol. 7. A. & C. Black, 1897, 427–56.

De Silva, Colvin R. *Ceylon under the British Occupation, 1795–1833.* Two vol. The Colombo Apothecaries Co., Colombo, 1953 and 1962.

Dixon, C. Willis. *The Colonial Administration of Sir Thomas Maitland.* Longman, Green & Co., 1939.

Dolapihilla, Punchibandara. *In the Days of Sri Wickramajasingha, Last King of Kandy.* Saman Press, Maharagama, Ceylon, 1959.

Elliott, C. Brooke. *The Real Ceylon.* H. W. Cave & Co., Colombo, 1939.

Ferrar, Major M. L. *A History of the Services of the 19th Regiment.* Eden Fisher & Co., 1911.

Ferrar, Major M. L. *Officers of the Green Howards.* W. & G. Baird, Belfast, 1931.

Ferriman, Z. D. *Some English Philhellenes.* Number 6. *Lord Guilford.* The Anglo-Hellenic League, 1917.

Fortescue, The Hon. W. J. *History of the British Army*, Vols. 5 and 11. Macmillan & Co., 1921 and 1923.

Glover, Richard. *Peninsular Preparation: The Reform of the British Army*. Cambridge University Press, 1963.

Godwin-Austin, A. R. *The Staff and the Staff College*. Constable & Co., 1927.

Goonetileke, H. A. I. *A Bibliography of Ceylon*. Two vols. Inter Documentation Company AG, Zug, Switzerland, 1970.

Hettiaratchi, D. P. E. *More About Major Davie*. C.A.L.R., 8 (2), Oct. 1922, 163–5.

Hettiaratchi, D. P. E. *The Chief Executioner of Major Davie's Detachment*. J.R.A.S.C.B., 26 (76), 1923, 182–5.

Hettiaratchi, D. P. E. *Note on 'Greeving's Diary'*. J.R.A.S.C.B., 29 (77), 1924, 323–7.

Hettiaratchi, D. P. E. *Johnston's Expedition to Kandy in 1804*. J.R.A.S.C.B., 30 (78), 1925, 146–55.

Hulugalle, H. A. J. *Ceylon of the Early Travellers*. 2nd ed. Wesley Press, Colombo, 1969.

Hulugalle, H. A. J. *British Governors in Ceylon*. Associated Newspapers of Ceylon, Colombo and London, 1963.

Kanapathypillai, V. *Dutch Rule in Maritime Ceylon, 1766–96*. Doctor of Philosophy Thesis, London University, 1969.

Keble, W. T. *Ceylon, Beaten Track*. 7th ed. Associated Newspapers of Ceylon, 1953.

Knighton, William. *The History of Ceylon*. Longmans, Brown, Green and Longmans, 1845.

Lawrie, Archibald Campbell. *Gazetteer of the Central Provinces of Ceylon*. Two vol. Government Printer, Colombo, 1896.

Lewis, Frederick. *Johnston's Expedition to Kandy in 1804*. J.R.A.S.C.B., 30 (78), 1925, 43–65.

Lewis, John Penry. *Tombstones and Monuments in Ceylon*. H. C. Cottle, Government Printer, Colombo, 1913.

Lewis, John Penry. *Ceylon in Early British Times*. 2nd ed. Times of Ceylon, 1915.

Lewis, John Penry. *The Tragedy and Problem of Major Davie*. C.A.L.R., 4 (4), April 1919, 179–80.

Lewis, John Penry. *More About Major Davie*. C.A.L.R., 5 (4), April 1920, 168–71.

Lewis, John Penry. *General Hay Macdowall.* C.A.L.R. 6 (1), July 1920, 1–6, and 7 (1), July 1921, 45–6.

Lewis, John Penry. *The Captivity of Major Davie.* J.R.A.S.C.B., 29 (76), 1923, 147–82.

Lord, Walter Frewen. *Sir Thomas Maitland.* T. Fisher Unwin, 1897.

Ludowyk, Evelyn F. C. *The Modern History of Ceylon.* Weidenfeld and Nicolson, 1966.

Ludowyk, Evelyn F. C. *The Story of Ceylon.* 2nd ed. Faber & Faber, 1967.

Mendis, G. C. *Ceylon under the British, 1795–1832.* The Colombo Apothecaries Co., Colombo, 1952.

Mendis, G. C. *Problems of Ceylon History.* The Colombo Apothecaries Co., Colombo, 1966.

Mendis, V. L. B. *The Advent of the British to Ceylon, 1762–1803.* Master of Arts Thesis. London University, June, 1966. Published by Dehiwela (Ceylon), Tisava Prakasakayo, 1971. (Ceylon Historical Journal, Vol. 18).

Mills, Lennox A. *Ceylon under British Rule.* Oxford University Press, 1933. (Reprinted London, Frank Cass, 1964.)

Neighbour, J. R. . . . *And See the World.* The Green Howards Gazette, 75 (884), Nov. 1967, 508–9; 75 (885), Dec. 1967, 526–32; 75 (886), Jan. 1968, 551–3.

Oman, C. W. G. *Wellington's Army, 1809–14.* Edward Arnold, 1913.

Pakeman, S. A. *Ceylon.* Ernest Benn, 1964.

Pearson, Joseph. *The Throne of the Kings of Kandy.* J.R.A.S.C.B., 31 (82), 1929, 380–3.

Pieris, P. E. *Ceylon and the Hollanders, 1658–1796.* American Ceylon Mission Press, Tellippallai, Ceylon, 1918.

Pieris, P. E. *Ceylon and the Portuguese, 1505–1658.* American Ceylon Mission Press, Tellippalai, Ceylon, 1920.

Pieris, P. E. *Tri Sinhala, The Last Phase, 1796–1815.* W. Heffer & Sons, Cambridge, 1939.

Pieris, P. E. *Sinhale and the Patriots, 1815–1818.* The Colombo Apothecaries Co., Colombo, 1950.

Pieris, Ralph. *Sinhalese Social Organization in the Kandyan Period.* Ceylon University Press, Peradeniya, Ceylon, 1956.

Raven Hart, R. *The Great Road*. Pts I & II. J.R.A.S.C.B., New Series, 4 (2), 1955, 143–212; 8 (1), 1962, 141–162.

Reith, Charles. *The 19th (Yorkshire) Regiment and its Connection with Ceylon*. J.R.A.S.C.B., 23 (66), 1913, 55–69.

Reith, Charles. *An Ensign of the 19th Foot*. Heath Cranton, 1925. (Fiction.)

Skinner, Major Thomas. *Fifty Years in Ceylon*. Ed. by Annie Skinner. W. H. Allen, 1891.

Still, John. *Jungle Tide*. William Blackwood & Sons, 1947.

Suckling, H. *Ceylon* by an Officer, late of the Ceylon Rifles. Two vols. Chapman & Hall, 1876.

Tennant, Sir James Emmerson. *Ceylon*. Two vols. 4th ed. Longman, Green, Longman and Roberts, 1860.

Tomlinson, Michael. *Kandy in 1820*. Times of Ceylon Annual, Colombo, 1958.

Toussaint, J. R. *Annals of the Ceylon Civil Service*. The Colombo Apothecaries Co., Colombo, 1935.

Turner, L. J. B. *Pilima Talawuwé; Maha Adigar: His Political Intrigues, 1798–1805*. C.A.L.R., 3 (3), Jan. 1918, 219–25.

Turner, L. J. B. *The Town of Kandy about the Year 1815 A.D.* C.A.L.R., 4 (2), Oct. 1918, 76–82.

Turner, L. J. B. *Notes on Some of the Authorities for the History of the British in Ceylon, 1798–1805*. J.R.A.S.C.B., 28 (72), 1919, 15–35.

Turner, L. J. B., *The Military Establishments in the Maritime Provinces of Ceylon, 1798–1805*. C.A.L.R., 5(2), Oct. 1919, 59–69.

Tylden, Major G. *The Ceylon Regiments, 1796 to 1874*. Journal of the Society for Army Historical Research, 30, 1952, 124–8.

Tylden, Major G. *The Accoutrements of the British Infantryman, 1640–1940*. Journal of the Society for Army Historical Research, 47, 1969, 4–22.

White, Herbert. *Manual of the Province of Uva*. H. C. Cottle, Government Printer, Colombo, 1895.

Wilson, Lt.-Col. W. J. *History of the Madras Army*. Vol. 2. Government Press, Madras, 1882.

Wylly, Colonel H. C. *History of the King's Own Yorkshire Light Infantry*, Vol. 1. Percy, Lund, Humphries & Co., *circa* 1925.

Zeylanicus. *Ceylon*. Elek Books, 1970.

SELECT BIBLIOGRAPHY

ABBREVIATIONS USED IN THE NOTES AND BIBLIOGRAPHY

If the bibliography contains only one book by an author, the name of the author only is given in the notes. An abbreviated version of the title is given if the author is mentioned more than once in the bibliography.

A.A.R.	Asiatic Annual Review.
C.A.L.R.	Ceylon Antiquary and Literary Register.
C.G.O.	Ceylon General Orders.
C.J.H.S.S.	The Ceylon Journal of Historical and Social Studies, New Series.
C.L.R.	Ceylon Literary Register.
C.O.	Colonial Office.
H.M.S.O.	His (Her) Majesty's Stationery Office.
J.R.A.S.C.B.	Journal of the Royal Asiatic Society (Ceylon Branch).
M.L.R.C.	Monthly Literary Register and Notes and Queries for Ceylon.
W.O.	War Office.

INDEX

INDEX

Malabars, 88, 89, 118, 215, 218, 219, 227, 231
Malacca, 82, 83
Malays: visit Ceylon, 22; troops fighting for Dutch, 37, 42, 43, 44; troops fighting for Kandyans, 88, 89, 123, 128, 204, 215
Malay Regiment: in first war, 78, 81–3, 95, 107, 110–19 passim, 124, 126, 127, 131–43 passim, 159, 164, 167, 181, 184; in second war, 209, 219, 220; in third war, 255, 258–9, 260
Manaar, 80, 137
Marchant, Colonel le, 171
Marshall, Dr Henry, 46, 57, 189, 290–1; writes about first war, 127, 130, 145, 169; writes about second war, 212, 223, 230, 231; his experiences in second war, 214, 217; writes about third war, 236, 255; his experiences in third war, 265, 266; retirement and later career, 273
Matale, 274; involved in first war, 110, 167; dissawa of, 205, 243; involved in third war, 249, 250, 252, 253, 257, 260, 261, 262–3, 267
Matara, 60, 80, 144, 173; fort attacked by Kandyans, 137–9
Mawilmada, 119
Medamahanuwara mountain, 220
Mercer, Lieutenant, 139, 140, 141
Meuron, Brigadier-General Pierre de, 43, 62
Meuron, Comte de, 43
Migastenna, 109, 155, 234; arranges truce with Macdowall, 106; attacks fort at Dambadeniya, 134–5; death of, 195
Minneriya, Lake, 90–1, 95, 168, 240, 243
Mohandiram, the Haji, 240, 241, 242
Moira, Lord, see Hastings, Marquis of
Molligoda, 195, 203, 207, 246, 248, 259, 265; invades Sabaragamuva, 204–5; discord between Ehelepola and Molligoda, 208, 243, 248–9, 263; on British side during Brownrigg's attack on Kandy, 214–16; becomes Mahadigar, 234, 243; death of, 271
Moore, Lieutenant-Colonel John, 78
Moormen, 56, 215, 241, 247, 258, 260
Moratota, 184
Mount Lavinia, 207
Mowbray, R., 158
Mozambique, 148
Mugurugampale, 104
Muttusamy, 102, 109, 118, 119, 131, 177; proclaimed heir to throne by North, 94–5, 97, 106; murder of, 120, 204
Muttusamy (cousin of Sri Wikrama), 219–20, 279
Mutwal, 190
Mylius, Lieutenant, 219, 220
Mysore War, 42, 80

Nalanda, 91, 210, 215, 217, 243, 250, 262

Narolle, M. de la, 39, 40
Nayaka, Kobbakaduva, 232
Negombo: captured by Portuguese from Dutch, 32; threatened by Kandyan invasion, 36; involved in first war, 80, 84, 104, 134, 139, 140, 143, 173; involved in second war, 210
Newman, Lieutenant, 241, 242
North, the Hon. Frederick, 77–86 passim, 128, 138, 139, 143, 146–50 passim, 179–84 passim, 192, 199, 209, 222; becomes Governor of Ceylon, 63–5; tackles problem of Kandy, 65–9; embarks upon war with Kandy, 75–6; writes to Sri Wikrama suggesting settlement, 94; proclaims Muttusamy heir to throne, 95, 97, 106; meets Pilima Talauva, 66–9, 109–11, 132, 134; gives order to evacuate Kandy, 113, 114; blames Davie for disaster at Kandy, 130; appeals for help from overseas, 137; disputes with Wemyss, 151–3; plans further offensive against Kandy, 154–6; asks to be replaced as Governor, 175–6; character study and achievements of, 176–8; later career, 272, death of, 272
Nouradin, Captain, 112, 116, 117, 127–8, 131
Nuwara Eliya, 266

Ode to an Old Camp Cloak (Anderson), 256
Onesicritus, 22
Ormsby, Lieutenant, 111

Palk Straits, 18
Pangaragama, 160
Paranagamma, 249
Parangi Hatana, 29
Paravi Sandesaya, 24
Percival, Robert, 53, 70, 73, 82, 172, 188, 192, 193
Persians, visit Ceylon, 22
Phrenological Society of Edinburgh, 266
Pierce, Captain, 279
Pieris, P. E., 24, 146, 206
Pitt, William, 78
Plenderleath, Lieutenant, 121
Pliny, 22
Point de Galle, 138
Pollock, Captain William, 141–3, 144
Polo, Marco, 88
Polonnaruwa, 22, 92
Polygars, 82
Portuguese; invasion of Ceylon, 18, 23–30, 33–4; driven out of Ceylon by Dutch, 32–3; their effect on commerce in Ceylon, 55–6
Proclamation of 1815, by General Brownrigg at end of third war, 261–2; text of, 281–2
Puttalam, 137, 139, 173
Pybus, John, 40–1, 49–52, 92

318

INDEX

Quiberon Bay, 179
Quin, Daniel, 163
Quoit social club, 192

Raja Sinha I, 26, 27
Raja Sinha II, 52, 88; at war with Portuguese, 28; at war with Dutch, 31, 32, 34–5; his menageries of Europeans, 39–40, 124; becomes embittered tyrant, 47; description of court ceremonial, 49, 50–1; visit of John Pybus to court, 49, 50–1; death of, 65
Rajarata, 21, 22
Rala, Levuke ,142
Raper, Captain, 250
Raymond, Colonel, 43
Regiments: 1st Ceylon, 81, 209, 241
2nd Ceylon, 81, 209, 239, 247
3rd Ceylon, 148, 209, 232, 239
4th Ceylon, 181, 209, 239
7th Foot, 252
10th Foot, 146
15th Madras Native Infantry, 252
18th Foot, 252
19th Foot, 17, 70, 72; in first war, 78, 79–80, 90, 91, 92, 95, 100, 107, 111, 115–26 passim, 134, 136–7, 146, 157, 159, 164, 167, 182, 186; in second war, 209, 216, 220; in third war, 239, 245, 246–7, 249, 250, 251, 256, 268; sails for England, 273–4
34th Foot, 146
51st Foot, in first war, 77, 78, 89, 90, 107, 108, 111, 117, 135, 136, 139, 146, 190, 194
65th Foot, 80–1, 103, 104, 108, 136
66th Foot, 147, 209
73rd Highlanders, 209, 226, 239, 251, 257, 267, 268, 274
75th Foot, 112
83rd Foot, 239, 246, 249, 251, 261, 264
86th Foot, 260
89th Foot, 260
Relic of the Tooth, 233–4, 259–60, 265
Ribeiro, Captain Joao, 17, 33
Rice, Lieutenant Samuel, 194
Robinson Crusoe (Defoe), 39
Rodiyas, 256
Romans, visit Ceylon, 22
Royal Military Academy, 172
Royal Military College, 171–2
Rumley, Captain, 123, 128, 142
Ruwanwella, 70, 72, 83, 143, 144, 213–14, 224

Saa, Captain General Constantine de, 28
Sabaragamuva: involved in first war, 95, 173, involved in second war, 201, 202, 203, 215, 220, 234; involved in third war, 238, 248, 252, 253, 257, 263
Salagamas, 55
San Domingo, 178–9
Sangunglo, 115, 116, 128
Saparamadu, S. D., 45
Sarr, Johann Jacob, 32
Sarum, Mudaliyar Abraham de, 197, 230
Sawers, Simon, 243, 244, 266
Scindia, 210
Senkadagala, *see* Kandy
Sepoys: in first war, 103, 104, 115, 135, 139, 140, 146, 151, 159, 161, 164, 167, 181, 184; in second war, 209, 210, 214; in third war, 239, 252
Seringapatam, 92, 194
Seven Korales, 274; involved in first war, 85, 94, 95, 110, 134, 195; countryside despoiled by British, 144–6; 173; involved in second war, 201, 205, 214, 216, 218, 234; involved in third war, 244, 249, 250, 257, 261, 262
Seven Years' War, 40
Shipp, John, 81, 99
Silva, Colvin R. de, 232
Sinhalese: history of, 20–3; way of life of, 45–58; social intercourse with British, 192–3
Sitawaka, 66, 70, 72, 143, 204, 208, 211
Slave Island, 190
Snow Minerva, 138
Sorikalmunai, 159
Sousa, Manoel de, 28
Spain, domination of Portugal by, 30
Spilbergen, Admiral, 31
Sri Wikrama Raja Sinha, 75, 88, 92, 107, 109, 110, 144, 145, 147, 225, 231, 283; becomes last Kandyan king, 66; description of, 73, 222–3; plans by Pilima Talauva to depose him, 68–9, 95–6, 106–7, 109, 110, 195–6; disputes with Pilima Talauva, 112, 132, 194–5; condemns Muttusamy to death, 119, 120; imprisons captives, 124, 127–8, 130; responsible for massacre, 132–3; attacks fort at Hanwella, 140–2; North wishes to depose him, 154–5; has Pilima Talauva beheaded, 196, 201; becomes unpopular after Pilima Talauva's death, 201–8, 236; uses terror to control kingdom, 204–6, 207–8; captured by British, 218–21, 255; taken to Madras, 222–3; death of, 223, 271; fate of his regalia and state treasures, 227–9
Stevenson, John, 226, 227
Stuart, Colonel, 42–3, 59–60, 99, 209
Suffren, Admiral, 41
Sumatra, 82
Sutherland, James, 230, 285

319